rhymes, the little verses that book owners
have inscribed in their books, and considers
what they reveal about the identity of the
inscribers as well as about attitudes toward
book lending, book borrowing, and the circulation of knowledge.

Solidly researched and venturing into
areas long neglected by scholars, *Folklore and
Book Culture* is a work that will engage not
only folklorists but historians and literary
scholars as well.

The Author: Kevin J. Hayes is associate
professor of English at the University of
Central Oklahoma and the author of *A
Colonial Woman's Bookshelf.*

Jacket Illustrations: *front cover and spine:* detail of bookplate by Joan Hassall; *back cover:*
ornamental border, artist unknown; *front
flap:* illuminated initial, artist unknown;
back flap: detail of bookplate by Walter
Crane.
Jacket design: Todd Duren.

Folklore and Book Culture

"Folklore

and

Book Culture"

Kevin J. Hayes

The University of
Tennessee Press / Knoxville

In memory of Ada Dreyer

First Edition.

The paper in this book meets the minimum requirements of the
American National Standard for Permanence of Paper for Printed
Library Materials. ∞   The binding materials have been chosen
for strength and durability.
⊕ Printed on recycled paper.

Library of Congress Cataloging-in-Publication Data

Hayes, Kevin J.
Folklore and book culture / Kevin J. Hayes.—1st ed.
        p. cm.
Includes bibliographical references and index.
ISBN 0-87049-978-5 (cloth: alk. paper)
1. Literature and folklore. 2. Books—Folklore. 3. Tales—History
and criticism. 4. Popular literature—History and criticism. I. Title.
GR41.3.H39 1997
398'.09—dc21   96-45802
                                                  CIP

Contents

Introduction

During the 1930s, members of the Works Progress Administration's (WPA) Georgia Writers' Project visited the coastal regions of Georgia and South Carolina for the purpose of locating beliefs, customs, and superstitions which could be traced back to Africa. At Tin City, a shantytown east of Savannah, the WPA interviewers encountered Nathaniel John Lewis, an elderly citizen and mayor of the town. They asked him about conjuring and spells, and he explained that his arm had been crippled and his wife killed through the efforts of a local conjure doctor. Not long after the interview had begun, Lewis showed the interviewers his "single treasured book," a copy of the twelfth edition of Lauron William De Laurence's *The Book of Magical Art, Hindu Magic and East Indian Occultism* (1914), which, the title page puffed, contained "the *Key* for the *Practice and Composition* of Hindu Amulets, Charms, Seals Requisite for the Perfection of all Talismanic, Ceremonial, Hindu and Celestial Magic, Invocation and Binding of Astral Spirits, Exorcisms, Enchantments, Benedictions, Conjurations, Clairvoyancy and Hindu Mediumship."[1] "This book has helped me some," Lewis told them, "but I didn't really need it. I was birthed with my wisdom because I was the seventh child an bawn with a caul."[2] The interviewers expressed little interest in the book and tried to direct the conversation to the spirit world. Lewis briefly told them about the ghost which haunted his property but then brought the conversation back to his prized volume. The interviewers recorded:

> Then he insisted on returning to the subject of his magic book. We evinced the proper interest and he showed us a strange recipe jotted down in almost illegible writing on the flyleaf of his book.
>
> Eggs—2
> carisin—1 pint
> turpentine—1 pint

vinegar
cy pepper
table salt—1 box

"That's a conjuh mixin," the old man explained. "I don't know what it's faw. It was in the book when Joe Fraser, a root doctuh, gave it to me."
"Where is Joe Fraser?"
"He is dead these long yeahs. All the real old root doctuhs are passin on to the beyon."[3]

The interview apparently ended shortly thereafter.

The encounter between the WPA interviewers and Nathaniel Lewis indicates two distinct attitudes toward the book. The interviewers, as government employees gathering folk beliefs and superstitions for the purpose of writing and publishing a collection of folklore, represented the established culture. Since they were looking for African survivals, they were not interested in collecting information about books. When they first met Lewis, they noted that "a certain amount of schooling was evident in his speech, which was extremely soft, slow, and careful."[4] In both his speech, therefore, and his act of showing them the book, Lewis demonstrated his education, letting the interviewers know that he belonged among the literate members of the established culture. The interviewers and Lewis related to each other in opposite ways. The interviewers' behavior deliberately differentiated them from Lewis (we are the collectors, you the informant), whereas Lewis sought to assimilate himself within the establishment.

Not only did the interviewers miss the importance of the book in terms of the relationship between folklore collector and informant, they also missed its importance to traditional magic practice. The description of their attitude when Lewis brought the conversation back to his prized book ("We evinced the proper interest . . .") seems condescending. Their purpose was to record surviving superstitions which could be traced back to Africa. They had little desire to hear about a book which had been published during their lifetimes. For Lewis, however, and for Joe Fraser, the root doctor who had previously owned the book, the twentieth-century magic book and the traditional superstitions and beliefs belonged together. It little mattered to them whether supernatural wisdom came from a book published in New York City or from a great grandfather in Africa or from being born with a caul. Lewis's use of the book shows the ease with which printed material could be integrated within the traditional folk culture. The interviewers' search for survivals, defined by Mary Granger, the project director, as "the customs and beliefs of what is left of a generation closely linked to its native African origin,"[5] suggests that they viewed the field collector's job as a kind of salvage operation. They saw folk culture diminishing in the face of modern society and technology. The process of gathering folklore, therefore, had to be accomplished before it disappeared or became contaminated by the stuff of modern civilization, such as the printed word or the mass media. Lewis's inclusion of the book as part of his folk belief system, on the other hand, shows the ease with which new objects, ideas, and technology could be made part of traditional folk culture.

Though Lewis was obviously proud of his book, it remains unclear how much he actually had used it. After explaining that it had helped him some, he stated that he had been born with his supernatural knowledge. Congenital wisdom, it seems, obviated the need for other sources of magical knowledge. The book's importance to Lewis comes, not from its individual magic spells and conjurations, but from the fact that it was formerly in the possession of Joe Fraser, a root doctor whom Lewis greatly respected and a person who had practiced a traditional way of doctoring which was fast disappearing. The conjuring recipe which Fraser had inscribed on the flyleaf held no intrinsic value for Lewis. He had no idea what it was for. The manuscript note, however, provided evidence that Fraser had once owned the book and that he had used it to work magic. Among hoodoo practitioners, a person's handwriting is considered a powerful manifestation of his individuality.[6] A manuscript note inside a printed volume serves as a reminder of the book's former owner. In a way, Lewis's copy of De Laurence's *Book of Magical Art*, though less than twenty-five years old, was also a "survival," an artifact handed down from a passing generation. Preserving Joe Fraser's magic book, Lewis helped keep his magic alive.

The encounter between the WPA interviewers and Nathaniel John Lewis reveals some of the complexities involved with folklore and book culture. While the two are often considered opposites—folklore involves orally circulated texts, while book culture concerns the transmission of written texts—there are many instances when they intersect. The acquisition of literacy and, concomitantly, the acquisition of books as personal possessions, far from expunging folklore, have given rise to new beliefs and superstitions. In other words, book culture has augmented folklore. Some books have generated new proverbs. Others have fostered their own legends. The ownership of books has prompted superstitions about spirituality as well as the acquisition of knowledge. Sometimes the book has become an important motif in the folktale, a curious situation in which written objects have become important parts of orally circulated tales, stories which reveal much about attitudes toward literacy in many parts of the world. The flyleaf rhyme, a folk genre which challenges the traditional assumption that folklore must be orally circulated, makes the book a place in which folklore occurs and thus indicates a lively interaction between folk, print, and manuscript culture.

For the most part, scholarship treating the relationship between folklore and the book has concentrated on the inexpensive, widely distributed books which proliferated from the turn of the sixteenth into the nineteenth century. The study of cheap print has been enlivened in recent decades by a number of important studies. Work on the German *Volksbücher* has been undertaken by Albrecht Classen, John L. Flood, and Bodo Gotzkowsky, to name a few.[7] Since Robert Mandrou's pioneering treatment of the *Bibliothèque bleue,* other insightful studies of the cheap-print trade in France have appeared, most notably, the essays by Roger Chartier.[8] For Great Britain, Margaret Spufford and Tessa Watt have both made important contributions to our knowledge of chapbooks, and Victor Neuburg has written an important essay on the chapbook trade in early America.[9] The list could go on—Hubert Seelow for Iceland, Joaquin Marco for Spain, Candace Slater for Brazil[10]—but suffice it to say that the scholarship on cheap books, though vast, is far from exhausted. The current enthusiasm for the history of the book promises to enliven the study of cheap print.

Depending upon their country of origin, these cheap books have received different labels—*Bibliothèque bleue,* chapbook, *Volksbuch.* Each label reflects a different orientation, and each has advantages and disadvantages. The term *Bibliothèque bleue* refers to the blue covers of the inexpensive French publications of the seventeenth and eighteenth centuries published at Troyes and elsewhere. The advantage of the French term is that it clearly denotes a specific set of books. The term has an added advantage in that it is the same term that was used by contemporary readers, though, as Roger Chartier has shown, contemporary use of the term was generally reserved for prose fiction, while modern usage of the term refers to all such inexpensive publications, including didactic and devotional works, some of which had covers which were not even blue.[11]

While the French term reflects the physical appearance of the book, the English term "chapbook" reflects the sale and distribution of inexpensive publications. In Great Britain and North America, chapbooks were sold by chapmen or itinerant booksellers, or as they were more colorfully called, flying stationers. Unlike the term *Bibliothèque bleue,* "chapbook" is anachronistic. Such cheap books were around for centuries before the term came into use. Instead, they were known as "chapmen's books," "small books," or "small histories." Harry B. Weiss, the pioneering scholar of the chapbook trade, suggested that a key part of the definition of chapbooks is that they are books sold by chapmen. While it is important to understand the relationship between itinerant book peddlers and the consumers who purchased their goods, not all chapbooks were sold by chapmen. Often the same books vended by the chapmen in rural areas could be had at urban book shops.

Rather than reflecting either the physical appearance of the cheap book or the condition of its sale, the German term *Volksbuch* places the emphasis on the reader. The term is most often used to denote a set of sixteenth-century fictional German prose narratives, specifically those listed by Paul Heitz and François Ritter in their ground-breaking bibliographical study and those which Bodo Gotzkowsky includes within his recent bibliography.[12] I like the orientation toward the reader, and the term *Volksbuch* seems capacious enough to hold other folk books beyond those early, popular German narratives. For the term to continue to have meaning during the era of mass production, however, its scope must be severely constricted. Otherwise, each nineteenth-century pamphlet novel, all pulp fiction, and, indeed, every cheaply printed book everywhere would have to be included. For works published through the eighteenth century, I use the term *Volksbuch* synonymously with chapbook. I will continue to use the term chapbook, but only when specifically treating the book as a commercial object. For works published after the stereotype and the steam press came about, I apply the term *Volksbuch* to those books, generally but not necessarily occult in nature, which have developed a reputation for powers which transcend their text.

Other than the *Volksbuch,* the topics I discuss in the present work have received little scholarly treatment. Of the preceding works which address my subject perhaps none are as relevant as Holbrook Jackson's classic *Anatomy of Bibliomania.* In his work, Jackson touches upon several topics which I treat in greater detail here. But Jackson's deliberately idiosyncratic work remains more of an omnium-gatherum, and its author carefully shies away from in-depth analysis. In "Hohman and Romanus," Don Yoder treats Johann Georg Hohman's *Long Lost Friend,* a nineteenth-century American *Volksbuch* which has fostered a significant reputation for its powers, but similar books have not been treated with such detail. More recent studies within the burgeoning field of study, the history of the book, have only just started addressing the relationship between folklore and book culture. Carlo Ginzburg's work *The Cheese and the Worms* brilliantly shows how one man's reading process was influenced by traditional oral culture. David Cressy's 1986 essay "Books as Totems in Seventeenth-Century England and New England" briefly treats some superstitions of the book. And David S. Shields has emphasized the importance of understanding the ongoing manuscript culture within a world of print.[13]

Perhaps the present study shares the greatest affinity with those works which stress the interrelationship between folklore and modern technology, specifically Hermann Bausinger's *Folk Culture in a World of Technology,* Linda Dégh's *American Folklore and the Mass Media,* and the numerous collections of photocopy lore assembled by Alan Dundes and Carl Pagter.[14] Bausinger's dichotomy between folklore and technology is not dissimilar to the relationship between folklore and the printed book. Dundes and Pagter stress that folklore cannot simply be considered as orally circulated material in the era of the photocopy machine. With my discussion of the flyleaf rhyme, I suggest that written folklore long predated the photocopier. In her recent study, Linda Dégh has emphasized the importance of accommodating print culture as part of the folk culture and has asserted the importance of drawing from multiple disciplines to study folklore.[15] The present work addresses some of her concerns.

Chapter 1 examines the *Volksbuch* in early America, an area of study which has received little scholarly attention compared to the treatments of *Volksbücher* in other countries. Harry B. Weiss contributed some groundbreaking articles in the 1930s and 1940s, but Weiss largely ignored the significance of imported chapbooks. Victor Neuburg has made the single most important scholarly contribution to date with his bibliographical essay "Chapbooks in America: Reconstructing the Popular Reading of Early America." Here, I look specifically at how the *Volksbuch* affected another folklore genre, the proverb. Though I concentrate my attention on the *Volksbuch* in early America, I do not mean to imply that the relationship between the *Volksbuch* and the proverb is a uniquely American phenomenon.

Chapter 2 takes an in-depth look at one particular *Volksbuch, The Sixth and Seventh Books of Moses,* and a passing glance at some of the other books of black magic which have entered the folklore. Not only have the various conjurations and recipes from these books become part of the practice of traditional magic from the Alleghenies to Trinidad, but the books themselves have become the subject of numerous legends.

Drawing on the major published collections of beliefs and superstitions—Frank C. Brown for North Carolina, Anthon S. Cannon for Utah, Helen Creighton for Nova Scotia, Harry M. Hyatt for Illinois, Newbell Niles Puckett for Ohio, Vance Randolph for the Ozark regions, Daniel Lindsey Thomas and Lucy Blayney Thomas for Kentucky—among many other smaller collections, chapter 3 looks at the numerous superstitions and beliefs associated with the book. While working on this chapter, I described to friends and colleagues the various beliefs and superstitions about books. They consistently responded with amused smugness: "Isn't it funny what people believed in olden days." They remained amused and smug, that is, until I asked: Haven't you ever heard that it is unlucky to leave a book unfinished? At which time they admitted, "Well, yes that's true." Don't you know that it is bad luck to read the last page of a book first? "Well, yeah." Isn't it bad luck to read over someone's shoulder? "Of course, everyone knows that."

Chapters 4 through 6 discuss folktales and legends. I began researching these chapters where all research on folktales and legends begin, with Stith Thompson's *Motif-Index*, Ernest Baughman's *Type and Motif-Index*, Antti Aarne's and Thompson's *Types of the Folktale*, and Reidar Christiansen's *Migratory Legends*. Admittedly, I was unsure what I would find. As my research continued, I discovered that a significant number of folktales and legends recorded in Iceland and in the Philippines contained the book as a motif. Furthermore, the legend type "Inexperienced Use of the Black Book" (*ML* 3020), which has been recorded widely throughout Scandinavia, is also known in Great Britain and the United States. Christiansen has studied the numerous variants of the type in Norway, but the English language variants have gone largely unstudied. Chapters 4 through 6 analyze these various folktales and legends, placing them within the context of book culture and the history of education and examining what they say about books, learning, and literacy.

One pseudonymous mid-nineteenth-century contributor to *Notes and Queries* known only as "Balliolensis" wrote, "It occurs to me that an interesting collection might be formed of the various forms and methods by which the ownership of books is sometimes found to be asserted on their fly-leaves."[16] To date, Fanny D. Bergen's brief

1900 essay remains the most detailed treatment of the subject.[17] Since then the subject has gone unstudied, and the flyleaf rhyme's significance has been ignored. One folklore dictionary characterizes flyleaf inscriptions as "mere identification rimes,"[18] but I cannot help but be unsettled by the brief definition. Should "identification" ever be described as "mere"? These traditional verses which involve the process of book owners inscribing their names say much about the way people think about themselves and wish others to think about them. Indeed, Alan Dundes has used the flyleaf inscription to introduce his important treatment of folklore and identity.[19] Chapter 7 explores what these traditional flyleaf inscriptions say about identity, but also what they say about attitudes toward book lending, book borrowing, and the circulation of knowledge.

Shortly after I began this study, I joined the electronic discussion group for rare book librarians and aficionados, ExLibris. After I sent out a message describing my project and asking for help, I received a letter from Edward H. Dahl, the Early Cartography Specialist at the National Archives of Canada in Ottawa, which contained several photocopied cartoons about books. I could not help but chuckle as I read the cartoons, because I recently had read Norman D. Stevens's review of Dundes and Pagter's first collection of photocopy lore, *Urban Folklore from the Paperwork Empire*. Stevens found it notable that the authors had taken none of their examples from the academic library bureaucracy: "Incidentally the total lack of any direct mention of libraries, academic or otherwise, is undoubtedly a reflection of our insignificance in the overall bureaucracy and not an exemption from the criticisms of the material. One almost wishes that there were specific library items of this kind no matter how harsh they might be."[20] Dahl's letter assured me that librarians do indeed have their own photocopy lore.

But are the items which Dahl sent me folklore? Dundes and Pagter rightfully have removed the oral transmission requirement from the definition of folklore, but they do suggest two other key criteria for folkloristic material, multiple existence and variation.[21] Two of the cartoons Dahl sent me are recognizably from the pages of the *New Yorker*. The source of the third, a delightful drawing which depicts a semi-tractor-trailer carrying gigantic books which extend from either side of the trailer with a sign reading "Caution Oversized" attached is less easily recognizable. Since it is the only one of its kind I have seen, however, I cannot verify its multiple existence or any variation. Dahl was the only one who responded to my query on paper. Everyone else responded using electronic mail. One person remarked,

"How about the really old cartoon from the *New Yorker* where the guy is walking past the book store, and on the window is: 'Rare, Out of Print, and Nonexistent Books.'" Another wrote, "On the earlier thread I assume everyone saw the *New Yorker* cartoon a while back? Man slumped in library chair surrounded by rows of empty shelves— wife in doorway saying 'Honey, maybe you shouldn't collect books that are so rare.'" Both items are attributed to the *New Yorker,* yet the medium of electronic mail has forced the informant to take a visual item and translate it into words, a process which leads inevitably to multiple existence and variation. The overall process is fascinating. A item of bookish humor gets printed in a magazine; a rare book librarian translates the visual medium to words and electronically disseminates the item to other librarians throughout the world; then the other librarians relate that item orally to their local peers. In my conclusion I further discuss the interrelationship between the folklore of the book and modern technology.

I am thankful to Peter Graham, the moderator of the ExLibris electronic discussion group, as well as the participants who have responded to my queries. Many other people deserve credit for making this work possible as well. I especially would like to thank Professor David Hoch, director of the University of Toledo Honors Program, for allowing me to return to my undergraduate alma mater, where I presented an overview of my study as part of the University of Toledo Honors Program Alumni Lecture Series in May 1995. At the lecture, I became reacquainted with Professor Tom Barden, my undergraduate folklore teacher and now chairman of American Studies at the University of Toledo, who invited me back in May 1996 when I presented a lecture in the "American Thought and Culture" series entitled "Zora Neale Hurston and *The Sixth and Seventh Books of Moses,*" a modified version of chapter 2 of the present work. I would also like to thank J. A. Leo Lemay for giving me the opportunity to present "Traditional Flyleaf Rhymes," an abridged version of chapter 7 at the 1995 Modern Language Association meeting in Chicago. The help of my research assistant, Jacquelyn Leonardi, was invaluable. Also, I am grateful to Doylene Manning and the interlibrary loan department at the Max Chambers Library, University of Central Oklahoma. I am also grateful to those I encountered while working at other libraries near and far: Columbia University, Indiana University, the University of Michigan, the University of Oklahoma, the University of Texas, the University of Toledo, and the University of Tulsa. Thanks also to Meredith Morris-Babb and Stan Ivester at the University of Tennessee Press. Karin

Kaufman deserves credit for copyediting the manuscript. My sister Kathleen entered many of my notes into the computer, for which I am grateful. Of course, I thank Richard and Carole Hayes for their encouragement and support. I would also like to thank Ada Dreyer, my grandmother and my first folklore teacher. This volume is dedicated to her memory.

Volksbuch and Proverb in Early America

Old Mr. Dod's Sayings, a short collection of religious maxims which Marmaduke Johnson reprinted at Cambridge, Massachusetts, in 1673, is one of the earliest known works printed in colonial British North America which can be considered a *Volksbuch.*Subtitled *Posies Gathered Out of Mr. Dod's Garden,* the work was a posthumous collection of individually numbered sententiae gathered from the writings of Puritan divine John Dod. In the collection, contemporary readers could find such nicely balanced sayings as "So much Sin, so much Sorrow; so much Holiness, so much Happiness" and "Either Prayer will make a man give over sinning, or Sin will make a man give over praying." The last item in the collection provides an indication that the brief work was designed for humble readers: "Brown-bread with the Gospel is good Fare."

According to surviving copies of London editions, *Old Mr. Dod's Sayings* first appeared as a broadside during the 1660s. The work proved popular enough that a broadside sequel, *A Second Sheet of Old Mr. Dod's Sayings,* soon followed. Marmaduke Johnson's edition, printed from one of the imported London editions, was a quarto pamphlet. London editions also appeared in octavo, duodecimo, and even smaller formats.[1] The various formats allowed Dod's text to be used in different ways. Pocket editions of *Dod's Sayings* provided convenience to and comfort from the printed word. Carrying a copy of the book made it easy to dip into its text during spare moments. Indeed, the very nature of the work lent itself to brief, occasional readings. Recalling one of the broadside editions of *Dod's Sayings* and its sequel, eighteenth-century historian James Granger wrote: "His Sayings have been printed in various forms: many of them on two sheets of paper, are still to be seen pasted on the walls of cottages. An old woman in my neighbourhood told me, 'that she should have gone distracted for the loss of her husband, if she had been without Mr. Dod's Sayings in the House.'"[2] The anecdote tells much about the value of print culture within the home. Pasted to the wall, the broadside version of *Dod's Sayings* could be casually read at anytime. Granger's neighbor may have paused occasionally as she swept her cottage floor to read a saying or two and then continued with her household duties. Used as a wall decoration, the printed *Sayings* also had iconographic value. Even when the old woman was on the opposite side of the room, too far away to read the text, she could still look to the wall, see the *Sayings* broadside, and feel comforted simply knowing that Dod's soothing words were nearby whenever she needed them.[3]

Old Mr. Dod's Sayings shares many characteristics with other *Volksbücher.* It is a brief work which was sold in conveniently sized, inexpensive editions. More important, the text of the work has much the same quality as other *Volksbuch* texts. In his treatment of the *Bibliothèque bleue,* Roger Chartier explained that many works made into such inexpensive editions formerly belonged to the learned tradition. As these works were appropriated for the cheap-print trade, their texts were abbreviated, modified, and rearranged for popular consumption.[4] The works of John Dod went through much the same process as did many of the French works which were digested for the *Bibliothèque bleue* editions. The anonymous compiler read Dod's works seeking pithy maxims which readers could immediately understand and apply to their own lives. The commercial success of the work verifies the editor's understanding of the book's potential readership.

Dod's Sayings was readapted for the popular audience when the work was turned from prose into verse. As the title page of the new adaptation explained, the rhymed sayings allowed for "the better help of memory, and the delightfulness of childrens reading and learning them . . . whereby they may the better be ingrafted in their memories and understanding."[5] The title makes clear that this new adaptation was an attempt to expand the readership of the work and make it appeal to adolescents as well as adults. While some chapbook verse adaptations of prose texts proved extraordinarily popular in early America—*The History of the Holy Jesus,* a metrical version of the New Testament, first comes to mind—Old Mr. Dod suffered at the hands of his versifier. *The History of the Holy Jesus* greatly condensed its biblical source into ballad stanzas, but Dod's versifier turned the pithy yet symmetrical maxims into rhyming couplets.[6] Some of the sayings actually became more verbose, for in order to make them rhyme, the one-line maxims were made into two lines. The saying about sin and sorrow clumsily became "And therefore so much sin, and so much sorrow, / If holy thou to day, happy to morrow." And the last one became "Though we have things below here, very rare, / Yet brown bread with the Gospel is good fare."[7]

Not only did the new edition attempt to expand the readership of *Dod's Sayings,* it also attempted to create new contexts for reading the book. Stressing the "delightfulness" of reading and learning, the title asserts that the versified sayings were intended to be read aloud and memorized. Once committed to memory, the rhymed couplets could be recalled any time they were appropriate. Thus they passed from the book into the oral culture. Of course, it was hardly necessary to versify the sayings for Dod's maxims to enter spoken discourse, for people read and reread the work so often that its most memorable sayings were easy to recall. Though many readers could remember and repeat Dod's sayings, the book retained its importance as a physical object. To return to the earlier example, Granger's old neighbor probably knew most of the sayings by heart, but the printed broadside remained an important part of her home.

Samuel Sewall was perhaps colonial America's most notable reader of *Dod's Sayings,* and his diary provides key information to show how the printed sayings entered the oral culture. In 1677, when Sewall was only twenty-four, he visited a man who curtly told his visitor that he had been a "careless Christian." The man's comment reminded Sewall of a passage from *Dod's Sayings.* Having read the work, perhaps multiple times, Sewall remembered Dod's words well enough to recall an appropriate saying, and he brought it into the conversation. According to Sewall's diary entry, the man found that the saying ideally suited his current disposition.[8] Years later, Sewall recorded reading *Dod's Sayings* again. One day, he heard some particularly harsh words spoken toward himself. In his diary, he recorded his reactions: "I had read in the morn Mr. Dod's saying; Sanctified Afflictions are good Promotions. I found it now a cordial."[9] Sewall was forty-eight at the time. The diary entry shows that the work he had read half a lifetime before was a work he had continued to read and to find relevant and comforting. Sewall's recollection of Dod's pithy phrase shows the ease with which a printed text could be remembered and could enter the oral culture.

Perhaps it is no coincidence that the saying Sewall recalled echoed a seventeenth-century proverb. A collection of proverbs published during the 1650s includes the following: "Afflictions are sent us by God for our good."[10] In his original work, Dod purposely may have integrated such traditional wisdom into his text. When the anonymous compiler of *Dod's Sayings* combed Dod's works looking for pithy quotations, he may have chosen the saying about afflictions simply because it contained a proverb he already knew. As the printed text and the compiler's memory coincided, he may have realized—consciously or not—that the same coincidence might occur in his reader's mind, too. The complete text of the maxim as it appears in *Dod's Sayings* reads: "Sanctified Afflictions are spiritual Promotions, and are far better for a Christian, than all the Silver and Gold in the world; being that the tryal of our Faith is much more precious than of Gold that perisheth." In his memory, Sewall truncated the saying to five words and substituted the word "good" for "spiritual." Sewall's comment, therefore, not only shows how a written text could enter the oral culture, it also shows how texts varied during the course of their transmission. Though *Dod's Sayings* was not responsible for creating the proverb, it did help to revive and perpetuate an old proverb. Sewall's diary entry suggests a tentative thesis: *Volksbuch* texts enriched traditional proverbs and proverbial phrases.[11]

Proving such a thesis, however, involves difficulties. Cheap print is ephemeral, and few of the chapbooks which circulated in early America survive. Furthermore, *Volksbücher* were so absolutely commonplace that even though many people read them, few recorded having read them. Many proverbs, proverbial phrases, and proverbial comparisons used in conversation daily may have never been written down. It is an irony of historical scholarship that some of the most commonplace things of the past are often the most difficult to recapture. Causality presents another problem. Even when documentary evidence testifying to the purchase or reading of *Volksbücher* survives and even where proverbs and proverbial phrases have been recorded, establishing causal links between a *Volksbuch* text and an orally circulated proverb may be tenuous.

The Massachusetts edition of *Dod's Sayings* attests to the work's extraordinary popularity in early New England. To be sure, numerous copies of British editions had reached the American strand before Marmaduke Johnson reprinted the work. Through most of the colonial period, British works were reprinted locally only when imports could not meet the demand. Otherwise, most chapbooks were imported from overseas, and relatively few have survived. Often, entire editions have disappeared completely, though they may have been printed in press runs in the thousands or tens of thousands. People bought such books to read and use, and they kept reading and using them until they fell apart, at which time they became tinder for starting fires, wrapping paper for dried goods, or, quite frankly, lavatory paper.[12] As Dr. Alexander Hamilton explained in *The History of the Tuesday Club,* pages from cheap romances and histories were highly preferable to the alternative, tree leaves. To such cheap print

> not . . . only the Tobacconists and spice Shops, but even the Houses of office, have been of late years so Infinitely Indebted, who, had they not been supplied from these vast piles of waste paper, would have been at a Sad loss how to wrap up their grocery and haberdashery, and besides, many honest well meaning Christians, must have run the risque of befowling their fingers, in using the tender leaves of vegetables, which are not of so tough a nature, as that same other Historical Stuff is, besides the risque they must have run, of getting that most grievous distemper called the piles, by means of the Corrosive down that often abounds upon the leaves of the said vegetables, which like so much low Itch, would vellicate in a dreadful manner, the Tender plicae of the Rectum, where it terminates in the anus.[13]

Well, enough said.

Estate inventories, the single most important resource for understanding the book culture of early America, almost never list chapbooks among their book titles. When chapbooks were mentioned at all, they were simply grouped under the title "small books." In 1657, for example, the estate inventory for John Mottrom of Northumberland County, Virginia, listed "39 small books."[14] A century later, estate inventories differed little in respect to chapbooks. In 1757, the estate inventory for Charles Christie, sheriff of Baltimore County, Maryland, listed titles of many books, but one of the final items simply reads "Small Books."[15] Few invoices for books imported from overseas survive, but those that do seldom list such inexpensive books by title. More often, they are simply listed as "chapmen's books" or "small histories" or, to confuse matters even further, as "histories."[16] One colonial Maryland store, for example, contained "29 Chapman's books," the largest number of printed items listed in the inventory besides horn books, and one surviving invoice from a Maryland importer lists "4 doz small Histories."[17] When an importer ordered chapmen's books, he usually ordered them not by title, but generically.

Since so little evidence survives to detail the *Volksbuch* in early America, the documents concerning the seventeenth-century Boston book market located by Worthington Chauncey Ford many years ago take on additional importance. Fortunately, some of the surviving invoices of the books imported from London list the titles and prices of both expensive and inexpensive books. Many of the listed titles belong to the *Volksbuch* tradition. When Ford first located and edited the Boston documents, he downplayed the importance of these traditional works in favor of the pious works sent along with them, but, as Roger Thompson noted in his follow-up study which corrected and yet appreciated Ford's work, the popular literature was much more important to the book culture of early New England than Ford gave it credit.[18] No inventories comparable to those located by Ford survive from early-eighteenth-century America. Instead, the surviving evidence concerning the *Volksbuch* for that period is largely anecdotal.[19] From the mid-eighteenth century, a handful of booksellers' catalogues and advertisements listing "chapman's books" survive to provide additional information concerning which *Volksbücher* were imported into colonial America. After the Revolutionary War, the local chapbook industry flourished, and American printers began issuing a variety of chapbooks in large quantities. Much fuller information, therefore, survives concerning the *Volksbuch* in late eighteenth and early nineteenth century America.

The evidence, spotty as it is, still permits some generalizations. The titles of the works imported to late-seventeenth-century Boston are remarkably consistent with those imported to mid-eighteenth-century America and those printed in early-nineteenth-century America and, for that matter, with those which had been popular in sixteenth-century Europe. The *Volksbuch* literature was a conservative literature. Many of the *Volksbuch* texts belonged to the medieval chivalric romance tradition, and some had roots in the traditional oral culture. One of the most widely known *Volksbuch* texts in early America, *Guy of Warwick*, was a medieval romance which described the adventures of a chivalric knight who wins the hand of the Earl of Warwick's daughter by accomplishing many feats of knightly prowess.[20] Other centuries-old *Volksbuch* texts such as *Fortunatus, Dr. Faustus, Reynard the Fox, Valentin and Orson*, as well as several works written specifically for the cheap-print trade, such as the verse and prose fiction of Thomas Deloney and Richard Johnson, retained their popularity throughout the colonial period and into the nineteenth century. Other genres of cheap-print literature available in early America included devotional manuals, voyages, biographies, midwifery books, and jestbooks.

In *The History of the Tuesday Club,* Dr. Alexander Hamilton mentioned a jestbook titled *Laugh and Be Fat,* which denoted one of several possible, similarly titled chapbooks.[21] Though Hamilton wrote deprecatingly of the *Laugh and Be Fat* jestbooks, he could not deny their popularity, a popularity which would continue into the nineteenth century. During the 1760s, Philadelphia booksellers William Bradford and Andrew Steuart both advertised the title. Massachusetts printer Nathaniel Coverly, who, with other members of his printing family, specialized in chapbooks, issued *Laugh and Be Fat: Or, An Antidote against Melancholy* (1799), *The New Laugh and Be Fat: Or, Fun for Everyday of the Week* (1813), and *Laugh and Be Fat: Or, Fun for Every Hour in the Day* (1816).[22] These collections of humorous anecdotes and facetiae repeat the proverb "Laugh and Be Fat" as part of their title. In this case, the proverb came first,[23] and the *Volksbücher* took advantage of a popular saying to familiarize potential purchasers with their contents in order to encourage sales. In a way, the printed object verified the proverb's truth. Purchase this book, laugh while reading it, and be fat, which back then was more or less construed as being healthy and prosperous. One of the Coverly titles, *The New Laugh and Be Fat*, shows that this proverb had become so closely associated with the *Volksbuch* that it had become a kind of generic name for jestbooks. While these various collections show one way the *Volksbuch* and the proverb could be associated, they really bring us no closer to verifying the notion that *Volksbuch* texts entered the language of the proverb.

Fortunately, Dr. Hamilton had more to say on the subject. Taking fellow club member, William Lux, to task, Hamilton suggested that the man's verbal wit fell short of what fellow club members expected. Hamilton wrote that the content and manner of Lux's speech

> inclines me to observe, that he is better read in the History of *Jeck and the Gyants, the wise men of Gotham, Tom Thumb, Laugh and be fat, Jeck Hicathrift . . .* in short, the froth and vanity of the rest of his Speech, his trite Simile of a dead weight and machine, with his *This here* and *That there*, are of a piece with all his other performances, and his latin quotations, would better become the pen of a Schoolboy than a grave Longstanding member, of the ancient and honorable Tuesday Club.[24]

The works Hamilton mentions were *Volksbücher: The History of Jack and the Giants; The Pleasant and Delightful History of Tom Hickathrift; The History of Tom Thumb;* and *The Merry Tales of the Wise Men of Gotham,* a title which incorporates a different kind of proverbial phrase, the *blason populaire*.[25]

Hamilton's reference to these *Volksbücher* reveals his disdain, but his comments clearly suggest that reading them could influence a person's spoken discourse. For Hamilton, the *Volksbuch* texts represented a lower level of intellect and sophistication, a level beneath that of the accomplished gentleman who should model his own spoken discourse on the writings of polite authors such as Joseph Addison and Sir Richard Steele. Elsewhere in *The History of the Tuesday Club,* Hamilton reaffirms his disdain for the *Volksbuch* texts. In the first chapter, he expresses hope that his own history will rise "some degrees ... above those celebrated authors, who have penned the Histories of *Tom Thumb, Jack and the Gyants* & *the wise men of Gotham.*"[26] Still, Hamilton himself was not totally averse to alluding to a *Volksbuch* character for an apt comparison. Describing some incomprehensible words William Lux used in his speech, Hamilton suggested that they were words "that one would think Invented by Dr Faustus to Conjure up the devil."[27]

Perhaps the most convincing evidence to show the impact of the *Volksbuch* on the traditional oral culture are the numerous proper names used in proverbs, proverbial phrases, and proverbial comparisons. A phrase used from the late sixteenth century was "Hobson's choice," which meant the opportunity to choose between one particular thing or nothing. Colonial Massachusetts clergyman John Wise, for example, used the proverbial phrase in his influential early-eighteenth-century tract *The Churches Quarrel Espoused,* in which he mentioned "a kind of Hobsons Choice, *One of these, or None.*"[28] This particular proverbial phrase has an anecdote behind it. As the story goes, a Cambridge carrier, Thomas Hobson, kept a large stable where every man who requested a horse was not allowed to choose among all the horses but instead was obliged to take whichever one stood nearest the stable door. It was that horse or none.[29]

A contemporary Hobson, known as Old Hobson, the Merry Londoner, had been gaining a reputation for his wit, a reputation which was significantly enhanced in the early seventeenth century with the publication of *The Pleasant Conceites of Old Hobson.* Edited by the prolific *Volksbuch* author, Richard Johnson, the work went through multiple editions before midcentury.[30] As Hobson the wit became known through the jestbook, the tale of Hobson the carrier faded, and origins of the expression "Hobson's choice" blurred. Of course, there's nothing inherent in the proverbial phrase to suggest that the understood reference shifted from the Cambridge carrier to the Merry Londoner, but a variant of the phrase makes the shift apparent. Thomas Morton used the variant in his tongue-in-cheek work *New English Canaan* (1637). He wrote, "And Scogans choise tis better [than] none at all."[31] Scogan was the purported author of another widely known seventeenth-century jestbook, *Scogan's Jests.*

Scogan's name could only be substituted for Hobson's in the phrase *after* the original identity of Hobson had blurred and people had begun associating the proverbial phrase with Old Hobson, the Merry Londoner. So the phrase "Hobson's choice" originated in the oral culture, but the publication of two *Volksbücher,* "Hobson's Jests" and "Scogan's Jests," shifted the original reference and therefore enriched the language of the proverbial phrase.

The History of Fortunatus, a narrative of the adventures of a man who acquired an inexhaustible purse and a magic cap which made him invisible and transported him anywhere he wished to go (AT 566), was popular in early America. Copies were imported into Boston during the seventeenth century, and later colonial booksellers also advertised the work for sale.[32] Two proverbial phrases can be directly traced to the *Fortunatus Volksbuch.* "Fortunatus's purse" indicates, often ironically, any seemingly inexhaustible supply of money, while "Fortunatus's wishing cap" referred to the ability (or, more precisely, the hope) to transport one's self anywhere instantly.[33] Thomas Jefferson was fond of using the second phrase. While in Paris serving as minister to France, Jefferson wrote an American correspondent who had written him previously and relayed information about his family. Jefferson responded, "The distance to which I am removed renders that kind of intelligence more interesting, more welcome, as it seems to have given a keener edge to all the friendly affections of the mind. Time, absence, and comparison render my own country much dearer, and give a lustre to all it contains which I did not before know that it merited. Fortunatus's wishing cap was always the object of my desire, but never so much as lately. With it I should soon be seated at your fireside to enjoy the society of yourself and family."[34]

In a letter written to a distant female correspondent some months earlier, Jefferson had used the same idea and, in so doing, provided additional context: "I wish they had formed us like the birds of the air, able to fly where we please. I would have exchanged for this many of the boasted preeminences of man. I was so unlucky when very young, as to read the history of Fortunatus. He had a cap of such virtues that when he put it on his head, and wished himself anywhere, he was there. I have been all my life sighing for this cap. Yet if I had it, I question if I should use it but once. I should wish myself with you, and not wish myself away again."[35] Though Jefferson's affectionate epistle to his lady friend has a deliberate literary quality, the witty litterateur-persona cannot mask Jefferson's genuine fondness for *The History of Fortunatus* or his continuing delight with the idea of Fortunatus's wishing cap. As the letter suggests, Jefferson first read *Fortunatus* during his youth. After reading the *Volksbuch,* he found the notion of a wishing cap which could transport him anywhere an attractive one, and the proverbial phrase entered his personal vocabulary. There's no telling how often he may have used the phrase. It may have remained dormant until Jefferson found himself engaged in the business of transatlantic diplomacy, when its aptness allowed him to recall the idea of Fortunatus's wishing cap.

One of the most notable chapbook titles issued during the eighteenth century was *Anson's Voyage Round the World.* Different cheap editions were imported from London, and there was also a locally printed one available. In 1760 and 1761, Boston printer Benjamin Mecom printed W. H. Dilworth's chapbook version, *Lord Anson's Voyage Round the World.*[36] The book became so widely known that Anson's name entered the figurative language, and "as far as Anson's voyage" became a proverbial comparison. Esther Edwards Burr, for example, found it a useful phrase to describe her feelings about moving her family from Newark to Princeton, New Jersey. She wrote a correspondent, "I find I was not settled till I had a Child, and now [that] I am effectually settled, a journey seems a Vast thing. I am to go to Princeton soon, which seems like Ansons voyage almost."[37]

The most important literary genre which early America contributed to the *Volksbuch* was the Indian captivity narrative.[38] Not surprisingly, Mary Rowlandson's *Soveraignty & Goodness of God,* the finest of all Indian captivity narratives, appeared in numerous chapbook editions. Retitled *The Narrative of the Captivity,* Rowlandson's account was revived in the early 1770s and went through many editions during the next several decades.[39] Chapbook publisher Nathaniel Coverly issued multiple editions of the work. The title page of Coverly's 1795 Amherst, New Hampshire, duodecimo edition contains a note which verifies that it was issued largely for the chapbook trade: "Great allowance by the gross or dozen." The traveling bookseller, Chapman Whitcomb, also had an edition printed.[40] Just as Anson's name had entered the figurative language, Mary Rowlandson's, too, became part of a proverbial comparison, "as many removes as Mother Rowlandson." In 1786 Jeremy Belknap, for instance, wrote his longtime correspondent, Ebenezer Hazard, "I remember, when you removed your family to New York, you complained of the inconvenience. I now can, more fully than I could then, adopt the same language and entertain the same feelings. Once I could be at home anywhere. From the time I went to college till my settlement at Dover I had near as many removals as Mother Rowlandson (this is a New England comparison, and will make Mrs. Hazard laugh)."[41]

Of the *Volksbuch* characters which have entered the proverb lore, perhaps none are as well known as Old Mother Hubbard. The proverbial comparison "As bare as Mother Hubbard's cupboard" remains applicable and continues in use today any time there is little food in the house. This folk simile is one of those which has been repeated often but seldom recorded. Bartlett Jere Whiting does not list it in *Early American Proverbs,* nor do Archer Taylor and Whiting list it in *A Dictionary of American Proverbs and Proverbial Phrases, 1820–1880,* nor does Whiting list it in *Modern Proverbs and Proverbial Sayings,* but, to be sure, it has been in use almost since *Old Mother Hubbard and Her Dog* appeared in chapbook form during the nineteenth century.[42] Growing up in the 1960s, I remember hearing it from my parents nearly every Thursday (Friday was grocery-shopping day). Often, they expressed it not as a simile but as a metaphor: "This place is a real Mother Hubbardsville."

While works such as *Anson's Voyage,* Rowlandson's captivity narrative, and *Old Mother Hubbard* enlivened the chapbook trade, some of the older titles lost popularity. The centuries-old narrative *Volksbücher* retained a large readership, but the seventeenth-century didactic works lost ground. One staple of the colonial American chapbook trade, *Old Mr. Dod's Sayings,* slowly lost popularity. A New Hampshire publisher retitled the work *Moral Reflections: Or Flowers Selected from the Garden of Mr. Dodd* to make it appeal to a more refined readership, but there was little that could be done to rescue the once popular work. One more edition appeared before Old Mr. Dod faded into oblivion.[43] The pious maxims which had seemed so useful and pertinent during the seventeenth and early eighteenth centuries seemed a little old fashioned by the later decades of the eighteenth century. Americans tired of brown bread and Gospel and wanted more in their diet. Fortunately, Boston printer Benjamin Mecom had the solution and published a different collection of pithy sayings to appeal to more modern readers.

For the 1758 *Poor Richards Almanack,* Benjamin Franklin had gathered many of his most memorable sayings into "Father Abraham's Speech." As Franklin later explained in his *Autobiography,* "These Proverbs, which contained the Wisdom of many Ages and Nations, I assembled and form'd into a connected Discourse prefix'd to the Almanack ... as the Harangue of a wise old Man to the

People attending an Auction. The bringing all these scatter'd Counsels thus into a Focus, enabled them to make greater Impression."[44] Mecom, Franklin's nephew, subsequently reprinted the essay separately as *Father Abraham's Speech*. That Mecom intended the edition for the chapman's trade is clear from a note on the title page: "NOTE, Very good Allowance to those who take these by the Hundred or Dozen, to sell again." The work became known as *The Way to Wealth* and was reprinted numerous times through the nineteenth century.[45] *Johnson's Almanac, for the Year 1808* reprinted *The Way to Wealth* with the following headnote: "Tho' the following may be an old story to old people, it may be new to their children, and be of as much service to them as it has been to their parents." Joshua Sharp, the compiler of *Johnson's Almanac,* need not have worried, for copies of *The Way to Wealth* were still being printed in large quantities and distributed wherever the itinerant booksellers went. A Massachusetts edition printed the same year as *Johnson's Almanac* carried much the same message on its title page as Benjamin Mecom's original edition had a half-century earlier: "A very great allowance to all travelling Traders, who take them to sell again."[46]

 The Way to Wealth is the single most important early American contribution to the international *Volksbuch* tradition. Like *Old Mr. Dod's Sayings, The Way to Wealth* presented a collection of pithy maxims which readers could use to help guide their lives, but Franklin offered a very different message from Dod. "God helps those that help themselves" and "He that lives upon Hope will die fasting" present a much different viewpoint from Dod's pious admonitions, but Franklin, acutely understanding his contemporary (and future) readers, cleverly shaped the work to avoid offending devout Christian readers. In fact, they embraced the work. In the early nineteenth century, *The Way to Wealth* was published in chapbook form by the Christian Tract Society as one of their "tracts designed to inculcate moral conduct on Christian principles."[47] Franklin's proverb "God helps those who help themselves" is often misattributed to the Holy Scriptures.

 The chapbook editions of *The Way to Wealth* were directed specifically to a humble readership. An 1816 edition also contained a brief sketch of Franklin's life. The preface to the biographical sketch provides a good sense of the intended readership for the book. It explains that the work is "designed almost exclusively to benefit the labouring part of community—those whose daily bread is the fruit of their daily toils." The preface goes on to explain that though "the affluent and the great ... may condescend to look into these pages," that "to the young farmer and mechanic is a thorough acquaintance with this little volume recommended."[48] To be sure, young farmers, mechanics, and other working-class men were not the only readers of the work. The American Antiquarian Society copy of the same edition is inscribed "Anna Allens Book." In much the same way as the different formats of *Old Mr. Dod's Sayings* had done a century and a half before, different formats of *The Way to Wealth* helped expand its readership. The work also appeared in small-format, profusely illustrated children's editions and as a broadside.[49] Benjamin Franklin explained in his *Autobiography* that the broadside editions were designed "to be stuck up in Houses."[50]

Though Father Abraham's speech and the Franklinian sayings it incorporated first appeared in *Poor Richards Almanac,* it is important to note that the numerous Franklin proverbs which entered the language did so largely through the *Volksbuch,* not the almanac. Almanacs were printed once and usually cast away at year's end, but the *Volksbuch* could be printed and reprinted as often as demand required. And demand required it often. Indeed, the text of *The Way to Wealth* was treated with such awe and respect that the work began taking on reverential qualities which earlier had been associated with pious works. In Herman Melville's *Israel Potter,* John Paul Jones discusses the work with Potter and remarks, "I must get me a copy of this, and wear it around my neck for a charm."[51] Melville, of course, was being facetious, but the words he put in the mouth of John Paul Jones should be taken seriously. Only the most powerful texts were so used.[52] In Western culture, both the Holy Scriptures, as chapter 3 will show, and black magic texts, as the following chapter will show, were used as charms. By the time Melville was writing in the 1850s, the influence of *The Way to Wealth* on American culture had become absolutely pervasive. Together, a *Volksbuch* and its proverbs helped shape the world view of an emerging nation.

The Sixth and
Seventh Books of Moses

"Moses," wrote Zora Neale Hurston after her experience among the hoodoo practitioners of the American South, "is honored as the greatest conjurer." Moses a conjurer? In the Bible, Moses does accomplish some astonishing feats—turning his rod into a serpent, bringing several plagues upon the pharaoh of Egypt and his people, parting the Red Sea—but no where does the Bible equate Moses with a conjurer, that is, a practitioner of the black arts. The word "conjurer" is not used in English translations of the Bible. The word "magician" is, but only to refer to the pharaoh's magicians, never to Moses. In order to understand how Moses could become known as a great conjurer, it is important to look beyond the biblical text and examine the oral tradition.

Hurston's comment originally appeared in her 1931 essay "Hoodoo in America."[1] Her experiences among the Negro conjure doctors of New Orleans taught Hurston Moses's importance within the African American oral tradition. She became fascinated with the figure of Moses and mentioned him several other times in subsequent writings. In 1934, she published a short story which presents a conversation atop Mount Nebo between Moses and a lizard.[2] *Mules and Men,* her fine treatment of African American folklore, reprinted her "Hoodoo in America" essay, which also included an impressionistic summary of the folk beliefs concerning Moses. *Tell My Horse,* which contained a lengthy section on voodoo in Haiti, reiterated the importance of Moses in the oral tradition—African, Caribbean, and American.[3] Hurston's fascination with Moses culminated in her third novel, *Moses: Man of the Mountain,* a retelling of the life of Moses which also serves as an allegory of the African American experience.[4]

Though classified as a novel, *Moses: Man of the Mountain* remains the fullest treatment of the African American folk beliefs concerning Moses. Indeed, the story closely follows the brief remarks

Hurston made about Moses in *Mules and Men*. It also closely follows the Bible. In terms of its basic plot, *Moses: Man of the Mountain* differs little from the biblical story. What does differ between the two are the individual details concerning how Moses accomplished what he did. The Bible says little about his youth, but Hurston treats Moses's boyhood activities in great detail. In the novel, young Moses urges the pharaoh's magicians to teach him their magic tricks. After he leaves Egypt for Midian, he encounters Jethro, who, himself a conjurer, imparts his knowledge to Moses, who ultimately exceeds Jethro's abilities. At one point, Jethro calls him "the finest hoodoo man in the world."[5] Moses's quest for magical knowledge culminates in his search for the Book of Thoth. Once he finds the book and reads it, he can "command the heavens and the earth, the abyss and the mountain, and the sea." He knows "the language of the birds of the air, the creatures that people the deep and what the beasts of the wilds all said."[6] Hurston's description of the Book of Thoth emphasizes the importance of books for the practice of magic. Among the hoodoo practitioners she encountered during her fieldwork in the American South, magic books often functioned as icons of power. Part of the charm of Hurston's novel comes from the way she blends hoodoo methods into Moses's behavior. After he reads the Book of Thoth, for example, Moses takes a piece of papyrus, copies out the book's text, washes off the writing with beer, and then drinks the beer to make sure he will never forget what he has read.[7] The process of dissolving a written message and then ingesting the solution was a common hoodoo practice. In *Moses: Man of the Mountain*, Hurston portrays Moses as he was understood within the African American oral tradition and therefore conveys several widely held yet seldom recorded beliefs.

The handful of comments which have been gathered from twentieth-century hoodoo practitioners echo Hurston's folk portrait of Moses. One of Harry M. Hyatt's New Orleans informants, known only as Hoodoo Book Man, claimed, "*Hoodooism* started way back in de time dat Moses days, [*sic*] back in ole ancient times, nine thousand years ago. Now you see, Moses, he was a prophet jis' like Peter, Paul an' James. An' den he quit bein' a prophet an' started de *hoodooism*."[8] As a conjurer, the Hoodoo Book Man thus placed himself in a direct line of descent from Moses. Thomas Smith, a Georgia Negro born into slavery, told an interviewer during the 1930s that the same magic power that Moses had used when he turned his rod into a snake before the pharaoh still existed among the Negroes. "Dat happen in Africa duh Bible say," he explained.

"Ain dat show dat Africa wuz a lan uh magic powuh since duh beginnin uh histry? Well den, duh descendants ub Africans hab duh same gif tuh do unnatchul ting."[9] Though brief, Smith's remarks express much. In three sentences, he wends his way through several dubious assumptions. First, he posits continuity between Egypt and sub-Saharan Africa. Next, he asserts that one act of magic performed by one person on the African continent endows all people throughout the continent, throughout all time with magical powers. Finally, he suggests that anyone whose ancestors came from Africa inherited those same magic powers as a matter of course.

Thomas Smith's remarks and, to a lesser extent, those of the Hoodoo Book Man show how contact with written culture can reinforce a deeply rooted oral culture.[10] Thomas Smith built his superstructure of assumptions on the authority of the Bible, but his Moses-as-magician idea derives from the oral tradition. The written text, therefore, both sanctions and helps perpetuate the folk legend. The authority of the Bible validates the folk beliefs, and common characters and motifs allow biblical stories to serve as a continual reminder of the folk legends. Much like Hurston's *Moses: Man of the Mountain,* the legends do not necessarily contradict the biblical text; instead, they embellish those aspects of Moses's life on which the Bible remains silent. Reading or hearing stories about Moses from the Bible, people keep his name familiar and provide the opportunity for alternative stories about Moses to circulate as part of the oral tradition.

In *Tell My Horse,* Zora Neale Hurston wrote that "wherever the Negro is found, there are traditional tales of Moses and his supernatural powers that are not in the Bible, nor can they be found in any written life of Moses. . . . All over the Southern United States, the British West Indies and Haiti there are reverent tales of Moses and his magic."[11] In the introduction to *Moses: Man of the Mountain,* she wrote, "Africa has her mouth on Moses. All across the continent there are the legends of the greatness of Moses."[12] The association between Moses and magic has long been part of the European oral tradition as well. In his *Natural History,* for example, Pliny listed Moses as an important figure in the development of magic, and Apuleius called Moses a magician in his *Apology.*[13] The offhand and undetailed references from these two ancient authors suggest that their contemporary readers were familiar enough with the Moses-as-magician idea that it was unnecessary for either to supply extra detail. Other surviving documents from the Greco-Roman tradition, magical papyri and spurious writings attributed to

Moses, reinforce the traditional link between Moses and magic. Summarizing the early written evidence outside of Scripture in his 1972 study, John G. Gager concluded, "Jewish tradition and Egyptian syncretism agreed that Moses possessed a higher knowledge of the divine than most mortals. For advocates of the magical arts, whether Jewish or not, the essence of this revealed *gnosis* was Moses's knowledge and transmission of the divine name, not the tenets of the law as in Jewish scriptures and much of rabbinic Judaism."[14] Gager's conclusion based on surviving documentary evidence from antiquity differs little from the conclusion based on African American oral tradition which Hurston had made forty years before him: "The names he knowed to call God by was what give him the power to conquer Pharaoh and divide the Red Sea."[15]

· · ·

A surviving papyrus dating from the third or fourth century A.D. bears the title "Holy Book Called the Monad or the Eighth Book of Moses Concerning the Sacred Name."[16] While there is no evidence that Moses himself had anything to do with the manuscript or that it is in anyway related to the Pentateuch, its existence raises an intriguing possibility. If there are five books of Moses (the Pentateuch) as well as an eighth book, then what has happened to the sixth and seventh books of Moses? The same question occurred during medieval times, and a *Volksbuch* purporting to be the sixth and seventh books of Moses long circulated in manuscript.[17] Manuscript copies of the work circulated in colonial America as well, especially in those regions of Pennsylvania settled by the Germans.[18] In 1849, an enterprising German bookmaker published *Das sechste und siebente buch Mosis* at Stuttgart. The work was reprinted in Germany during the following decade, and copies of the German work were brought to America. The German version was republished in the United States during the 1850s and 1860s.[19] By 1880, the book had been translated into English, and editions of *The Sixth and Seventh Books of Moses* were published at Chicago, New York, and Philadelphia that year.[20] Another late-nineteenth-century edition was published at Cleveland. Undated English editions have been published at Chicago, Hackensack, Memphis, and Philadelphia.[21]

Numerous other editions have been published bearing neither dates nor places of publication, but anecdotal evidence helps supply what the bibliographical evidence does not. From the 1880s, copies could be found among the Obeah men of the West Indies.[22] An early-twentieth-century correspondent from Reading, Pennsylvania, remarked that the *Sixth and Seventh Books of Moses,* along with a local *Volksbuch,* Johann Georg Hohman's *Long Hidden Friend,* vied for popularity among the Pennsylvania Germans: "It is a fact that there are a number of 'witch doctors' in eastern Pennsylvania, and they do a flourishing business. Hohman's book and the 'Seventh Book of Moses' are, I understand, the foundation of their practice."[23] Lauron William De Laurence, the author of *The Book of Magical Art, Hindu Magic and East Indian Occultism,* published a new edition of *The Sixth and Seventh Books of Moses* at Chicago in 1910.[24] Arthur H. Lewis recorded an African American hoodoo practitioner from York County, Pennsylvania, using a copy during the second decade of the twentieth century.[25] During the mid-1920s, Newbell Niles Puckett reported that the sale of the book was "enormous" and its use widespread among Negroes in the American South.[26] A new American edition appeared in 1938.[27] In *Moses: Man of the Mountain,* published the following year, Zora Neale Hurston wrote, "In America there are countless people of other races depending upon mystic symbols and seals and syllables said to have been used by Moses to work his wonders. There are millions of copies of a certain book, *The Sixth and Seventh Books of Moses,* being read and consulted in secret because the readers believe in Moses."[28] Reviewing Hurston's novel, Louis Untermeyer confirmed the widespread knowledge of the book among white Americans.[29] Though Hurston's "millions" seems hyperbolic, it is important to note that the numerous recorded copies represent only a small portion of the total number of editions. Library copies are rare now because the book gets stolen almost as soon as it reaches the shelves. The standard bibliographical references list no new editions or reprintings between 1938 and 1970, yet during that period Harry M. Hyatt recorded numerous instances of its use in the American South, including those of the Hoodoo Book Man whose reputation, even his identity, depended on the work.[30] In the early 1960s and again in the 1970s, a ska and reggae group recorded a song called "Six and Seven Books of Moses," an indication of the work's popularity in Jamaica.[31] The book was reprinted again during the 1970s. The following decade one edition was published in New York and another in Arlington, Texas.[32] The book is currently in print in no less than four separate editions.[33] As proof of the work's continued use, the newest editions have been designed and edited to make it as user-friendly as possible. One edition, available as an inexpensive pamphlet, explained in its preface that "the issue of a cheap edition will be more serviceable than the formerly expensive productions on sorcery, which were only circulated in abstract forms and sold at extortionate rates."[34] A different edition is spiral-bound so that it will lie flat during use. In another edition, *The New Revised Sixth and Seventh Books of Moses,* the work's contents have been rearranged and simplified to make it easier to use, just as the contents of the seventeenth-century *Volksbücher* were often simplified and rearranged.[35] Though I largely focus on the book in North America, it is important to note that copies have been located through much of Europe well into the twentieth century. During the 1970s, Hans Sebald found evidence of its use in Franconian Switzerland, East Prussia, the Upper Palatinate, and Saxony.[36]

The Sixth and Seventh Books of Moses, often simply called the Seventh Book of Moses, purportedly contains the secrets of Moses's magic as well as other magical practices derived from the Kabbalah and the Talmud. Basically, the work is a compilation of seals, tables, and talismans with kabbalistic engravings to use when calling forth spirits. Accompanying the various seals and symbols are explanations of their powers, directions to be followed, and conjurations to be recited in order to evoke those powers. The Sixth Table of Jupiter, for example, assists in overcoming lawsuits and can help win games of chance. Also included is a section on the magical use of the psalms. Psalm 72 ("He shall judge thy people with righteousness . . ."), for instance, explains, "This Psalm will free anyone from prison if prayed by him reverently seven times daily."[37]

Describing the book's contents, a hoodoo practitioner from Memphis, Tennessee, said, "You know you heard of the *Seventh Book of Moses.* . . . That book contains symbols. There's the symbol of Jupiter, Jupiter being the god of lawsuits and financial plenty. You cut that symbol, before you go to trial you bury that symbol and you recite the 72nd Psalm . . . which is supposed to forset all lawsuits."[38] This informant's remarks provide one reason why many copies of the book have escaped the bibliographer's attention—because the book has been victim of the scissors during the course of its use.[39] Many of the directions for using the various seals and talismans contained within the book require the practitioner to inscribe facsimiles of the seal on a piece of cloth placed on the floor and recite a conjuration above the seal, yet this user, instead of redrawing one of the elaborate seals, simply snipped it from the book. Here, the hoodoo practitioner has used the book to work magic, yet instead of following its instructions, she has devised her own method of using it by conflating it with other hoodoo practices. Frequently, other written texts—most often individual psalms—were copied onto slips of paper and buried in the ground or carried as amulets. She has thus made the book more useful because she has made its magic easier to use. Furthermore, in so doing she has given the printed page added significance. The act of redrawing a seal, as the book's directions stipulate, suggests that the magical power resides in an image which could be replicated with no loss of power. Snipping a page from the book, on the other hand, suggests that the magical power is inherent to the printed page.

While some users of *The Sixth and Seventh Books of Moses* situated the book's power in the seals it reprinted, others placed the book's power within its verbal conjurations. Sometimes the power came from reciting these conjurations, while others found that the written text could act as a charm. One early-twentieth-century reporter from Pennsylvania explained, "One [charm] that serves as a fair sample consists of a small muslin bag, intended to be hung around the neck. On the outside of the bag appear the letters, 'I.N.R.I.' and some meaningless characters. Inside is contained a scrap of paper, on which was written a charm, made up, as are many of the incantations of the witch doctors, from a curious book which many of them possess, and which is called the 'Seventh Book of Moses.'"[40] This practice suggests that the written text possessed powers which did not need to be read but only to be brought into close proximity with the human body for its magic powers to work, a notion which many other bookish superstitions reiterated.[41]

Since *The Sixth and Seventh Books of Moses* provides access to supernatural powers, owners of the book have generally kept its contents secret. Those who own copies have often denied it. For example, one old man from Carbon County, Pennsylvania, who had practiced powwowing through much of the twentieth century and whose magic clearly had been influenced by the work denied that he owned a copy of it when he was confronted.[42] While book owners have been reluctant to discuss the work, rumors of its powers have frequently been circulated in the oral tradition. Indeed, many, if not most, of the folk beliefs surrounding the book have been propagated by people who have never seen a copy of it.

Ideas about the purported origins and contents of *The Sixth and Seventh Books of Moses* vary greatly. In the mid–twentieth century one woman simply called it a "mysterious old book" and remembered "hearing grown men whisper about" it when she was a child.[43] A New York informant called it "a book of mystic facts about the hex and lessons in how to put the hex on people."[44] An Ohio informant suggested that the book referred not to the biblical Moses but to a different person named Moses: "It's a German origin, but this [is] not from the authentic Bible. It's a magician Moses, and a lot of people think it's from the Bible, but it's not." Another Ohio informant explained, "The Seventh Book of Moses was lost from the canon, and was never incorporated in the Bible. Some people have copies. It tells how to call up spirits, contact the dead, and gain the powers of sorcery." Yet another suggested that "the Seventh Book of Moses is supposed to be part of the Bible expurgated because of its dangerous powers."[45] In Jamaica, the book is associated with other books of the Old Testament.[46] Hyatt's Hoodoo Book Man attributed its authorship to Moses and dated the foundation of hoodooism to Moses's composition of the book.[47] As these various attitudes indicate, ideas about the book's purported origins vary greatly. Some assert that it was never part of the Bible, others that it once was part of the Bible but since has been expurgated, and still others that it is indeed part of the Bible.

Such divergent opinions have resulted from a combination of rumor, gossip, curiosity, and fear. A female informant from a Pennsylvania German background explained that she had heard something about the book but readily admitted she knew little about it: "There's a certain book in the Bible that you would read backwards to become a witch. It's something to do with Moses but I never was that inquisitive to find out what it was. . . . It was considered the book of the devil. What it was I don't know."[48] The woman's fragmented information, brief as it is, seems contradictory. How could something be a "book in the Bible" as well as "the book of the devil"? Well, one way a religious text could be diabolically perverted was for it to be read backward. It was a commonplace superstition that reading sacred texts in reverse would call forth evil spirits. In a magician's legend from Iceland, for example, a sorcerer writes the Lord's Prayer backward on a piece of paper and then chants it to raise a ghost. In a British legend, to cite one further example, some schoolboys call forth the devil by reciting the Lord's Prayer backward.[49] Another informant also emphasized the importance of reading in reverse. In order to read *The Sixth and Seventh Books of Moses,* he explained, you must start at the "back of the book—at the bottom of the last page and read it upward, every word backwards, else you would become insane."[50] Though the female Pennsylvania German informant does not explicitly mention *The Sixth and Seventh Books of Moses,* her description leaves little doubt. Her remarks show that she was curious about it but hesitant to express too much curiosity about a devil's book.

Stories of the supernatural feats which a person could accomplish using *The Sixth and Seventh Books of Moses* are as varied as the ideas about its origin and its contents. A Cleveland woman simply stated that the book gave its owners "great supernatural power."[51] Legends recorded in New York and Texas suggest that the book could be used to call forth evil spirits.[52] Other beliefs are more specific. One man, it was said, could turn another into any animal or serpent he wished.[53] One person who admitted having never seen a copy stated that the book could "put spells on man and beast, from boys to bumble-bees."[54] Another stated that quotations from it could stop bleeding.[55] A New York man claimed that he knew a person who, by using the book, could milk a neighbor's cow "merely by squeezing a dish towel."[56] An African American informant born during the late nineteenth century stated, "If you walk along a cemetery at a certain time in a certain direction and read from the Seven Books of Moses, things will happen."[57]

These suggestions clearly come from the oral tradition, not from firsthand experience with the book itself. *The Sixth and Seventh Books of Moses* contains nothing so bizarre or specific as directions on how to milk a cow from a distance or how to hex a bumblebee. And none of its directions require a person to walk past a cemetery as he reads the book. These sometimes elaborate rumors about *The Sixth and Seventh Books of Moses* suggest that an actual book, much like a historical personage, could enter the oral tradition and, in so doing, be transformed into something very different. Just as it is important to distinguish between the historical Moses and the legendary Moses, so too is it important to distinguish between the actual *Sixth and Seventh Books of Moses* and the legendary *Sixth and Seventh Books of Moses*. In its transformation from the actual to the legendary, the book's ordinary qualities have disappeared while its supposed powers have been greatly exaggerated.

Some went so far as to suggest that *The Sixth and Seventh Books of Moses* could be lethal. A young American woman of German ancestry explained, "When anyone died in the area . . . they stated it was because the woman in the county had a copy of this book, and wanted this person dead."[58] A New York informant also described the book's deadly possibilities: "If you had the book, you could kill an enemy without being near him, or you could put a curse on a person in a hundred different ways."[59] One Illinois story detailed how a book owner read his victim to death:

> A man came to our house one day. He was a south-Quincy farmer who used to bring us chickens, eggs and butter. He trembled as he sat

there, and as he sat there his eyes dilated. He had an obsession and we could not dissuade him into a saner way of thinking. He said, "I can't live long," held up his shaking hand as evidence that he had been *ferhexed.* The strange part that came from his conversation was that a man possessed a *devil book* from which he read backward. This man had said to our farmer, "*I shall read you to death out of my devil book.*" And when our farmer asked him from where he got the book, he said that he had inherited it and that originally and years ago it had come from Germany. When plowing the man was unable to control a straight furrow. Always when these spells were upon him he would look up and find this man reading from the road across the way in a field or perhaps sitting on horseback. As time went on he received a phychic [*sic*] communication which told him his blood, sinews and muscles were drying up. You could trace the muscles and veins up his arm and see where they were drying up. Life's pump was beginning to fail. As he pitifully gazed into my face he said, "I shall not be with you long, for the spell of the *ferhexing* will carry me to the next world." And he never came back any more. He died.[60]

Some of the stories about *The Sixth and Seventh Books of Moses* concern the book owner's responsibilities. In part, the text of the work has contributed to its superstitious handling as it cautions the reader: "He who refuses a copy of this book, or who suppresses it or steals it, will be seized with eternal trembling like Cain, and the angels of god will depart from him."[61] The tales and beliefs about the book, however, have greatly elaborated on the ways it should be handled. One owner was said to be unable to read the book until two of its pages had been glued together with blood.[62] Some believed that special precautions were necessary to properly dispose of the work. A New York storyteller described two neighbors who argued over a copy of it, and, in order to settle their dispute, decided to get rid of the book by burying it "in the cellar of a neighbor's house . . . where it was never to be disturbed again."[63] An Illinois man from a German background explained: "A man in the south part of Quincy had the *Seventh Book of Moses* and he gave it away to a man one day downtown, and when he got back home the book was on the table. After you have that book you just can't give it away, for it will always come right back to you" (motif D1602.10).[64] In Scandinavia, similar beliefs are held toward the *Cyprianus Volksbuch,* a dreaded volume of sorcery analogous to *The Sixth and Seventh Books of Moses.* The owner of a *Cyprianus* "can never get rid of it, for whether he sells it, burns it, or buries it, it always returns to him—and yet, if he cannot rid himself of it before his death, things will go badly with him then."[65] Though recorded during the twentieth century from an

informant with a German background, the following story dates
back to the 1870s:

> My aunt years ago near Columbus [Illinois] had the *Seventh Book of
> Moses.* My daughter's husband's grandmother took it. She bewitched
> my son-in-law's mother. She took sick and was sick a long time. They
> did everything for her but nothing done her any good. Then someone
> told her to take her urine and put it in a bottle and hang it up in the
> chimney, and that would make whoever bewitched her suffer so they
> would come and confess. So she put her urine in the bottle, put it in
> the chimney, and the old woman did come and confess, and brought
> the book back, too. Just as soon as the book was in the house she got
> well again and didn't have any more trouble.[66]

Time and again the stories of *The Sixth and Seventh Books of Moses*
emphasize the power which comes from possession. Owning the
book means having the power.

. . .

Though few books have developed as colorful a reputation as *The
Sixth and Seventh Books of Moses,* others have become part of the
folklore in similar ways. Johann Georg Hohman's *Der lang verbor-
gene Freund,* a Pennsylvania German *Volksbuch,* was first published
at Reading, Pennsylvania, in 1820 and republished several times
throughout Pennsylvania during the following decades.[67] The work
was subsequently translated as *The Long Lost Friend* (1856) and
The Long Hidden Friend (1863) and has more recently been published as *Pow-Wows.* Unlike *The Sixth and Seventh Books of Moses,*
The Long Lost Friend provides remedies to cure specific ailments. It
has been printed and reprinted numerous times, and its influence has
extended well beyond the borders of nineteenth-century Pennsylvania.[68] Like *The Sixth and Seventh Books of Moses, The Long Lost
Friend* has been published in many more editions than the number
recorded. E. Grumbine mentions a 1903 Lancaster, Pennsylvania,
edition for which the demand was "very considerable," yet the
standard bibliographies do not list the edition.[69] Arthur H. Lewis
estimated that around 150 editions totaling perhaps half a million
copies of the work had been published during the century and a half
since it first appeared. In York County, Pennsylvania, during the late
1920s, the book became the center of a sensational murder trial as a
self-confessed witch and his two teenage accomplices were convicted
of murdering another witch because he refused to surrender a lock
of his hair and his personal copy of *The Long Lost Friend.*[70] During
the last third of the twentieth century, a Chicago informant described

The Long Lost Friend as the only medical book, besides the almanac, a person needed to stay healthy.[71] The book was reprinted not long ago and has since remained in print.[72]

Another *Volksbuch* which achieved a significant reputation in nineteenth-century France and was not unknown in twentieth-century America was *Le Dragon Rouge, ou L'art de commander les esprits célestes, aériens, terrestres, infernaux, avec le vrai secret de faire parler les morts*. Though surviving editions are dated 1521 and 1522, these imprint dates are fictitious. The book was first published during the early nineteenth century, reprinted into the second half of the century, and also translated into Italian.[73] One of Richard Dorson's informants from Michigan's Upper Peninsula had much to say about the book:

> The "Red Dragon" is a powerful book. You can do everything that you wish with it. It is in nine volumes. It is only the priests who can have the ninth, no one else. An extraordinary secret! With it you can put out the fire a hundred miles away. It is a book which possesses the Devil.
>
> Fifty-four years ago, the proprietor of a hotel in Escanaba was a man who made no practice of religion, who owned this book. One day I went up into his room, I saw this book there. It was written in red, as if with blood. It was stamped, "printed in London." In that city are published many indiscreet books, books the most secret. It is forbidden to read that book. It gave me a fright. I started to read the book; I could not make it out! "Black magic" is something that you cannot understand.[74]

This informant's description of the book contains much misinformation. *Le Dragon Rouge* was a one-volume work published in several places throughout France; there are no recorded multivolume, foreign-language editions printed in London. Having told and retold his story for over half a century, the man had liberally embellished his original tale. Still, the extraordinary powers he attributes to the book are not dissimilar to powers attributed to *The Sixth and Seventh Books of Moses*, such as the idea that only priests could possess powerful books of magic. One informant suggested that both priests as well as witches owned copies of *The Sixth and Seventh Books of Moses*, but a priest dared not read it unless the pope had given him special dispensation for research into "psychical research or other approved profound reason."[75]

Similar *Volksbücher*, popularly known as "Le Grand Albert" and "Le Petit Albert," have been popular in France and other French-speaking parts of the globe. Le Grand Albert, or, more precisely, *Les admirables secrets d'Albert le Grand,* was first published during the early seventeenth century and republished numerous times during the eighteenth and nineteenth centuries.[76] Though nominally the work of Albertus Magnus, the work is spurious. Le Petit Albert, specifically *Secrets merveilleux de la magie naturelle et cabalistique du Petit Albert,* a work published under the pseudonym Lucius Albertus Parvus, first appeared during the last third of the seventeenth century and was reprinted numerous times during the eighteenth and nineteenth centuries.[77] Copies of Le Petit Albert have been located among the nineteenth-century French peasantry, the hoodoo practitioners of New Orleans, and the Obeah men of the French West Indies.[78] During the nineteenth century, the popularity of Le Petit Albert outstripped that of Le Grand Albert, but the earlier work was by no means forgotten. *Le grande et veritable science cabalistique,* a three-part work published in Paris during the 1860s, contained Le Grand Albert, Le Petit Albert, and *Le Dragon Rouge.*[79]

Another *Volksbuch* which has fostered a significant folk reputation in the United States and the West Indies is *Albertus Magnus; Being the Approved, Verified, Sympathetic and Natural Egyptian Secrets; Or White and Black Art for Man and Beast,* a work attributed to, but, like Le Grand Albert, not actually written by Albertus Magnus. Rather, it is a compilation made in Germany during the early nineteenth century.[80] The preface explicitly states the book's raison d'être: "For the purpose of rendering a great service to mankind, this book was issued, in order to bridle and check the doings of the Devil."[81] The book contains a variety of spells and recipes for curing physical ailments. Perhaps most striking is the cure for cancer: "When a human being takes hold with his right hand of a live mole, and keeps the mole so long with a tight grip until it dies, such a hand obtains by dint of this miraculous proceeding, such marvelous power, that cancer boils, repeatedly rubbed, by moving up and down with this hand will break open, cease to form again, and entirely vanish."[82] *Albertus Magnus* went through numerous editions during the last third of the nineteenth century and the first third of the twentieth, including one edited and published in Chicago (1910) by Lauron William De Laurence. During the 1920s, the Chicago edition could be found as far away as Trinidad.[83] One undated copy, whose place of publication is given as Toledo, indicates the secret quality of the book's contents. Strips of paper, mounted along the edges of the first and last pages and sealed with wax, indicate that the volume had been sealed, presumably before purchase.[84] *Albertus Magnus* remains in print and in demand. When I went to my local bookstore here in Oklahoma City to order a copy, the clerk informed me that several other people had the book on order.

Like *The Sixth and Seventh Books of Moses, Albertus Magnus* undoubtedly has been published in many more editions than have been recorded, but the recorded editions reveal much. Perhaps the University of Pennsylvania copy of the 1875 Harrisburg, Pennsylvania, edition of *Albertus Magnus* is the most revealing. A printed slip pasted over the first line of the title page reads "The Seventh Book of Moses."[85] The actual contents of *The Sixth and Seventh Books of Moses* and *Albertus Magnus* were quite different. Where *The Sixth and Seventh Books of Moses* contained symbols and talismans with accompanying conjurations, *Albertus Magnus* contained sympathetical and magical recipes and cures for man and animal. That *Albertus Magnus* could be sold as the Seventh Book of Moses verifies how secret the contents of both works were kept. People who did not own the book had little idea what it contained. All they knew about it is what they might have heard from the oral tradition. The secret contents of *The Sixth and Seventh Books of Moses* made it easier for the publisher to sell another work as the Seventh Book of Moses. That a publisher could market *Albertus Magnus* as the Seventh Book of Moses suggests that the actual contents of either book were much less important than their symbolic and iconographic value. *The Sixth and Seventh Books of Moses,* in other words, was more important for the magic potential it embodied rather than for any of its individual spells.

That *Albertus Magnus* could be sold as the Seventh Book of Moses also indicates Moses's selling power. The publisher obviously had surplus copies of *Albertus Magnus* to unload, so what better way to do so than to give it the title of a much more ominous and powerful book which had many more folk legends about it. This copy of *Albertus Magnus* further substantiates that, though other books have become part of the North American folk tradition, no other book has generated as much folk belief, superstition, and legend as *The Sixth and Seventh Books of Moses*—that is, no other book except that which contained the first five books of Moses, the Holy Scriptures. As Zora Neale Hurston explained in "Hoodoo in America": "All hold that the Bible is the great conjure book in the world."[86] Some of the many folk uses for the Bible will be taken up in the following chapter.

Superstition and the Book

Book ownership has given rise to numerous beliefs and superstitions. While some involve the act of reading, others treat the
book as a physical object with an authority which transcends
the text contained inside its covers. Some superstitions respect the
book's physical integrity, but others require their owners to purposefully deface volumes. Still others assert that mishandling a book can
cause enormously bad luck. Used knowingly, however, books can
help tell the future, increase intelligence, heighten spirituality, scare
away ghosts, exorcise the devil, and guard against some illnesses
while curing others. Folk beliefs about books touch every aspect of a
person's life, from birth through childhood and adolescence, court-
ship and marriage, and illness and death.

Some of these folk beliefs affect the infant's development even
before birth. When a woman is carrying her child, one superstition
has it, she should place a book on her stomach to make sure the
newborn baby will be intelligent. According to another, if a woman
reads educational material during pregnancy, her child will be smart.[1]
While both of these superstitions supposedly produce the same ends,
their means differ significantly. The first stipulates that physical
contact between an expectant mother and a book is sufficient to
make the child smart, while the second requires the mother to take a
more active role and read during pregnancy in order to affect the
child's intelligence. The second superstition emphasizes the sense of
sight and the powers of cognition, while the first privileges the sense
of touch. Superstitions about books often place the sense of touch
above the sense of sight. According to many, simply touching a book
can dramatically effect both knowledge and spirituality.

Bringing the newborn in physical contact with the Bible can pro-
foundly influence the child's future. One Illinois woman believed that
just after a boy is born but before he is dressed, his head should be

placed on a Bible to assure he will become a preacher. An Ohioan similarly believed that a Bible should be placed in a newborn's hands to make him a minister.[2] While these two superstitions provide for the child's future career, others are less specific. Some suggest that bringing the infant in physical contact with the Bible will allow him to lead a more exemplary life. To make sure your child will be kind, honest, and good throughout his life, another stipulates, place his umbilical cord between the pages of a Bible.[3] These practices do not require the text of the Bible to be read or even acknowledged. There is no need for the infant to know how to read or even to have cognizance of the Bible for them to have an effect. Physical contact alone permits the child to receive its spirituality.

Other superstitions are associated with early phases in the infant's development. Many concern the moment the first louse appears on a baby's head. While these may only last as long as bad hygiene persists, the numerous superstitions which call for a mother to crack her baby's first louse on a book suggest that book ownership does not necessarily imply good hygiene. Some say that as soon as a mother finds the first louse in her baby's hair, she should crack it on a Bible, for the child will then become a preacher.[4] A Kentucky belief stipulates that cracking the baby's first louse on the Bible will enhance the child's reading abilities.[5] Cracking it on a songbook or a hymnal will guarantee that the child will be a good singer.[6] An Ozark superstition suggests that the mother should make a wish about a baby boy's future profession as she cracks the louse on the family Bible.[7] A more detailed practice calls for the mother to open a Bible at random, drop her baby's first louse into it, and close the book. The verse on which the louse gets smashed foretells what will happen to the baby. Reading biblical text as individual prophecy may sometimes require considerable interpretive efforts, while other times the text's meaning may be disturbingly apparent. Pity the poor mother whose child's first louse end up smashed on a passage from Psalms: "Let his children be continually vagabonds." Or Revelation: "I will come on thee as a thief."[8]

While book ownership is essential for carrying out the practice of louse cracking, enacting these superstitions actually defaces the book. Using a Bible to smash bugs—even if it is for purposes of divination—hardly seems to respect the book as a physical object or, for that matter, the Deity its text represents. Understood as a symbolic gesture, ritual louse-cracking, while it may stain the cover or even the pages of a Bible, is a cleansing process. The louse, both literally and figuratively, represents the world's filth. The moment a mother finds the first louse on her baby's head marks the first time the world's filth evidences itself on the infant. Head lice essentially indicate the child's movement from innocence to experience. Removing the first louse and cracking it on a Bible's cover or within its leaves provides a way to restore—albeit fleetingly—the child's innocence. While the smashed bug may physically sully the Bible, the Bible's transcendent purity cleanses the child, guaranteeing that he or she will lead a more exemplary life. The worst thing a parent can do (or rather, the worst thing short of not removing the lice at all) is to crack lice on the baby's head. Doing that, superstition says, will make the child a simpleton.[9]

A more widely practiced superstition involves a ceremony which takes place on, or sometimes before, a child's first birthday. Several objects—usually three—are placed in front of the infant. The first object the child touches indicates his future. A frequent combination is a dollar bill, a bottle, and a book. If the infant takes the dollar, he will be rich; if he touches the bottle first, he will become a drunkard; and if he touches the book, he will become a scholar or, if the book placed before the child happens to be the Bible, a preacher.[10] While most of the superstitions recorded in North America use the masculine pronoun "he" to refer to the child, one belief supplied by a woman of Polish Catholic descent in mid-twentieth-century Ohio suggests that baby girls also participated in this divination ritual: "On a child's first birthday have a relative come over to the house and place various objects in front of the child. If the child reaches for a rosary, she'll become a religious person. If she reaches for a glass, she'll become a drinker; if money, she'll be rich; if for a book, she'll become a scholar. People used to put out dirt under the belief that if the child reached for it, she would soon die."[11] This informant's last remark suggests that during her lifetime the ritual had undergone a change in its level of seriousness. No longer, she suggests, do people use objects which may foretell an early death. While similar superstitions have been recorded from North Carolina to Utah, the stipulated objects often vary. If the child chooses a hammer, he will become a carpenter.[12] A hat, a snappy dresser.[13] An apple, a farmer.[14] Pen and paper, an artist.[15] A button, a tailor. A piece of bread, a baker.[16] And a deck of cards, a gambler.[17]

The different combinations offered to the infant are puzzling. Why would parents deliberately select objects which would predict that their child would become a drunk or a gambler? Or that she would soon die? One Illinois belief stipulates that if the child touches a pair of scissors first, he will become a murderer![18] Why use any objects which portend a wicked future? Why not use only those objects which anticipate the child's future success? I believe these superstitions, with the possible exception of the scissors, indicate a healthy sense of reality. Using only those items which predict wealth or prestige may establish unrealistic expectations for the parents or set unrealistic goals for the child. If a dark future were portended and the son or daughter turned out okay, then the parents could be thankfully relieved.

Why do so many of these superstitions stipulate a book as one of the possible items? Does the book, like the dollar bill, have positive connotations? The wording of the child's future occupation within the recorded beliefs may help answer these questions. While the superstitions use the word "scholar" for the book-touching child more often than any other, some use "bookworm," a pejorative label which indicates a person who has a love of learning but little cognizance of the real world. While it may be difficult for some—me, for example—to understand how the prospect of a child with his nose always stuck in a book could be a bad thing, less bookish parents may dislike the idea. A recent bumper sticker—yet another way print culture can help perpetuate folklore—provides additional support. On the bumper of an Oklahoma pickup truck, I recently read the following: "My kid can beat up your honor student." This bumper sticker reacts to the numerous others which begin "My child is an honor student" and end with the name of the child's school. It indicates a code which devalues intellectual accomplishments in favor of more physical ways of proving one's superiority. Of course, there's an important difference between the one-year-old's prediction and the bumper-sticker message. The prediction indicates one possible future for a child who has yet to prove himself, while the bumper-sticker message provides an after-the-fact way to accept a child's less than exemplary performance in the classroom.

The bookworm prediction also indicates the possibility that the child will differ from other members of the family. By touching the book and therefore indicating that he will become a scholar, the child shows that he will become learned and, consequently, may stop believing and practicing the superstition. As a scholar, the son or daughter thus becomes a threat to the superstitious family. A scholar might debunk the superstition or refuse to perpetuate it with his own children. Such an explanation reconciles the apparent differences between the murderer and the scholar. Becoming a murderer, the scissors-touching child would fulfill the prophecy yet destroy the social basis of the ritual. Normally, this divination ritual takes place on a child's first birthday, a festive occasion celebrating life during which many family members eagerly gather to watch the child make his choice. A murderer's act is antithetical to this celebratory superstition. Both the murderer and the scholar, therefore, threaten this superstitious practice, and, as a result, both threaten the cohesiveness of the folk group which practices such superstitions.

. . .

More people are involved with books during their schooling than in any other time of their lives, and numerous superstitions concern the relationship between the book and the act of learning. The sometimes arduous process of studying, combined with the uncertainty of doing well in school, has given rise to superstitions which guarantee scholastic success. Perhaps the most widely known schoolbook superstition requires the student to put his textbook beneath his pillow before going to bed to make sure he will know his lesson in the morning.[19] Sleeping with a book beneath the pillow suggests that proximity to the book is sufficient to acquire its knowledge. The folk expression for this process, "learning by osmosis," supplies an especially apt metaphor. Just as nutrients pass from one cell to another through the cell membrane during the organic process of osmosis, knowledge passes through the medium of the pillow from the book to the mind. The metaphor thus treats the book as a living thing which can impart its knowledge to anyone nearby.

Studying from a smart person's book or reading a used book, some believe, can also help a student do well in school.[20] To continue the metaphor, this superstition suggests that the process of osmosis between book and reader works in both directions. Just as information could flow from the textbook to the student, a smart person's intelligence could flow into the book. Since smart people are generally associated with books, studying from one of their schoolbooks, a less-gifted student might hope for wisdom by association.

After a person finishes studying for the night, another belief stipulates, he should not, under any circumstances, leave his book open, or else he will forget what he has read.[21] This superstition suggests a different organic process. Here, the book and the reader share a symbiotic relationship. The book and the mind are attached, and the state of one depends on the state of the other. The book becomes an outward manifestation of the mind, and its physical state reflects the inward condition of the memory. Literally closing the book, the student gives the studying process closure. The act of closing the book seals the knowledge inside the brain so that it cannot escape. Perhaps not surprisingly, a slang expression for a person who seldom speaks or shares little of himself is "a closed book."

No matter how carefully a person studies the night before a test, things can still go wrong on test day. Dropping a book, according to a common superstition, means that the student will do poorly on an exam.[22] Other superstitions, however, provide ways to avert such bad luck. Stomping on the book before picking it up is one way to cancel the bad luck.[23] Picking up the book and immediately kissing it can also counter the bad luck.[24] Stomping on a book seems to denigrate the book, while the act of kissing it suggests veneration. It may seem unusual that two such different acts—one violent, the other affectionate—could produce identical results, but neither respect nor disrespect for the book motivates these two superstitions. Though they treat the book differently, each allows the student to reestablish the physical contact with the book which was lost when it was dropped. Much like the superstitions associated with infancy, these also stress the importance of touch.

. . .

Many superstitions and practices concerning the Bible and other religious books are similar to those schoolchildren hold toward textbooks. "Never leave a religious book open on the table," one cautions, or "you will forget what you read."[25] Dropping the Book of Mormon, a Utah superstition has it, will cause bad luck.[26] A dropped Bible or prayer book must be picked up and kissed in order to avert bad luck.[27] Unlike those for schoolbooks, religious book superstitions show respect for the book. I have located none which require the book owner to stomp on his Bible before picking it up.

Other superstitions concerning the Bible further emphasize such reverence. For good luck, a Bible should be one of the first things new homeowners bring into their home.[28] Furthermore, placement of the Bible within the home is crucial. It should never be put on the floor.[29] Rather, it should be kept on the center of a living room table.[30] Also, no other book should ever be allowed to rest on top of the Bible. If you place something atop the Bible, you will have bad luck until the object is removed.[31] One informant, recalling her mother's attitude, explained that it was "tragedy" when her father would sometimes forget the superstition and set his newspaper on the Bible.[32] Conveying the relationship between the two printed items, this informant's recollection makes the father's absentmindedness understandable. The newspaper was something that family members read everyday, whereas the Bible had stopped being regular reading material and instead had become part of the furniture, a coffee table decoration. Though it may have been read seldom, the Bible remained important within the household as an icon. Just as other coffee table books—usually lavishly illustrated art books—attempt to signify a family's cultural sophistication to their guests, the prominently displayed Bible similarly attempts to show a family's piety. In turn-of-the-century Pennsylvania, some rural families kept copies of Johann Georg Hohman's *Long Lost Friend* on the table in the parlor or best room of the house, a gesture which demonstrated a family's supernatural power to visiting members of the community yet also served as an amulet to guard the home from misfortune.[33]

It was crucial to protect the Bible from physical harm. Damaging it could cause bad luck.[34] For example, one Illinois informant reported, "My grandfather used to say it was bad luck to tear leaves out of a Bible."[35] This superstition appears so obvious that it hardly seems necessary to be said. Why would anyone deliberately tear leaves from a Bible, or any book for that matter? The grandfather's superstition, however, counters others which do indeed require people to tear leaves from the Bible for purposes of protection, healing, or divination. Much like the seals from *The Sixth and Seventh Books of Moses* or the individual charms from Hohman's *Long Lost Friend,* biblical verses—most often psalms—were sometimes snipped from the Bible and used as amulets (motif G271.2.5 [c]).[36] While dropping the Bible could be remedied with a kiss, I have located no folk remedies to reverse bad luck created by damage to a Bible. Even when Bibles or other religious books were worn out from normal usage, they should not be thrown away or incinerated: "Don't destroy a book with God's name in it. Bury it, or you will have bad luck."[37]

Bedtime superstitions often make use of the Bible. Reading before bed has long been a way to promote sleep, but books could also counter insomnia even if they were not read.[38] Sleeping with a Bible under the pillow, superstitions recorded from Nova Scotia to North Carolina say, prevents bad dreams.[39] According to other beliefs, the Bible under the pillow can also prevent snoring,[40] talking in sleep,[41] sleepwalking,[42] convulsions,[43] and other kinds of restlessness.[44] Most of these superstitions specify the Bible, but any book containing the Lord's name could be substituted in a pinch.[45] While sleeping with the Bible or another religious book may seem to impart spirituality in the same way that sleeping with a schoolbook could impart knowledge, these superstitions are not motivated by hopes for devotion "by osmosis." Rather, the belief underlying such practices concerns thwarting witches or devils during their nighttime visits.[46] In order to render a devil helpless, he must be given an impossible task. When a person goes to sleep with a book nearby, the devil must read the volume cover to cover or count every letter of its text prior to working his mischief. With the Bible or other religious books, the devil simply cannot read past the name of the Lord (motif K211.1). In a British legend, an inadvertently summoned devil is given the seemingly impossible tasks of counting the blades of grass in a meadow and the grains of sand on a beach, which he accomplishes with no problem. It is only when he is asked to count the letters in the Bible that he falters.[47]

A superstition recorded in both the American Midwest and South suggests that it is lucky for a person to sleep with a newspaper under their bed.[48] This superstition says much—I had almost said, speaks volumes—about folk attitudes toward print culture. The idea that a newspaper can guard against the devil suggests how intimidating a newspaper could be. The sheer amount of text in a daily newspaper is enough to overwhelm even the ablest devil. Counting the letters of its text has become an impossible task analogous to counting blades of grass or grains of sand.

· · ·

No one can completely avoid illness, but aches and pains sometimes can be prevented and other times alleviated with books, according to many superstitions. Many consider the Bible the great cure-all. The ways the Bible can prevent or treat illness differ significantly from one ailment to another. Sometimes physical contact between a patient and a book is sufficient to effect a cure. Other times, specific passages of text must be read before the patient can get well. Often, book and text must be used in combination to produce an effective cure.

Soldiers have tried to avoid life-threatening battle wounds by carrying a Bible. Family legends frequently tell stories of ancestors saved from certain death during battle by a strategically carried Bible. Retelling his experiences as a rare book dealer, A. S. W. Rosenbach wrote, "Among the hundreds of Bibles offered to me each year there is one type which blooms eternal. It is the bullet-hole Bible: the Bible which saved grandpa's life in the Civil War, or the Revolution— as you will. . . . Some people have fondly believed that a tale of sentiment, plus a dash of bravery, mixed with their own simulated reverence, would bring value to the family Bible."[49] Rosenbach's comments suggest that the Bible needed to be carried in front of some

vital organ for it to effectively prevent a deadly bullet. Others, however, asserted that simply carrying a Bible anywhere on the person
would guard against enemy fire.[50] Still others believed that carrying
the whole Bible was superfluous; all the soldier needed to do was to
pin a copy of the Ninety-first psalm over the heart.[51] The psalm concerns the Lord's protection in times of conflict. Its seventh verse
reads: "A thousand shall fall at thy side, and ten thousand at
thy right hand; but it shall not come nigh thee." Whether a soldier
pinned a copy of the Ninety-first psalm over his heart or whether
he placed a whole Bible in a chest pocket indicated the degree of
his superstition or, perhaps, his level of faith. For the believer, the
Ninety-first psalm—either torn from a copy of the Bible or inscribed
on a separate sheet of paper—was sufficient. For the skeptic, a good,
thick Bible kept in a chest pocket might more effectively stop a
bullet. During World Wars I and II American soldiers could easily
practice these superstitions. In both wars, Bibles were distributed to
servicemen in huge quantities.[52] The relatively small number of surviving copies may be attributed to the fact that certain pages and
passages of Scripture were torn from the Bible and the rest of the
volume discarded. During World War I, steel-plated Bibles were sold
to people in the United States to send to their relations at the front.[53]
If one leaf from Psalms indicated a different level of belief than a
whole Bible, the idea of armor-plated Scriptures indicates a third.
Though many stories of armor-plated Bibles may be apocryphal, the
whole idea implicitly questions the value of God's word in itself for
providing protection from enemy gunfire.

Many superstitions for curing physical maladies rely on the Bible
as a magic talisman. Its curative properties, in other words, depend
on its physicality, not on any specific passages of text. Much like
those concerning newborn babies, the superstitions for illness often
require physical contact with the book. If a person is ill, place a
Bible to the temple, and he will get well.[54] To get rid of a bursa, drop
the family Bible on it.[55] Hit a wart with a Bible and it will go away.[56]
To get rid of a lump on the back of your hand or wrist, slam a Bible
on it (cf. motif G271.2.5 [b]).[57] One Hawaiian healer particularly
attributed sickness to a person's failure to read the Holy Scriptures
and used the Bible to effect her cures. She would "take her Bible and
put it on the head of the sick person, saying, 'In the name of Jesus
Christ.' The demons within would be tormented by the presence of
the Bible, which tells of Christ, and so the sick person would back
away and try to push the Bible away."[58] For each of these supersti-

tions, simply placing the Bible in physical contact with the afflicted area is sufficient to affect a cure. Of course, the Bible did not always heal injuries. In *Huckleberry Finn,* Mark Twain spoofed such superstitions. After Boggs is shot, the townspeople place one Bible under his head and an opened Bible across his chest. The Bibles cannot save him, for Boggs soon passes away.[59] Even for the terminally ill, however, a nearby Bible could be a comfort. One informant reported, "A man's wife was dying hard. Someone told him that her last hours would be eased if they put a Bible under her pillow. He did this and said it sure worked, for she died in about ten minutes."[60]

Other superstitious cures combine the idea of physical contact between patient and book with a specific passage of text. Opening the Bible to the Twenty-third Psalm and placing it on the head can alleviate a headache.[61] The Twenty-third remains one of the most memorable of all the psalms ("The Lord is my shepherd . . ."), yet it also contains a specific reference which might help relieve a headache ("Thou anointest my head with oil . . ."). With this particular superstition, however, reading or understanding the psalm is unimportant. What is important is the physical contact between the afflicted head and the printed page on which the psalm occurs. Here, a sheet of paper, once printed with a magical psalm, takes on powers which transcend the printed page.

No other Bible cure has been more widely recorded throughout North America than blood stopping, but no others have been surrounded by so much confusion. The amount of information and the precise details about how the Bible could be used to stop the flow of blood differ greatly. Most informants stated that reading a specific Bible verse could stop a bleeding wound, but many did not know or would not say which verse.[62] Some diligent folklorists who have collected numerous tales and superstitions in the field have been unable to identify the specific verse. In Alabama, Carl Carmer recorded multiple instances of the blood-stopping superstitions but could find no one who would tell him which biblical passage.[63] In Michigan's Upper Peninsula, Richard Dorson recorded many stories about blood stopping without precisely identifying how the process of blood stopping worked.[64] Knowing which verse can stop blood, however, would usually not be enough to work the cure because, according to superstition, only people who have the power can stop the blood flow.[65] Furthermore, this power was a fickle thing. If a person with the power told another person which Bible verse stopped the flow of blood, he or she would lose the power or it would be transferred from the teller to the listener.[66] One old woman told a friend that she already had told the secret to three persons, and that if she ever told a fourth, she would lose her power.[67]

These beliefs about losing the power explain one reason why so many people who knew about the superstition did not know which Bible verse worked. The power required secrecy. The practice of this superstition also has helped healers protect their secret. The healer would ask the name and age of the bleeding, go into a room alone, and recite the Bible verse and possibly some additional magic words. Once the magic verse had been recited, the victim's bleeding presumably stopped.[68] This superstition suggests a somewhat different relationship between supernatural power and the book. With other superstitions and beliefs, especially those concerning *The Sixth and Seventh Books of Moses,* power came with possession of the book, but in this case, the power exists separately from the book. By the way, the blood-stopping verse is Ezekiel, chapter 16, verse 6: "And when I passed by thee, and saw thee polluted in thine own blood, I said unto thee when thou wast in thy blood, Live; yea, I said unto thee when thou wast in thy blood, Live."[69]

• • •

Bibliomancy, the practice of using books for divination, dates back to classical times. The ancient Romans practiced what was known as *sortes Virgilianae.* A copy of the *Aeneid* would be opened and a pin stuck randomly into a passage of text. The selected text would foretell the future (motif D1311.14). The practice of seeking *sortes* continued through the Middle Ages, into the Renaissance, and even beyond. In *Gargantua and Pantagruel,* for example, Rabelais had Pantagruel supply Panurge advice about his forthcoming marriage using the technique. "Bring me the works of Virgil," Pantagruel commands, "and, opening them with your fingernail three times running, we'll explore, by the verses whose numbers we agree on, the future lot of your marriage."[70] To convince Panurge of the method's worth, Pantagruel describes several historical instances when Homer's *Iliad* and Virgil's *Aeneid* had been used similarly for divination purposes. A few chapters later, Pantagruel completes the procedure. The three passages from Virgil, as Pantagruel interprets them, indicate that Panurge's future wife will beat him, rob him, and cuckold him.[71] Though Rabelais makes fun of the practice, he clearly delights in this intersection of book culture and folk belief.

The attitudes toward poets embodied within the ancient Roman culture made Virgil's works appropriate for divination. As Sir Philip

Sidney best explained, "Among the Romans a Poet was called *Vates*, which is as much as a diviner, foreseer, or prophet . . . so heavenly a title did that excellent people bestow upon this heart-ravishing knowledge. And so far were they carried into the admiration thereof, that they thought in the chanceable hitting upon any such verses great foretokens of their following fortunes were placed."[72] If all poets had some prophetic ability, it made sense that the most highly regarded poets, Virgil and Homer, had the greatest ability to see the future. Indeed, it was not unusual for people to carry pocket editions of Virgil for such purposes. Describing an episode when King Charles consulted Virgil for the purpose of seeking *sortes,* John Aubrey wrote that he obtained a copy of Virgil from Abraham Cowley, who "alwaies had a Virgil in his pocket."[73] The practice of *sortes Virgilianae* remained popular through the Renaissance and into the nineteenth century, gauging by the sporadic references of its use. In Robert Louis Stevenson's *Ebb Tide,* for example, Robert Herrick carries "a tattered Virgil in his pocket" with which he would "dip into the Aeneid, seeking *sortes.*" In a pinch, other works from classical antiquity could be pressed into service for divination. In Herman Melville's *Confidence-Man,* for instance, the man with the weed discovers the young collegian who holds a copy of Tacitus: "'Pray, now, my young friend, what volume have you there? Give me leave,' gently drawing it from him. 'Tacitus!' Then opening it at random, read: 'In general a black and shameful period lies before me.'"[74]

While the practice of seeking *sortes* continued after the Renaissance, the Bible largely supplanted the *Aeneid* as a more appropriate book to use for divination purposes. The shift from the ancient classic to the Bible during the history of this superstition reveals much about attitudes toward the book in Western culture. With the dissemination of print technology, literacy, defined as the ability to read the vernacular, increased while simultaneously a smaller percentage of the literate population learned to read classical languages. In other words, more and more people learned to read as fewer and fewer learned to read Latin. Protestant reform took the Bible from Latin, Greek, Hebrew, and the other Near East languages into the vernacular and thus made its text accessible to the people. During the course of its history, the printed Bible has become increasingly affordable and easier to handle. Prior to the Protestant reformation, the Catholic hierarchy feared blasphemous lay interpretations and long kept the Bible from the hands of the people. The reformers, however, held that the Bible belonged to the people and made Bible reading an important part of salvation. After the invention of printing, vernacular Bibles became available throughout Protestant regions. The Catholic leaders kept the Bible in Latin and in the hands of the priests for some time, but their conservative efforts could not be maintained indefinitely, and bandit vernacular translations began circulating among the Catholic population.[75] As vernacular Bibles began to be printed in huge quantities and disseminated throughout the Christian world, however, it became impossible to punish the blasphemous use of the Bible while sanctioning its use for private and family devotion. With little fear of punishment for blasphemy, people put the Bible to use for such profane purposes as divination rituals. *Sortes Virgilianae* largely disappeared as *sortes sanctorum* emerged.

The divination rituals associated with the Bible have become more varied and elaborate than the traditional practice of seeking *sortes*. Make a wish, then open a Bible at random. If you see the words "And it shall come to pass," the wish will come true.[76] Sometimes the wisher must open the Bible three times in a row and see the phrase "It came to pass" each time for the wish to come true.[77] If you open the Bible and your finger rests on the words "Verily, verily," then you will have good luck.[78] The Bible could also be used to solve personal problems and to make decisions. Worry could be treated using the technique: "If worried open the Bible. The first verse the eyes fall upon will tell whether your worry is necessary or not."[79] Confusion and uncertainty could also be dispelled: "Well you know when you are real puzzled about something, that you can't find the answer, you just say the Lord's Prayer and open the Bible and put your finger on a verse, and usually that will answer the question for you."[80] Decisions, too: "If you have to make a decision, open the Bible and point to a word without looking. Open your eyes; if the word is 'Yea,' go ahead, but if the word is 'Nay,' then do not go ahead with what you may be considering, because it would be unwise."[81]

Some have made it a New Year's Day tradition to open the Bible at random in order to foretell their future for the year,[82] a process known in Great Britain as "dipping": "A Bible is laid on the table at breakfast time, and those who wish to consult it open it at random, and it is supposed that the events of the ensuing year will be in some way described by the contents of the chapter contained in the two open pages."[83] The following episode was recorded in Great Britain during the mid–nineteenth century.

About eight years ago [c. 1853], I was staying in a little village in Oxfordshire, on the first day of the year, and happening to pass by a cottage where an old woman lived whom I knew well, I stepped in and wished her a happy new year. Instead of replying to my salutation, she stared wildly at me, and exclaimed in a horrified tone: "New Year's Day! and I have never dipped." Not having the slightest idea of her meaning, I asked for an explanation; and gathered from her that it was customary to *dip* into the Bible before twelve o'clock on New Year's Day, and the first verse that meets the eye indicates the good or bad fortune of the inquirer through the ensuing year. My old friend added: "Last year I dipped, and I opened on Job; and, sure enough, I have had nought but trouble ever since." Her consternation, on receiving my good wishes, was in consequence of her having let the opportunity of dipping go by for that year, it being past twelve o'clock.[84]

Words and phrases such as "It came to pass," "verily," "yea," or "nay" make the divination process unambiguous, because their meanings are determined before the ritual begins. Other methods which require a person to interpret whatever passage of text they happen upon, however, may require considerable imaginative effort before a personal problem is solved or a personal future foretold. Rabelais's humor in the fortune-telling episode of *Gargantua and Pantagruel,* after all, comes not from the passages selected by the *sortes Virgilianae* but from Pantagruel's convoluted interpretations of those passages. Sometimes interpreting a biblical text would present no problem. An adolescent girl who happens upon a passage from the Song of Solomon ("Let him kiss me with the kisses of his mouth . . .") would have no trouble discerning its meaning. But other passages may not be so clear cut.

One of the most elaborate yet most widely known divination rituals is the Bible (or Psalter) and key. This ritual predates the invention of print and has been recorded numerous times since the Middle Ages.[85] Originally, the ritual provided a way to detect a thief. A Bible or Psalter would be opened to the Fiftieth psalm ("When thou sawest a thief . . ."), and a large door key placed there with its head protruding from the top. Next, the book would be closed and tied securely with a piece of string or, alternatively, fastened with a garter. Two people would then balance the key by their fingertips with the book suspended below. After reciting the psalm, they would recite the names of the suspects. When the real thief's name was recited, it was believed, the key would turn and the book would fall to the floor. More recently, the Bible and key ceremony has been used to determine the name of someone's future spouse. The process is much the same, but instead of the Fiftieth psalm, the key should be placed on Ruth 1:16 ("Intreat me not to leave thee, or to return from following after thee: for whither thou goest, I will go; and where thou lodgest, I will lodge . . .".). Or the Song of Solomon 2:16–17 ("My beloved is mine, and I am his.") Two people suspend the Bible between their fingertips and recite the verse, followed by the letters of the alphabet. The letter on which the Bible and key turn represents the initial letters of the future wife's or husband's name.

An analogous use of the book and key was recorded in late-nineteenth-century England. It seems a Shropshire woman visited a local conjuror in order to locate her husband. With no Bible handy, he placed a key between the pages of *Guy of Warwick*, a *Volksbuch*, and thus performed the ritual.[86] Though the Shropshire conjuror used a *Volksbuch* in place of the Scriptures, his gesture by no means denigrates the Bible. Rather, it shows the value of any and all printed material. He just as easily could have put the key between a pair of old shoes placed sole to sole, but he did not. The printed text, any printed text, had the potential to provide supernatural information in a way which other material objects could not.

Still, the Shropshire conjuror's use of a *Volksbuch* for the ritual was rare. Nearly always, either the Psalter or the Bible was used to identify husbands and thieves. The book and key ritual for detecting thieves predates its use for predicting spouses for two main reasons. The first concerns the history of the book. Psalters were available to the people long before entire Bibles were available, indeed long before the invention of printing. In fourteenth- and fifteenth-century England, Richard Rolle's *English Psalter* was the only part of the Bible which the laity could use without license.[87] Even after the invention of printing, when vernacular Bibles became available, they were first printed in weighty, expensive formats, while the Psalter was available in lightweight, small-format editions. (After all, the book had to be light enough for the friction between the pages of a book and the surface of a key to suspend it temporarily.) The shift from theft detection to spouse prediction also signals a change in the demographics of the ritual's practitioners from adults to adolescents. This is not to say that the use of Bible and key for theft detection disappeared. Numerous instances of its use for locating thieves were recorded in late-nineteenth-century Great Britain and among twentieth-century hoodoo practitioners of the American South.

Dissemination of the Bible and key ritual has differed remarkably from the dissemination of the blood-stopping superstition. Though the precise way of using the Bible for blood stopping must be kept secret to safeguard its practitioner's powers, knowledge of the Bible-and-key ritual must be shared in order for it to be practiced. Of the numerous recorded instances of this superstition, I have located none which stipulate that an individual could suspend the key between the tips of the right and left hands, though it is physically possible. The Bible and key requires two people. Performing it is a social activity. The fact that knowledge of the ritual must be shared before it can be practiced, however, has limited its powers. Besides detecting thieves and predicting spouses, the Bible and key can do little else. Secrecy, it seems, is a necessary precondition for fostering a book's legendary powers.

Once the word of God became available in inexpensive, portable, vernacular Bibles, people began seeking God's knowledge by using the Bible in other ways besides merely reading its text. The countless superstitions about the Bible suggest that literacy and book owner-ship, far from expunging superstitions, has fostered additional beliefs. As the word of God has been made available to the people in a physical, tangible way, that physical object has lent itself to numer-ous superstitious rituals. The superstitious uses of the Bible are based on the belief that it can reveal divine knowledge in many ways, some of which do not require its text to be read. Reading the Bible allows partial access to divine knowledge, but since that knowledge is infinite, it cannot be circumscribed by or merely contained within human language. The superstitions suggest the popular belief that there are facets of God's knowledge which are accessible to men and women which have nothing to do with reading.

The Book in Icelandic
Magicians' Legends

Though Iceland officially adopted Christianity in the year 1000, magic and religion long continued to be associated within Icelandic belief. The church outlawed pre-Christian religious rituals, but many were modified for Christian purposes. Similar attitudes toward the word—both spoken and written—made possible this blending of pagan ritual with Christian liturgy. After all, both the traditional magic spell and the Paternoster provided their speakers or readers with the opportunity to contact the spirit world in order to effect change upon the earthly.[1] Icelandic folklore reflects this meeting between traditional Icelandic belief and Christian practice. The master magicians of Icelandic legend are nearly always priests or, at least, students training for the priesthood. The clergyman's special relationship with God gave him privileged access to the spirit world, which, according to belief, also permitted him to contact devils, ghosts, and other spirits. Supernatural power was supernatural power, and the process of communicating with a benevolent God or a malevolent spirit differed little to believers. Furthermore, the priest's superior learning, people assumed, increased the likelihood that he knew the black arts. Learning can intimidate. Whenever one person's learning far exceeds that of others, then rumor and legend exaggerate it all the more. Since words, as Kirsten Hastrup has convincingly shown, were "the most important instrument of supernatural power in Iceland,"[2] it should not be surprising that the book occurs as a prominent motif in many Icelandic magicians' legends.

Each legendary master magician has a real-life counterpart from Icelandic history. Sæmundur Sigfússon, known as Sæmundur *fróði*, or Sæmundur the Wise, studied in France during the eleventh century and eventually returned to southern Iceland, where he became priest at Oddi.[3] Sæmundur established a reputation for his learning and apparently wrote the first history of Iceland, though no copies survive.[4] During and immediately after Sæmundur's tenure at Oddi, the place developed a good reputation as a school. Little is now known about the Oddi school, but subsequent Icelandic magicians' legends are usually set around the important schools. Many of the legendary priests studied at or lived near Iceland's traditionally recognized centers of learning, Hólar and Skálholt. Gottskálk Nikulásson served as bishop of Hólar during the early sixteenth century. Hálfdán Narfason served as vicar of Fell in the diocese of Hólar through the first half of the sixteenth century. In legend, Gottskálk would become known as Iceland's most powerful and malevolent magician, whereas Hálfdán, his contemporary, would become known for his benevolent magic.[5] By the mid–sixteenth century, the Danish, who had governed Iceland since the fourteenth, had exerted their influence on Iceland's worship to such an extent that the country adopted the Lutheran faith. Even with the shift from Catholic to Protestant, however, legends of the master magicians persisted. Jón Guðmundsson, also known as Jón *lærði,* or Jón the Learned, was born during the last third of the sixteenth century. Much of his learning was self-taught; he eventually mastered German, Dutch, and Latin. His numerous writings reveal his wide reading. The powerful magic songs Jón used to exorcise a ghost at Snæfjallaströnd did much to advance his reputation as a *kraptaskáld,* that is, a bard whose verse was capable of potent magic. In 1631, Jón was convicted of witchcraft and outlawed for his authorship of a pamphlet describing how to guard against the attack of evil spirits.[6] Eiríkur Magnússon attended school at Skálholt during the middle years of the seventeenth century. He became vicar of the parish of Selvogsþing, where he served until his death during the second decade of the eighteenth century. Galdra-Loftur Þorsteinsson, Eiríkur's contemporary, attended the cathedral school of Hólar and died under mysterious circumstances during the early 1720s.[7] Though few historical documents survive to detail the real lives of these men, each has developed an important legendary history.

One of the earliest legends about Sæmundur concerns his education at the Black School, a place where students supposedly learned witchcraft and magic which the Scandinavian legends generally locate near Wittenberg.[8] "Sæmundur at the Black School" (*ML* 3000) begins: "Sæmundur the Wise travelled abroad and went to the Black School, and there he learnt strange arts. There was no schoolmaster to be seen in the Black School, but whatever the students might say one evening they wanted to know about, books about it would be provided by next morning, or else it might be written up on the walls."[9] This description of the learning process which took place at the legendary Black School says much about the importance of the word within Icelandic culture. In order to make a book appear, the student must first say what he wants. Learning depends upon the book, but the book depends upon speech. The spoken and the written word are thus inextricably linked. The apparent interchangeability between the books and the writing which appears on the wall suggests that the written text is more important than the way that text is conveyed to its reader. The absence of teachers at the Black School adds further importance to writing as a source of knowledge. With the usual schooling process, teachers served as a medium between the student and the book. Without teachers, students at the Black School had to rely on their own interpretations of the text. In "Last Man Out," a variant of "Sæmundur at the Black School," the school is described as "pitch black inside. There were no teachers, either, and the students learned from books written with fiery red letters that could be read in the dark."[10] Another Icelandic legend similarly describes the book from the Black School as "grey and inscribed with fiery letters that shone throughout the room, where there was no other light."[11] These descriptions of reading at the Black School provide a negative image of the traditional reading process. Reading the Bible, the word of God, required an exterior source of light, but the devil's words burned from within, unilluminated by God's light.

A very different legend further associates the power of the book with that of the spoken word. "Ima the Elf-Girl" tells how Jón *lærði* acquired his ability as a *kraptaskáld*. While herding sheep, the story goes, he meets Ima, who quite forwardly tells him all about her family, their home, and her father's magic book "in which there was much marvellous lore, and from which one might learn much." She further explains to Jón that "anyone who read it would become a poet with magic powers in his verse, and few things would come on him unawares."[12] The magical possibilities intrigue Jón, so he asks Ima to borrow it. She agrees to let him have the book for a few weeks. When she returns to reclaim it, he tells her he will never let it go. Despite her desperate efforts, she cannot persuade him to relinquish the magic volume. Soon, another elf warns Jón in a dream that the elves will try and regain the book on Christmas Eve. So he arms himself with a large knife, and when four elves, including Ima, approach him at midnight, he slays them all and keeps the book. Jón's violent efforts both to keep the book and, subsequently, to compose power-wielding verse demonstrate the power of the word. Furthermore, the legend stresses the importance of book ownership. It was not enough for Jón to read from the text to acquire its magical power. Otherwise, he could have returned the book after he had read it. His power came from both reading and possessing the book.

Another legend takes up Sæmundur's story from the time he left the Black School. "How Sæmundur Got the Living of Oddi" tells how Sæmundur and two fellow students, Kálfur and Hálfdán, were each anxious to obtain the clerical position at Oddi which had recently been vacated. Together they ask the king of Norway for the opportunity. He tells them that whoever reaches Iceland first would receive the position. Sæmundur immediately leaves the king and summons the devil ("Old Nick"), telling him, "Swim with me to Iceland, and if you can get me ashore without wetting the skirts of my coat in the sea, you can have me." Success seems sure to Old Nick; Sæmundur certainly cannot avoid getting wet someplace between Norway and Iceland. Old Nick agrees to the bargain, turns himself into a seal, and has Sæmundur climb on his back. Throughout the journey, Sæmundur reads his Psalter, but, as they near Iceland's coast, he raps the seal's head with the book. The seal pitches forward, throwing Sæmundur into the water. Sæmundur then swims ashore by himself and therefore cheats Old Nick of his bargain and successfully obtains the clerical position at Oddi.[13]

Though "How Sæmundur Got the Living of Oddi" makes Hálfdán one of Sæmundur's classmates, their real-life counterparts actually lived five centuries apart. Independent legends concerning Hálfdán, however, also make him a graduate of the Black School. Furthermore, some of the legends told of Hálfdán are remarkably similar to those of Sæmundur.[14] Hálfdán often tricks the devil into working for him and also thwarts him using a Psalter in "The Devil Mows a Meadow." In this legend, he lets Old Nick know that he can have his soul if he mowed the whole meadow at Fell in one night, finishing no later than midmorning. The bargain seems virtually certain, so Old Nick agrees, and, one evening soon after, he begins mowing. As Old Nick comes close to finishing, Hálfdán takes a Psalter from the church and places it on a hillock in the unmown part of the meadow. Old Nick finishes mowing the entire meadow except for the hillock on which the Psalter rested. When Hálfdán returns in the morning, he sees Old Nick making little rushes at the hillock, hacking at it, and then darting away. By midmorning the hillock remains unfinished, and Old Nick loses the bargain.[15]

In these two legends, Sæmundur and Hálfdán demonstrate their power to make the devil work for them. To persuade Old Nick, both must make bargains and presumably put their souls on the line as an enticement, but their souls never really seem in peril. The humorous tone of both legends reassures the listener that Old Nick never really has a chance with either Sæmundur or Hálfdán. In both stories, the Psalter represents the priest's ultimate control over the devil. In each, Old Nick is sure of himself, yet in neither does he pause to consider that the priest has a book which he can never overcome. These two legends convey the same belief as those superstitions requiring sleepers to put Bibles beneath their beds to guard against restlessness.[16] The devil cannot succeed because he cannot read the Lord's name (motif K211.1).

Though the book ultimately thwarts the devil in both legends, it functions differently in "The Devil Mows a Meadow." Hálfdán specifically takes one of the church Psalters and places it on the hillock. The Psalter thus functions as an icon for the church. In "How Sæmundur Got the Living of Oddi," Sæmundur reads his personal copy of the Psalter during the trip across the sea. The legend thus conveys the idea that the Psalter could be carried as a protective charm. Though the tone, theme, and final result of "How Sæmundur Got the Living of Oddi" is much different than the story of Jón lærði in "Ima the Elf-Girl," both legends emphasize the act of reading and the importance of book ownership. Sæmundur's behavior during the passage suggests that reading the Psalter protected him from the devil's evil ways. Given the humorous and light-hearted tone of the legend, however, Sæmundur's act of reading may convey little else but his nonchalance. In other words, he has no trouble leisurely reading during the passage because he knows he can overpower Old Nick at any moment. When he does, the Psalter literally becomes what it had always been figuratively, a weapon to overpower the devil.

Taken together, the stories of Sæmundur and Hálfdán use the book in several different ways. In the Black School, Sæmundur and Hálfdán read and learn from books of black magic. After the two graduate from the Black School, they use the Psalter to control the devil. Neither "How Sæmundur Got the Living of Oddi" nor "The Devil Mows a Meadow" explains how the priest-magicians conjure up the devil. The storyteller simply takes for granted that they can. Sæmundur and Hálfdán may have learned from books of black magic, but they no longer need to rely on them. The prominence of the Psalter in the two stories emphasizes the ultimate benevolence of the two priests. Though both are on intimate terms with the devil, they only use him for beneficial or, at least, practical ends. In other stories of Sæmundur, for example, Old Nick builds a bridge and cleans out the cow barn.[17] The Psalter represents a barrier which protects the two priests from the devil.

Another legendary master magician, Eiríkur Magnússon, while ultimately benevolent, takes much greater chances with the devil than either Sæmundur or Hálfdán. The book appears in many of the Eiríkur stories, but it functions differently than in the stories of the other two. Far from being a barrier between magician and devil, Eiríkur's book seems to provide a conduit through which they communicate. "How Eiríkur Learned His Arts at School" requires much background information before Eiríkur appears in the story.[18] It seems that an old cottager had a reputation as a heathen and a loner. The old man valued two possessions far above all others: "a book, of which nobody else knew the contents, and a heifer which he fed lavishly."[19] Falling ill, the old man sent for the bishop of Skálholt. After the bishop arrived, the old man asked him if he could be buried with his book and his cow. "If not," the old man vaguely threatened, "it will be the worse for everyone."[20] Fearing that the old man would indeed haunt the earth after his death, the bishop agreed to his wishes and carried them out upon his death.[21]

Many years pass, and new students enter the cathedral school at Skálholt. Eiríkur, along with Bogi and Magnus, his fellow Skálholt students, make up their minds to learn magic. The story of the old man intrigues them, so they decide to try and raise him from the dead in order to obtain his mysterious book. Unsure precisely where he had been buried, the three raise the entire churchyard before the old man appears, carrying his book and leading the heifer. The boys attack the old man, but he vigorously fights back. Still, they manage to snatch a few leaves from the first part of his book. The old man attacks again, but the three hold their own. The old man continues to struggle against them until dawn, but at daybreak, he vanishes into his grave. The three friends keep the leaves from the old man's book and use them to compile the manual of magic called *Gráskinna* (Greyskin), an occult book written in secret runes describing evil spells.[22] Eiríkur and his two friends are eventually ordained, and each receives their own parish. Though they keep their magic learning a secret, it is soon rumored that Eiríkur understands witchcraft. After summoning him, his bishop shows Eiríkur the *Gráskinna* and orders him to say whether he knew what was in the book. Eiríkur flips through the pages and then swears to the bishop that he does not understand any of the text. Afterward, however, he tells his friends that he knew all the magic signs it contained, except one.

Eiríkur's quest for supernatural knowledge clearly goes far beyond that of Sæmundur or Hálfdán. "How Eiríkur Learned His Arts at School" mentions two different books, *Gráskinna* and the old man's much more powerful book. An alternative version of the story has Eiríkur take the old man's book and read from it until just before dawn, at which time he returns it to the old man, who then quickly sinks back into his grave. Later the other boys ask him what he had read. "Enough," he tells them, "to know that if I had read any further I would have lost my soul to the Devil."[23] Though Sæmundur and Hálfdán repeatedly put their souls on the line, they never really seem threatened with eternal damnation, but the tone of "How Eiríkur Learned His Arts at School" is much more serious, and Eiríkur genuinely appears to endanger his soul for the opportunity to read about and practice magic.

Though the two versions of the Eiríkur story suggest that no one could achieve complete knowledge of the black arts without sacrificing their souls in exchange, the treatment of the book differs significantly from one to the next. One version places the emphasis on the act of writing, whereas the alternate version stresses the act of reading. The two different emphases affect Eiríkur's portrayal in each story. As an author of the *Gráskinna* in the first version, he achieves an extraordinary level of magic learning as well as tremendous confidence toward his supernatural knowledge. In the second version, Eiríkur learns much from reading the old man's book, but his confidence has been shaken. He frightens before finishing the book and then returns it to the old man without attempting to keep it for himself—which, according to belief, he could have done had he only kept it until sunrise, at which time the old man would have had to return to his grave without it. Eiríkur the author achieves a level of self-confidence and bravado which Eiríkur the reader does not. Writing ability combined with reading ability allows him to achieve a level of power which reading ability alone cannot.

Eiríkur's magic books play a prominent role in many of the stories about him. In "Eiríkur's Pupil and the Book," he uses a magic book as a way to test a boy's capacity for magic power before taking him on as a student.[24] In "Eiríkur Rescues a Woman from the Otherworld," a magic book precipitates the rescue.[25] Before his death, legend has it, Eiríkur buried his magic books under a cairn in Kálfsgil, a ravine among the Urdarfellir Mountains north of Svörtubjörg. Like the old man with the heifer, the legendary Eiríkur did not want anyone else to use his magic books after his death, but, unlike the old man, Eiríkur did not want to be buried with his occult books. In Iceland, it was commonplace for religious men, bishops especially, to be buried with their holy books. One seventeenth-century Lutheran bishop, a contemporary of the real-life Eiríkur, for example, was interred with "his New Testament, Psalter and the Four Evangelists."[26] This burial custom further emphasizes the importance of book ownership within Icelandic culture, but it also suggests that interment with evil books would mean certain doom. Relinquishing his magic books before death, the legendary Eiríkur demonstrated his hope for salvation. Still, he died unsure whether or not he would be saved. Another legend, "The Burial of Eiríkur the Priest," describes the elaborate instructions Eiríkur left his pallbearers. At his funeral, he predicts, there will be a great storm, and then two birds, one white and one black, will fight over which will perch on the ridge of the church roof. The victorious bird will indicate Eiríkur's fate. The story concludes: "All this turned out to be true when Eiríkur died, both about the storm and about the birds, and the white one was victorious over the black, and so Eiríkur was buried inside the churchyard."[27]

Neither version of "How Eiríkur Learned His Arts at School" specifically names the old man's book, but it seems much the same as another book often mentioned in the Icelandic magicians' legends, the *Rauðskinna* (Redskin). Legend generally credits the authorship of the *Rauðskinna* to Gottskálk Nikulásson, the early-sixteenth-century bishop at Hólar. Bishop Gottskálk developed a reputation as the greatest sorcerer of his day. According to legend, he gathered together all the black spells, none of which had been used since heathen times, and compiled them as the *Rauðskinna,* a supposedly magnificent volume bound in red and written in gold-lettered runes. The legendary Bishop Gottskálk taught no one all his lore and unabashedly had his book buried with him.[28]

Knowing the story of Bishop Gottskálk and the *Rauðskinna* is a prerequisite for understanding the story of "Loftur the Magician," the finest of all the Icelandic magicians' legends. Two centuries after Bishop Gottskálk's time, the story goes, Loftur arrives at the Hólar cathedral school, where he spends all his time studying magic. He has his fellow students help him practice magical tricks and often goads them into helping him play pranks on others. After mastering the *Gráskinna,* Loftur seeks knowledge from other magicians only to realize that he already knows more than they. Soon, Loftur's temper sours. He so intimidates and frightens his fellow students that they dare not oppose anything he wants. One day in early winter, Loftur asks another student to help him raise all the ancient bishops of Hólar from the dead. When the other boy hesitates, Loftur threatens to kill him. The boy reluctantly complies without really understanding how he can be any help since he knows no magic. Loftur tells the boy to stand motionless in the bell tower with his hand on the bell rope, stare at him until he gives the proper hand signal, and then ring the bell.

Next, Loftur explains to the boy the motivation behind his plan:

> Those who have learned as much magic as I have can only use it for evil, and must all be lost whenever they die. But if a man knows enough, then the Devil will have no power over him, but must serve without pay as he served Sæmundur the Wise, and whoever knows as much as that is also his own master, free to use his arts for any purpose he wishes. It is not possible to attain to this degree of knowledge nowadays, since the Black School closed down, and Gottskálk the Cruel had his book Red Skin buried with him. That is why I want to raise him up and force him by spells to let me have Red Skin. But the old bishops will all rise with him, for they will not be able to resist such powerful enchantment as well as Gottskálk, so I will make them tell me all the sorcery they knew in their lifetimes—that is no trouble to me, as I can tell by their faces whether they knew magic or not. I cannot touch the later bishops, because they were all buried with the Bible on their breasts. Serve me well and do as I bid you, ring neither too soon nor too late, because my life and my eternal welfare both depend on it, and I will reward you so well that no man shall be your superior.[29]

Loftur's speech sounds like a harangue on the downfall of the modern magician as it harkens back to the glory days of Sæmundur the Wise and the Black School. Like Eiríkur in the second version of "How Eiríkur Learned His Arts at School," Loftur recognizes that learning too much magic imperiled the soul, but, unlike Eiríkur, Loftur does not stop short. Remembering the stories of Sæmundur, Loftur imagines that it could be possible to attain a level of knowledge which could ultimately overpower the devil. Loftur laments that the Black School was closed and Gottskálk buried because the most important sources for magical knowledge, the school and the *Rauð-skinna*, were no longer available. Loftur foolishly imagines the old days of the Black School as a halcyon time when priest-magicians could learn the black arts without taking dangerous chances and risking their souls.

After bedtime, Loftur and the boy leave their beds and quietly enter the cathedral, the boy to the bell tower and Loftur to the pulpit, where he begins to conjure. Soon a man rises through the floor, probably the first bishop of Hólar, and warns Loftur to cease his activities. Loftur, however, persists. One by one, all the ancient bishops rise from their graves, even the three crowned bishops. All, that is, except Gottskálk. Loftur begins addressing his incantations to Gottskálk alone. He turns the penitential psalms of David to the devil's name and confesses all the good he had ever done as if it were a sin. After a tremendous rumbling, Bishop Gottskálk arises through the floor with the *Rauðskinna* under his right arm. He grins at Loftur, taunting him that it will be impossible for him to acquire the *Rauðskinna*.

Gottskálk's taunts anger Loftur and throw him into a berserk fury. He conjures with all his might, reciting the Lord's Prayer to the devil and giving the blessing in the devil's name until the whole church shakes as if in an earthquake. The boy, who had been watching the proceedings from the bell tower in a kind of stunned awe, thinks he sees the bishop teasingly offer the book to Loftur, who seems to extend his hand to take it. The boy then faints, pulling the bell rope as he falls to the floor. The peal of the bells immediately sends the dead bishops through the floor with a great whoosh!

As if paralyzed, Loftur stands in the pulpit for a moment and then eventually staggers to the boy, sighs, and says:

> This went worse than I intended, but I don't blame you. I could well have waited for the dawn, when he would have had to give the book up, and would have laid it on the pulpit himself for me to take, since he would not have paid for it by being kept out of his grave, nor would the other bishops have allowed him to do so. But he won the contest between us, because when I saw the book and heard his mockery I went mad and thought I could get it at once by force of conjurations; I came to my senses when, if I had chanted just one verse more, it would have sunk the whole cathedral into the ground, which was what he intended. In that moment I saw the faces of the crowned bishops, and so stumbled, but I knew that you would turn faint and grasp the bell-rope to sound the bell, while the book was so close to me that I felt I could grasp it. As it was, I touched one corner, and I really did think I had got a grip on it and would never drop it! But what must be, must be, and now my salvation is lost for ever—and your reward too. We must both keep quiet about it.[30]

Loftur has lost the chance to save his soul. The book might have saved him, as he imagined, but, more likely, he never really had the chance to save himself. As the legendary Eiríkur had recognized, achieving complete knowledge of the black arts doomed the magician. Loftur hopes for powers akin to those of Sæmundur the Wise, but he never really understands the sources of Sæmundur's magic. While the legendary Sæmundur had used his Psalter as a weapon

against the devil, Loftur reads the psalms in the devil's name to conjure forth the evil spirit of Gottskálk.

. . .

Few other national legends collectively place as much emphasis on
the book as those from Iceland. The importance of the book within
Icelandic legend mirrors the importance attached to literacy within
Icelandic culture. The prevalence of runes and magic verse in pre-
Christian times shows the Icelander's respect for both the written and
the spoken word. Just over a century after Christianity had been of-
ficially adopted, the see at Hólar was established. Its first bishop, Jón
Ögmundsson, soon founded the school there and hired a man named
Gísli Finnason to teach as well as to help lead the congregation. The
surviving comments about these pioneering educational efforts provide a glimpse into early Icelandic attitudes toward the book. The
"Saga of Bishop Jón," which provides the only substantive description of Icelandic schools during the period of Catholicism, describes
Gísli's preaching technique: "Always when Gísli preached before the
people, he had a book lying in front of him and took from it what
he said to the people. This he did chiefly for the sake of prudence
and humility, because he was young and those who listened to him
put greater value on it when they saw that he took his teachings from
sacred books and that it was not altogether from his own ingenu-
ity."[31] This twelfth-century description emphasizes the importance
the medieval Icelanders attached to the authority of the written page.
They accepted teachings from a book which they were reluctant to
accept via word of mouth. Despite the Icelanders' respect for the
book's authority, it is important to note that their only experience
with books occurred in an oral context. They did not touch the book
or read it themselves. They only experienced the book through the
cleric's mediation.

Two additional anecdotes told as part of the "Saga of Bishop Jón"
demonstrate the respect for learning among the Icelanders during the
early Christian period. One time, Bishop Jón hired a man named
Thórodd to construct the church building: "It is told about this man
that he was so quick at learning that while attending to his work he
listened when the theological students were taught that discipline
which is called *grammatica;* and so well did it stick in his ears
because of his quickness to learn and his attentiveness that he became
most skillful in such learning."[32] Elaborating upon the "Saga of
Bishop Jón," Gunnlaug Leifsson, monk at Thingeyar, supplied a
similar story:

A chaste maiden was also studying there whose name was Ingunn. She was inferior to no one in these studies. She taught *grammaticam* to many and instructed anyone who wished to learn; consequently many men became well educated by her guidance. She expounded Latin books which she [had] had read to her while she herself sewed or weaved or was engaged in other needlework upon the lives of the saints, making the glory of God known to men not only by her words but also by the work of her hands.[33]

These two anecdotes may be apocryphal, yet both assert the compatibility of physical labor and literacy. Thórodd's duties as a responsible laborer did not prevent him from learning nor did Ingunn's domestic responsibilities prevent her from learning or from sharing her knowledge with others. Indeed, her needlework provided a way for her to express what she had read. Both anecdotes convey the hope for widespread literacy extending both to women and the working class, a hope which, however, would take several hundred years to accomplish.

Still, during the twelfth and thirteenth centuries, Iceland's leading classes were generally more literate than their contemporaries in other European countries. Halldór Hermannsson attributes the literacy of the early Christian Icelanders to unique conditions not found in other contemporary European countries. After Christianity had been established and officially adopted, the churches were owned by the chieftains who were responsible for providing priests. Indeed, many of the chieftains were ordained as priests. As community leaders, the chieftains were responsible for maintaining the traditional values. As spiritual leaders, they were responsible for disseminating the Christian beliefs. So, Icelandic tradition and the newly introduced religious beliefs were sustained simultaneously, often in the same person.[34]

Literacy greatly declined during the fourteenth and fifteenth centuries, and it was not until the first half of the sixteenth when Iceland adopted the Lutheran faith and when printing was introduced that literacy began to improve.[35] The Danish Church Ordinance of 1537, accepted in Iceland during the 1540s, provided for new school systems and specifically named the books the Lutheran ministers were required to own. After about 1560, a contemporary observer remarked, books became increasingly common throughout Iceland.[36] During the seventeenth century, the Icelandic press, under the management of Bishop Þórður, published many small-format books for people to carry in their pockets.[37] Þórður's innovation, though it may seem little more than a bibliographical curiosity, actually provides evidence to show the country's increasing literacy during the 1600s. Inexpensive, portable books always signal greater reading opportunities for the masses.

Though the bibliography of Iceland would have us believe that the people who could read directed their attention to devotional works, such a belief is far from the truth. In the introduction to his list of seventeenth-century Icelandic books, Halldór Hermannsson expresses a hunch that the people's literary interests and the products of the press did not precisely coincide.[38] The recent work of Hubert Seelow confirms Hermannsson's hunch. From the mid–sixteenth century, as Seelow has shown, numerous German *Volksbücher* began circulating throughout the country in Icelandic manuscript translations.[39] To understand Icelandic book culture during the period, it is crucial to recognize the coexistence of print and manuscript. People read the printed devotional manuals, but they also had access to the fictional German prose narratives translated into their own language. Reading script, however, was not necessarily the same as reading print; the two were often considered different skills. With a limited literacy, further constrained by an even more limited ability to read script, it seems likely that many of these manuscript *Volksbücher* were read aloud among groups of people.

Perhaps the most important event in terms of Iceland's history of literacy took place during the first half of the eighteenth century. In the 1740s, the Danish king sent a Lutheran clergyman, Ludvig Harboe, to Iceland to survey the reading ability and the knowledge of Christianity among its adolescents. Harboe returned to Denmark and reported that the spiritual education of Iceland's youth was seriously inadequate. Soon, local pastors were ordered to visit the homes of their parishioners regularly and to make sure the children were learning. The subsequent efforts of Iceland's clergy had an astounding effect on the country's education. Remarkably, Iceland achieved near-universal literacy before the eighteenth century ended, the first nation to accomplish the feat.[40] During the last third of the eighteenth century, the traveler Uno von Troil wrote, "You will seldom find a peasant who besides being well-instructed in the principles of religion, is not also acquainted with the history of his country, which proceeds from the frequent reading of the traditional histories (sagas) wherein consists their principal amusement."[41] Also, studies of probate records and estate inventories have shown that nearly all of Iceland's late-eighteenth-century households contained books. Out of some one thousand homes surveyed in the 1780–1800 period, only seven were without books.[42] In an urgent plea for books for Iceland's public and academic libraries made during the last third of the nineteenth century, Willard Fiske wrote, "To no spot can books be sent with so much certainty of their being intelligently and eagerly read as to Iceland. No country reads so many books in proportion to its population, and none is so ill able to purchase them."[43] The fact that most households contained books and that most Icelanders could read them is reflected in an Icelandic riddle: "'What is it in the house that keeps silent and yet speaks to all?' A book."[44]

Though the Icelanders had achieved near-universal literacy by the end of the eighteenth century, it is important to understand how it was achieved and what it meant. The Danish educational reform of the 1740s made local pastors responsible for the education of Iceland's children, but it did not mandate schools. Those children whose parents were illiterate and could not teach them were taught by the pastor. The local ministers, therefore, were responsible for both the minds and souls of their parishioners. Generally, the pastors taught the children to read, but not to write. Iceland's universal literacy meant the ability to read, not necessarily the ability to write. The ability to read combined with general inability to write made the book commonplace, yet helped it to retain an aura of mystery.

With widespread literacy and book ownership, books entered traditional folk practices. For generations, Iceland's families gathered on winter evenings for the *kvöldvaka,* a custom dating from medieval times. As more and more Icelanders learned to read during the eighteenth century, reading aloud became an important part of the *kvöldvaka.* During this winter evening's entertainment, Icelandic families read a wide variety of materials: traditional sagas, devotional books, newspapers, magazines, novels, *Volksbücher,* and, even, published collections of folktales.[45] The idea of printed folktales seems most intriguing. Tales which had first circulated orally and since been collected and published were reintroduced into the traditional storytelling ritual via the medium of print. To be sure, reading did not supplant storytelling, but it did supplement it. As books were assimilated into the *kvöldvaka,* reading became an oral performance within the home. Formerly, reading aloud had been associated with the church, but the use of books in *kvöldvaka* made reading aloud a secular experience as well.

The treatment of the book within the Icelandic magician's legends reflects the unique place the book has held in Icelandic culture. The legends continually associate the book with the spoken word. In the Black School, Sæmundur must vocalize his wish before a book appears. Jón *lærði*'s ability to compose power-wielding verse depends upon his ownership of a magic volume. Loftur addresses incantations to Bishop Gottskálk in an attempt to acquire his powerful book of magic. The numerous instances in which the book occurs as a motif shows the respect for books among the Icelandic people, a respect which near-universal literacy and widespread book ownership only enhanced.

Inexperienced Use of the Black Book in Great Britain and America (*ML* 3020)

Chapter Five

One of the Icelandic legends tells how master magician Eiríkur leaves behind his magic book only to have his aspiring pupil get hold of the volume and create all kinds of mischief. The story belongs to the legend type which Reidar Christiansen has labeled the "Inexperienced Use of the Black Book." Christiansen studied numerous instances of the legend in Norway, and it has been recorded throughout Scandinavia. The British and American versions, however, have gone largely unstudied. Indeed, of all the different types of folktales and legends in which the book occurs as a motif, none have been more widely circulated in Great Britain and North America than those which describe how some unwitting churl gets hold of a book of black magic, sometimes with disastrous consequences.

The legend commonly begins by describing a person who owns and has usually mastered the black book. In Norway, the book owner is most often a farmer or minister. Several Norwegian versions specifically name real ministers who supposedly had mastered the powers of the black book. The book owner keeps the volume well hidden so that no one else can gain access to the book and abuse its powers, but when he is temporarily absent or when the book has been loaned to another, a person unaware of how to use the black book happens to acquire it. In Norway, the inexperienced person is most often a maid or servant but might also be a spouse, son, daughter, neighbor, friend, or even the book owner himself. Looking into the book, the inexperienced person accidentally summons the devil and then must give him some task to keep him busy and out of mischief. Most often, he has the devil twist a rope from sand, but in the Norwegian versions, the devil is sometimes asked to empty a lake, carry water in a sieve, count the strands of hair on a bullock's skin, count the trees in a wood, turn water upward in a waterfall, move a great stone, or even row a boatload of empty barrels against the wind. The book owner returns, either because he was summoned or because he instinctively knew what had happened. The book owner then exorcises the devil, though traces of the devil's activities often remain as testament to his activities.[1]

This migratory legend has analogues in the folktale tradition. "The Sorcerer's Apprentice and the Demon" (AT 325*), a tale type which Walt Disney made use of in *Fantasia,* tells the story of an apprentice who conjures up a demon while his master is away. He has the demon carry in buckets of water. As the room begins to flood, however, the boy cannot make the demon stop. Ultimately the master returns and speaks the words which send the demon away. In "Making a Rope of Sand" (AT 1174), the person who summons the devil must give him an impossible task in order to make him go away. The black book is not an essential part of these two tale types, though it sometimes appears as a motif.

The English fairy tale "The Master and Pupil" tells the story of a learned man and his pupil and servant, a foolish boy. The master reputedly knows all the mysteries of creation, a knowledge he largely obtained from his book (motif G224.3). The big book, bound in black calf with iron corners, is fastened with an iron clasp which requires a key to unlock it. Furthermore, the book is chained to a table which is in turn bolted to the floor. Only the master can read from the book, for it contains all the secrets of the spirit world. The master strictly prohibits the boy from looking into the book, but after the master leaves the house one day, the boy sneaks into the room where the book is kept and happily discovers that his master had neglected to lock the book's cover before he left. Unable to control his curiosity, the boy rapidly opens the volume. Though he understands little of its contents, he manages to put his finger on a line of text and spell it through.

All of a sudden the room darkens, the house trembles, and a clap of thunder sounds. The devil appears before him and asks the boy to give him a task. After considerable hesitation, the boy manages to tell the devil to water a potted geranium in the room. The devil then leaves the room but quickly returns shouldering a large barrel of water and pours its contents over the flower. Again and again, the devil leaves and returns, pouring so much water that the room begins to flood. The boy urges him to stop without realizing that only a special command from the book will send the devil away. The devil continues to pour and the water to rise. The boy gets on top of the table to save himself, but still the water level rises. It soon reaches his chest and nears his chin as the master returns. Partway through his journey, the master had remembered that he had not locked the book, so he had turned around, reaching home just in time to speak the words which return the devil to his fiery domain.[2]

The book's physical description within the tale tells much about its importance. It is a weighty tome decorated with corner bosses and a clasp. Such attachments, generally known as furniture, convey the book's age. The corner bosses and clasps suggest that the book dates back to the sixteenth century or earlier, back to a time when books were stored flat instead of upright. Bosses helped protect the binding of a book laying on its side while clasps helped stop the vellum leaves from curling.[3] Beyond the sixteenth century, as books began to be stored upright, such furniture became unnecessary, but the clasp sometimes survived to decorate Bibles or other important religious works. Though the clasp had lost its practical function, it retained a symbolic one. Clasps indicated that a precious text was contained inside the book's covers. The locking clasp in the tale helps emphasize the forbidden nature of the text within the master's book. Chains, too, were not unusual. Valuable books were often chained to prevent theft. English churches sometimes had valuable old folios chained to desks or shelves for their parishioners to read if they so desired.[4] According to one legend, the devil himself often stole pious books to prevent people from reading them, so the church installed chains to prevent the devil from stealing books.[5]

While the chain, the locking clasp, and the bolted-down table reveal that the master securely protected his book from theft, the story gives no indication how or why the master first acquired his black book. Why has he been privileged with the key which opens the book of supernatural knowledge? Has he, like Faustus, made a pact with the devil? There is no explicit reference to any Faustian agreement in the recorded variants, but the master may have acquired the book from the devil who was—always ultimately but sometimes directly—the source of the black book. A surviving contract with the devil written by an early-eighteenth-century Swedish student, for example, reflects this belief as it stipulates that, upon signing the agreement, the devil would provide the student with the black book.[6] Furthermore, among the peasants of Franconian Switzerland, becoming a witch depended on two conditions: entering a pact with the devil and consulting a secret book of black magic. Access to the book's power required a commitment to the devil.[7] Some of the beliefs concerning actual books of black magic such as the Scandinavian *Cyprianus* or *The Sixth and Seventh Books of Moses* suggest that the owner of the black book often had little choice in the matter. When offered a copy of the book, a person had to accept it.[8] Scandinavian legend also has it that only those who attended the Black School could effectively use the Black Book.

"The Master and the Pupil" is vaguely reminiscent of the Scandinavian legends of the Black School, but stories of the legendary school have not had that much impact on the British tradition. "The Master and the Pupil" suggests a less institutionalized way of learning, more like an apprenticeship than formal schooling. Since the master has a pupil of his own, it is logical to assume that he himself had once been pupil to another master of the black arts. If, as the tale suggests, the black arts were learned as a kind of apprenticeship, the question remains: Why would someone choose to follow such a career? Another folk belief may help provide the answer and also help explain why the black book is bound specifically with iron furniture instead of the more usual brass. Some believed that if a child touched cold iron, he would take up the profession the iron represented. In other words, if a child touched an iron-bound book, he would become a scholar.[9] This folk belief allows the possibility that the master, simply by coming in contact with the volume's iron corner bosses, determined his future as master of the black arts. According to another folk belief, once a magic book was used, it compelled person to do evil (motif D1678). I am not saying that merely by touching the book that the master achieved the power to use it. The touch simply destined him to his profession. His title, master, implies that the knowledge he possessed was something he had to study and ultimately master.

The story itself shows his mastery. As he returns home, he discovers the boy standing atop the table to which the book was chained with the water level nearing the boy's chin. The master quickly recites the words which send the devil away, but he does not use the book at the time. He could not have. The book was underwater; the boy was probably standing on it. (In *Fantasia,* Mickey Mouse desperately thumbs through a large book, but unable to find the text to stop the flood, he uses the book as a flotation device.) The episode shows that the master had so fully internalized the book's knowledge that it was no longer necessary for him to read or even touch the book for him to work its magic. The same incident which proves the boy's foolishness also proves the man's expertise.

Though "The Master and the Pupil" does show the boy's naïveté, it hints that he will not remain so. In a way, the tale is an initiation story. The boy has made his first contact with the book—and survived. His near-total immersion in the water reiterates the initiation motif. Indeed, one might say he has been baptized by the devil himself. Furthermore, the master-apprentice relationship establishes a parallel between the boy's life and the master's. While the tale does not explicitly indicate that the master had made a pact with the devil, the boy's demoniacal baptism, triggered by first touching the book, hints that the process of learning how to use the book involved a devilish indoctrination.

An Irish version of the story casts Oliver Cromwell in the master's role. Cromwell's Irish exploits long have made him a prominent though nefarious character in Irish folk legend. After invading Ireland, he undertook a reign of terror, mercilessly slaughtering innocents and dispossessing many Irish of their lands. He appears in several different legends, but nearly always he is depicted as incompetent, grasping, or merciless.[10] One, for example, begins, "Cromwell was a big English general and a bad man. He'd stick the bayonet in the child and hold it up in the air until one of his officers would fire a shot through it."[11] As "Oliver Cromwell and the Wall" begins, Cromwell has just become the leader of England and is beginning to devise ways to secure the country against invasion.[12] Soon he decides to erect a stout stone wall along England's perimeter and heads for the nearest coast, accompanied by a footman who carries his "Black Bible." Walking there on a warm summer day, Cromwell reaches the coast tired and sleepy. He tells his footman that he will take a nap before erecting the wall. He then puts his footman in charge of the Black Bible, warning him not to open it on any account. Cromwell soon falls asleep and begins to snore loudly. When the footman discovers his master asleep, curiosity seizes him, and he opens the Black Bible. Suddenly, a crowd of little men emerge from the open book, each shouting, "Give me work." Afraid their shouts will awaken Cromwell, the footman tells them to start making ropes from sand. The little men tell him the task is impossible, so he replies, "Well, if you can't . . . get right back here again into the Bible."[13] Once the last little man is back inside the book, the footman slams the Black Bible shut. After Cromwell awakens, he orders the footman to hand him the book. Cromwell opens it, but no little men come forth. "Ah, my good man," he tells his footman, "I'm afraid you opened the Bible while I was asleep. And that will leave England forever without a protective wall."[14]

Though Cromwell's book frequently is called a Bible in the story, it is first called a "Black Bible." In the seventeenth century, the word "bible" did not necessarily mean the Holy Scriptures. It sometimes meant any weighty tome. A contemporary of Cromwell's used the phrase "Black Bible" to refer to the book which contained the list of sinners.[15] The story's events make it obvious that Cromwell's Black Bible is much the same as the Black Book of Scandinavian lore or the master's iron-bound book in the English fairy tale. The fact that he has a footman to carry the book further emphasizes its weight. A variant describes the book as so huge that "it would take a horse to draw it!"[16] Such a description reveals the storyteller's literalism. Since he knows that several little men must emerge from the book, he makes the volume large enough to accommodate them.

"Oliver Cromwell and the Wall" depicts Cromwell as a bungler. While he established his reputation as a warrior and a man of action, here he is shown as someone who cannot accomplish anything without taking a nap first. His loud, uncouth snoring further denigrates his character. Just as in the Norwegian legends, the servant is forbidden to open the book, but overcome by curiosity, Cromwell's footman opens it anyway. The master's pupil has to read and pronounce one line of text to summon the devil, but here the footman needs only to open the book for its black magic to work. In other words, literacy is not a precondition for summoning the devil within the Cromwell legend. Instead of the devil himself, several little men appear. Like the pupil's devil, the little men demand a task. Somewhat shrewder than the pupil, however, the footman requests an impossible task, and they return to the book, the task unaccomplished.

The greatest deviation from the Scandinavian versions of this legend occurs with the ending. In Norway, for example, the story usually ends with the book owner reasserting his mastery. Upon waking, Cromwell is unable to summon the little men. The magic is gone, and the intended wall goes unbuilt. The explicit theme of Cromwell's political and strategic inefficacy is reinforced by the story's sexual innuendo. Postsomnial tumescence (or, in folk parlance, waking up with a stiffie) is a commonplace occurrence among normal adult males. Cromwell's inability to "erect" the wall after his nap, reinforced by his inability to get a "little man" to work, links his political ineptitude with sexual impotence. Among his Puritan followers, Cromwell was a forceful leader, but in Irish legend he remains ineffectual and impotent.

A local legend from Sutherlandshire, England, recorded during the late nineteenth century ends much the same way as the Cromwell story. Donald-Duival McKay, the legendary wizard of the Reay Country, was said to have learned the black arts in Italy. The story of his education is a variant of the Scandinavian legend of the Black School (*ML* 3000). As the story begins, Donald has loaned his magic book to another wizard, who has a servant return the book. Like Cromwell's footman, the servant's curiosity gets the better of him, and he opens the volume, releasing hundreds of little men who cry, "Work, work!" The servant first has them twist ropes of heather, but they accomplish the task in no time. He next asks them to make ropes of sand, but, unable to accomplish the impossible, they plunge into the sea, never to return. With the loss of the little men, Donald loses the ability to accomplish difficult tasks with his book, though he can still "draw rain or snow from the skies with a wave of his hand."[17] Like Cromwell, Donald can no longer summon the little men once they have been given the impossible task of turning sand into rope. He still retains some power, but the book itself has been rendered useless by the churl's actions. Those powers Donald does retain are nonverbal. He can change the weather with a physical gesture, but the book and its text are powerless.

The theme of different conjurors sharing a black book also appears in an English legend from the Gwent region. The beginning of "Two Conjurors/One Book" is much the same as the story of Donald-Duival McKay. One of the conjurors entrusts the book to a messenger, who pauses during the errand and opens the volume. An evil spirit appears immediately and asks for work. The man, though frightened, has enough presence of mind to have the spirit level a nearby hill. The evil spirit begins to move the earth. The messenger then accidentally turns over another page, and another evil spirit appears looking for work. "Stop that evil spirit who is levelling the hill," the man tells him, "and replace the soil as it was." The second evil spirit tackles his fellow spirit and, after an intense struggle, carries him off and replaces the soil. The messenger shuts the book and carries it to the conjuror without further mishap.[18] Like Cromwell's footman, the conjuror's trusty messenger does not need to read the book to work its magic. He need only open it to summon forth an evil creature eager for work. Here, however, the number of devils summoned depends on the act of turning pages. Turn a page, get a devil. Thus the book's physical qualities contribute to the plot development.

Other variants of this legend type recorded in Great Britain feature schoolmasters and their pupils. A Herefordshire version is brief: "There was also a Dr. C. who lived at Jewry Cottage; he used to have a lot of boys with him. One day he was called out. The boys got his books and rose His Satanic Majesty; but they had not learnt the art, and they could not lay him again. When Dr. C. returned in the morning, he found a fine state of affairs!"[19] A considerably more detailed variant was recorded in the late nineteenth century in Bury, England, but dates at least as far back as the early nineteenth century. "Schoolmaster Hodgson" tells the story of old Mr. Hodgson, master of the grammar school at Bury. While eating his midday meal, his wooden trencher begins to spin around, and he becomes convinced that something was going wrong at the schoolhouse. He returns immediately and discovers that the schoolboys had recited the Lord's Prayer backward, raised the devil, and could not get rid of him. Hodgson knew that the only way to get rid of the devil would be to give him a task which he could not perform, yet he also knew that if they could not assign him an impossible task in three tries, they would be doomed. First, Hodgson asks the devil to count the blades of grass in the Castle Croft, and he does so. Hodgson then orders the devil to count the grains of sand on the school brow, and he easily does. With only one chance remaining, Hodgson commands the devil to count the letters in the large Bible in the parish church (motif K211.1). Instantly, the devil descends through the schoolroom floor to the lower regions, leaving a great crack on the hearthstone where he passed through, to attest the truth of this story to future generations.[20]

The ending of "Schoolmaster Hodgson" is closer to the Norwegian versions of the legend than the British. The master returns and restores order, and the devil departs, leaving evidence of his visit to the earth's surface. "Schoolmaster Hodgson" differs from its Scandinavian precedents, however, in its use of the book. There is no black book. The boys call forth the devil by reading the Lord's Prayer backward, and the schoolmaster uses the church Bible to send the devil away. During the transmission of this legend, in other words, two widely known superstitions about the book were introduced as motifs while any reference to books of black magic disappeared. In a way, "Schoolmaster Hodgson" is more frightening than the other stories because it emphasizes that no special book was necessary to summon the devil, that sacred text could be manipulated with diabolical results.

Despite the differences between how the book is used in "Schoolmaster Hodgson" and other British versions of the legend, the story retains the hierarchical relationship between the experienced and the inexperienced users of the book. Indeed, each of the numerous versions of this legend which have been recorded throughout Great Britain embodies the master-servant or -pupil hierarchy. To further generalize, while the masters possess profound knowledge of the supernatural, the servants are illiterate or nearly so. "The Master and the Pupil" is the only British version which requires the inexperienced user to read the book's text, and, even then, the pupil needs only to sound through one line of text to summon the devil. Overall, the legends express the servant's desire to get hold of the book, yet they simultaneously suggest the dangers involved as books are placed in the hands of the folk. Within the context of the story, the inexperienced use of the book can result in the appearance of mischief-making and soul-taking demons. Within the larger social context, the servant who gets hold of the master's book can strip away his powers. Placed in the hands of the servant, books threaten to topple the longstanding social hierarchy.

．　．　．

Versions of the "Inexperienced Use of the Black Book" recorded in the United States differ significantly from the British versions. The works of Vermont novelist Daniel P. Thompson are most remembered for his use of folk humor and legends in his fiction.[21] In *Gaut Gurley; The Trappers of Umbagog* (1857) Thompson retells the story:

> There was once a curious sort of a fellow, whose land was so covered with stones, which had rolled down from a mountain, that little or nothing could grow among them; and the question was, how he should ever remove them. Well, one day, when he was thinking on the matter, he found in the field an old Black-Art book, on the cover of which read, "*One chapter will bring one, two chapters two, and so on; but set and keep them at work, lest a worst thing befall.*" So, to see what would come of it, he read one chapter; when a great, stout, dubious-looking devil made his appearance, and asked what he should go about? "Go to throwing these stones over the mountain," said the man. The devil went at it. But the man, seeing the poor devil was having a hard job of it, read on till he had raised about a dozen of the same kind of chaps, and set them all at work. And so smashingly did they make the stones fly that, by sunset, the last were disappearing; and the man was about to set them to pulling up the stumps on his newly-cleared land. But they shook their heads at this, and, being pretty well tuckered out, agreed to quit even, if he would, and go off without the usual pay in such cases made and provided in devildom; when, he making no objections, they, with another squint at the green gnarly stumps, cut and run; and all the chapters he could read after that—for he began to like the fun of having his land cleared at so cheap a rate—would never bring them back again.[22]

Clearly, Thompson is indebted to the oral tradition, and his anecdote belongs to the legend type. Unclear, however, is whether the story changed significantly at Thompson's hand or whether it had already metamorphosed as part of the New England storytelling tradition. There are several crucial differences between Thompson's anecdote and the British versions. Most important, the story contains no hierarchical relationship between the book owner and the person whose curiosity prompts him to open the book. In other words, the story has neither master nor servant. Instead, the curious fellow is his own churl to do with the book what he will. Unlike the servants in the British legends, Thompson's Yankee farmer is never intimidated by numerous evil little men. Rather than giving them an impossible task which would remove them as quickly as possible, he gives them the difficult but by no means impossible chore of removing the stones from his field. The task completed, the Yankee farmer next asks them to remove the tree stumps from the field. This task, however, they do find impossible and consequently run away.

Thompson's Yankee farmer is more reminiscent of Sæmundur and Hálfdán of Icelandic legend. Just as Sæmundur and Hálfdán used the devil for such tasks as cleaning the cow barn and mowing a meadow, this Yankee farmer uses his devils to clear his field. In place of the master and servant, the Yankee farmer performs both their roles. As the story begins, the Yankee farmer plays the servant's part. In other words, he is a curious fellow who serendipitously discovers a book of magic which he uses to summon forth spirits. Once the first spirit appears, however, he takes on the role of master. He is not intimidated by the devilish spirits; he knows how to summon forth additional ones, and he is able to provide them with useful, practical tasks for his benefit rather than giving them an obviously impossible task simply to get rid of them. The story's denouement is similar to the British versions, at least in form if not tone. Once the spirits have been given an impossible task, they disappear.

The humorous tone is more pronounced than in any of the other versions. While Cromwell is portrayed humorously at the beginning of "Oliver Cromwell and the Wall," by the end of the story, he seems rather pitiful. The Yankee farmer has no special powers as Thompson begins the episode, but the book endows him with power during the course of the story. His ability to summon spirits is gone by the end, but he is no worse off in the end than he was at the beginning. Rather, he is much better off because his field is no longer filled with stones. It still has stumps in it, but that really did not matter too much. Most pioneer farmers left the stumps in anyway and simply plowed around them. Perhaps most importantly, the devils "go off without the usual pay," that is, the Yankee farmer gets his stones cleared yet does not have to pay for the labor with his soul. Thompson thus takes the characteristic idea of Yankee thrift to its ultimate extreme.

The process of using the book also differs greatly from the way the book is used in British versions. The Yankee farmer's successful use of the book directly depends on his literacy. Since he finds the book purely by chance, he has no way of knowing the book is a black magic book unless he can read. The volume's cover provides instructions on how to use it: "*One chapter will bring one, two chapters two, and so on' but set and keep them at work; lest a worst thing befall.*" The more he reads, in other words, the more devils he is able to summon. The explicit directions concerning how to use the book are reminiscent of the practical self-help books which had been immensely popular among early American readers. Books such as *Every Man His Own Lawyer* and *Every Man His Own Doctor,* for example, achieved a level of popularity, which prompted Benjamin Franklin to place a joke ad in the *Pennsylvania Gazette:* "Note, in a short time will be published, *Everyman His Own Priest.*"[23] The book which Thompson's Yankee farmer finds might be called "Every Man His Own Conjuror." The only power required to use the book was the power of literacy, something which had become nearly universal throughout America's European population well before Thompson wrote his book.

Another version of the legend, "Nick Gort's Demon," survives in the oral tradition of upstate New York. Nick Gort, a resident of Croghan, New York, had a reputation for being able to call forth the devil with "a little trying." The story begins as Nick Gort is drinking at a nearby tavern:

> He wasn't much good, and down at the tavern they got fed up with him one night and kicked him out. He was so mad he went home and got out an old book of black magic that he owned, and looked up the part where it told how to call up the Devil—I suppose he had some notion of getting even with the tavern keeper. He read the directions carefully and made his arrangements accordingly; we have to take Nick's word for what happened as he told it later on. Then he said the magic words, the ones he found in the book, and the Devil came popping right out of the stove: bright red, had a long tail, and he kept dancing all over the room with a big pitchfork in his long claws. By this time any ideas of vengeance Nick may have had were routed by his own terror. The only thing he could think of was getting rid of the demon; fortunately he had enough presence of mind to remember that

further on in the book there was advice on how to get rid of the Devil, once you had him on your hands. The trouble was, you needed a big fire in the stove to do it. Nick piled the stove full of kindling and lit a match, but no sooner was it lighted than the Devil spit it out. Nick tried and tried again, but his unwanted guest had perfect aim and limitless spittle. It took two boxes of matches before Nick could get that fire lit; after that he said his magic words, and finally he was alone again. But the whole business was too close a call for comfort, and after that Nick let magic and such strictly alone.[24]

Like Thompson's Yankee farmer, Nick Gort's magical abilities also depend on his literacy. To call forth his demon, Nick must do much more than merely open the book of magic. The story describes in some detail how he uses the book. First Nick opens the book to a particular chapter and reads the directions carefully. Then he recites the magic words from the book. Like Thompson's Yankee farmer episode, "Nick Gort's Demon" contains no hierarchical master-servant relationship. Nick himself is both master and churl. As the story develops, however, the roles Nick Gort plays are reversed from those of the Yankee farmer. At the start, Nick is the master, someone who can summon the devil with minimal effort. Once the devil appears on the scene, however, Nick becomes the cowardly churl who is terrified at the devil's sight. Unlike the other spirits, Nick Gort's demon cannot be removed simply by giving it an impossible task to perform. Indeed, this devil seems to have no plans to do any work whatsoever. Fortunately, Nick recovers from his initial terror, remembers that the book contained further advice concerning how to get rid of the devil and, after much effort, manages to reread that particular section of the book, recite the magic words, and send the devil back to Hades. Though Nick loses his power, the ending of the story differs from the endings of "Oliver Cromwell and the Wall" and the story of Donald-Duival McKay. Nick voluntarily relinquishes his power rather than having it taken away from him. The book still retains its capacity for summoning the devil. Nick simply decides not to make use of it any more.

Both the Yankee farmer's tale and "Nick Gort's Demon" eliminate the master-servant relationship, but other versions of the legend recorded in North America preserve it. Emelyn Gardner includes one in her fine collection of folklore from New York's Schoharie Hills:

I knew a young feller that hired out to a farmer who had great power over people. Sometimes the young feller would come on the man reading a big black book that looked something like a Bible. The boy watched to see where the man put the book when he was done reading. One day when the man had gone to the village, the young feller thought he would examine the book for himself. He opened it where a leaf was turned down and begun to read, because he was smart enough to read. And it told how to witch people, houses, animals, and everything. Before he had got half way down the page the doors of the house begun to bang, the windows flew up and down, and he felt an icy blast sweep down on him. He put that book where he found it almighty quick and, without stopping to pack his duds, just cleaned out of that place faster than I'm a-telling you.[25]

The description of the book—"a big black book that looked something like a Bible"—is similar to the book's description in the British legends, but the young feller's treatment of the book is closer to the other American versions. The young feller can only summon the evil forces because he is "smart enough to read." Furthermore, the amount of evil force appears to depend on the amount of text read. Reading half a page was enough to bring forth the icy winds which prefigured the devil's appearance. Unlike the other inexperienced users of the book, this young feller hightails it from the house before the devil appears. He may be criticized for his cowardice, but in running away he handles the situation on his own. Unlike the servants in the British versions, the young feller does not wait for his master to come back and save him from the devil. He saves himself.

Among the German Wendish people in Texas, one informant told the following story of his great-grandfather's boyhood experience in Germany:

Great-grandfather Schneider was a blacksmith, but he learned his trade in Germany. Usually the *Meister* or teacher would take several boys and teach them the trade as they worked without pay. One Sunday when the *Meister* was at church the boys looked around the shop and in some of the cupboards which the teacher kept closed. In one they found a book, supposedly the Seventh Book of Moses, which they began reading. Soon a crow flew in through the window and lighted on a beam. The boys continued reading, and another crow flew in. More crows came until there were crows outside as well as inside the shop. When the boys noticed this, they became frightened and replaced the book. At the same time the teacher came out of the church and saw the crows. He went to the shop, took the book, and began reading it backward. As he did so the crows flew away in the same order in which they had come, and when he reached the first word all were gone.[26]

This legend is close to the story of the young feller in New York. While it preserves the master-pupil relationship common to the British versions of the legend type, it reflects the importance of reading common to the American versions. The number of crows which appear and later disappear directly depends on the amount of text read. The specific mention of *The Sixth and Seventh Books of Moses* reinforces that work's importance, and this legend incorporates the superstition about reading it backward. The reference to *The Sixth and Seventh Books of Moses* also signals another difference between the British versions and the American. In Great Britain, the black book was usually described as a weighty tome, but *The Sixth and Seventh Books of Moses* was a small, inexpensive book often sold in chapbook form. Just as the explicit directions on the Yankee farmer's self-help magic book made that work accessible, the cheapness of this book helped make this book available to a wider segment of the population.

While this is the first story discussed which mentions crows, the motif is not so unusual. Another American version also has children read *The Sixth and Seventh Books of Moses* and conjure up crows.[27] Actually, the crows add a touch of realism. In other words, while it is difficult for most to believe the possibility of summoning evil spirits simply by opening a book, it is not impossible to imagine a flock of vicious birds pecking at unprotected children, a motif Alfred Hitchcock used so effectively in *The Birds*.

· · ·

The legend type "Inexperienced Use of the Black Book" began in Scandinavia, and from there it extended west into Great Britain and south into other parts of Europe. The story entered America from both Great Britain and Germany. The migratory pattern of the legend, however, is less important than the changes in plot and motif as it migrated. British variants retain the master-servant relationship, which had been an important part of the Scandinavian versions. As an implement of power, however, the black book lost ground during the legend's transmission through Great Britain. In some British versions, the master begins firmly in control of his supernatural powers, but by the story's end, he often loses his power to use the book. Once the book is rendered useless, the master also loses his power over his servant. His literacy no longer differentiates him from his servant. As the book changes hands from master to servant, it threatens to break down their traditional relationship.

Some of the American versions of "Inexperienced Use of the Black Book" preserve the master-servant hierarchy, while others do not. The most important theme common to the American versions concerns the act of reading. All of the protagonists are literate, and the number of evil spirits summoned directly depends on the amount of text read. In several of the American versions, dismissing the demons also requires the book's text to be read. The American versions suggest that the power does not inherently reside in the master. Whoever can read can make the book work for them.

Three Brothers in the Philippines
(AT 653, 653A, and 654)

There's a Filipino proverb which goes, "A person who does not read is like a frog inside a well; he thinks that the sky is only that narrow." This is just one of several proverbs recorded throughout the Philippines which emphasize the importance of reading, an emphasis which can be found in other genres of Filipino folklore but perhaps none as noteworthy as the folktale.[1] "The Four Skillful Brothers," "The Rarest Thing in the World," and "The Three Brothers" are types of closely related tales which have been transmitted to the Philippines over hundreds of years. The Filipino versions which have been recorded, however, differ significantly from other versions recorded throughout the world. To be sure, variations within the same tale type are a normal and necessary part of a tale's transmission from one place to another over a lengthy period of time. During the oral transmission of these three related tales, however, one motif has become an important part of several Filipino variants: the book.[2]

"The Four Skillful Brothers" (AT 653), generally begins with a father sending his four (or three or five) sons away to learn trades.[3] After their education, the brothers return home where their father tests them. The brother who has learned stargazing points his telescope to a distant tree branch and counts the eggs in a bird's nest. The brother-turned-thief then steals the eggs. The huntsman shoots the eggs to pieces, though they had been arranged in a pattern which might have defied the most expert marksman. The tailor stitches them back together so they can be returned to the nest. The birds hatch, and a red line around each of their necks, representing the tailor's thread, provides the only indication of the brothers' activity. After proving themselves to their father, the brothers learn that a king has offered his daughter's hand in marriage to whoever rescues her from her captors. The astronomer uses his telescope to locate the kidnapped princess on a rocky island in a distant sea. Together the brothers sail to the island, and the thief steals her away. The huntsman shoots the dragon that had been guarding her. As they escape the island, their boat breaks into pieces, but the tailor manages to stitch together the vessel's shattered planks. Upon their return to the kingdom, each brother claims to have rescued the princess, and they dispute who shall have her. The ending of the tale varies. Either the dispute remains unsettled, or the king proposes that the princess be divided into parts to reveal the true lover, or the king awards the brothers half the kingdom instead.

While the astronomer and his telescope play an important role in the story, this tale predates the telescope, which came into use during the early seventeenth century. Prior versions, therefore, required a different motif to convey the essential information about the princess. In the *Vetálapanchavinsati* (*Twenty-Five Tales of a Demon*), one brother has "supernatural knowledge," but how he acquired his extraordinary knowledge is not specified.[4] In Basile's *Pentamerone,* the story of "The Five Sons" follows the standard plot of "The Four Skillful Brothers," except that the youngest brother, Menicuccio, has learned to understand the language of birds. His father challenges him to prove his skill by asking him what a nearby sparrow had chirped. "He was saying," Menicuccio replies, "that an ogre has stolen the King of Altogolfo's daughter and has carried her away to a rock, and no one can find out anything about her, and her father has issued a proclamation that whoever finds her and brings her back to him shall have her in marriage."[5] While the idea of a news-carrying sparrow has survived in the circumlocution "A little bird told me," a phrase most often used by rumormongers to avoid revealing the sources of their information, the little bird largely disappeared from versions of "The Four Skillful Brothers" once the use of telescopes for astronomy and navigation became widespread.

The replacement of the telescope for the sparrow says much about how a tale can change over the course of time. The telescope reveals the tale teller's fascination with emerging technology and his willingness to incorporate new motifs within a traditional tale. Quite simply, the optical possibilities offered by the telescope make for a more intriguing story. As Hermann Bausinger has shown, when new technology first enters the folklore, it often has magical associations.[6] As it becomes part of a folktale, the technological marvel often takes on characteristics yet more marvelous. In many versions of "The

Four Skillful Brothers" the telescope lets its viewer see everything that is happening throughout the world.

The change from sparrow to telescope also indicates a shift in the way information is conveyed and received. In Basile's "The Five Sons," Menicuccio *hears* the information from the bird, translates it from bird to human language, and then tells it to his father. The astronomer-brother knows the princess is in trouble because he *sees* her. As the tale has changed, seeing has become privileged over hearing. The shift from aural to visual perception also shifts the brother's behavior from passive to active. Menicuccio overhears whatever the sparrow happens to sing. The telescope, however, requires more involvement. The astronomer-brother must place the telescope to his eye and look through it before he can learn about the princess. As an information provider, the telescope allows its user closer contact with events taking place. The telescope lets its viewer *see* the princess with his own eye, while the sparrow's report must be taken on faith. In other words, the information about the princess's whereabouts is mediated through the sparrow. With the telescope, the astronomer-brother can witness events as they happen rather than relying on an intermediary.

"The Rarest Thing in the World" (AT 653A) shares attributes of "The Four Skillful Brothers." A princess is offered to the person who brings her the rarest thing in the world. Three brothers set out to acquire magic objects. Much like the astronomer of the other tale, one brother obtains a telescope which shows everything that is happening throughout the world. The second brother obtains a magic carpet which transports its passengers wherever they wish to go. The third brother acquires an apple (or some other object) which has the power to resuscitate someone from the dead. With the telescope, the three brothers see that the princess is either dead or near death. With the carpet they go to her immediately, and, using the apple, they restore her to life. As in the previous tale, the three dispute who will get the princess.[7]

The most basic version of "The Three Brothers" (AT 654) begins the same way as "The Four Skillful Brothers" and may have originated as an outgrowth of the other tale.[8] A father sends three sons away to receive training and, upon their return home, holds a trial to test their level of skill. The brother who has learned swordsmanship goes out in a heavy rainstorm and swings his sword so quickly that he does not get wet. The second brother has trained as a barber;

he proves his skill by shaving a running hare. The third brother, now a blacksmith, manages to shoe a horse while it is galloping.

. . .

One Filipino tale titled "The Three Brothers" when it was recorded and published during the early years of the twentieth century closely resembles "The Four Skillful Brothers." Told by an Ilocano man who first heard the story from his mother when he was a small boy, this Filipino tale begins by describing the plight of an old woman who must raise her three sons by herself after her husband's death.[9] An-no, Berto, and Tito grow to be sturdy young men, but eventually their mother must send them away to learn trades. They leave home, continuing together until they come to a place where the road forked in three directions. Each decides to take a different branch, but they agree to meet at the crossroads in nine years before returning home to rejoin their mother. After the time has elapsed, they meet one another at the crossroads and discover what each has learned. The oldest brother, An-no, has learned the art of glassmaking, and Berto has learned shipbuilding. Tito, the youngest brother, has become a thief.

Soon after the family has been reunited, the brothers learn that the king's daughter, Princess Amelia, has been kidnapped and that anyone who contributes to her return will be allowed to marry her. An-no had brought home "a spy-glass in which everything hidden from the eyes of men could be seen."[10] With this instrument, he tells his brothers, he can locate the princess. He looks through his glass and sees her imprisoned in a tower on a distant island. Next, Berto builds a ship which the three brothers sail to the island. Once there, Tito eludes the armed guards and successfully steals the princess from the tower. The three brothers and the princess then sail to the king's palace. The grateful king asks which of the three would like to have his daughter's hand. When the brothers begin quarreling, the king decides that rather than giving his daughter to any one of them, he would give them half his wealth divided equally.

The similarity of this version to the recorded Indo-European versions demonstrates that the tale was transmitted to the Philippines largely intact. The most important difference concerns the occupation of the oldest brother, An-no. In the Grimm version, for example, one brother trains to be a stargazer. When he has finished studying, his master gives him a telescope, telling him, "With this you'll be able to see everything that happens on the earth and in the sky, and nothing can remain hidden from you."[11] In the Filipino version, An-no trains as a glassmaker, not a stargazer. The Filipino version, in other words, emphasizes that the brother learns a practical craft rather than the more erudite and less tangible practice of stargazing.

In "Pablo and the Princess," a Filipino version of "The Rarest Thing in the World," the telescope disappears altogether. This tale was recorded in the early years of the twentieth century from a Tagalog woman who had originally heard the story from her father.[12] One morning, three friends, Pedro, Juan, and Pablo, meet at the junction of three roads, where they each decide to follow a different path to find their fortunes. Before parting, they agree to return to the crossroads and rejoin one another. After taking the road to the right and traveling through sometimes rugged terrain for three months, Pedro meets a hungry old man and gives him some food. The grateful old man gives Pedro a magic carpet in return for his kindness, telling him, "Whoever sits on it may be transported instantly to any place he desires to be."[13] Pedro thanks the old man, sits on the carpet, and instantly returns to the crossroads to wait for his friends. Juan, taking the road to the left, travels for three and a half months until he, too, meets an old man with whom he shares his bread. As a return for Juan's generosity, the old man gives him a book, telling him, "This book may seem to you of no value; but when you know of its peculiar properties, you will be astonished. By reading in it you will be able to know everything that is happening in the world at all times."[14] Juan thanks the old man and returns to the crossroads. Pablo takes the middle road, travels for four months, also meets a hungry old man, shares his meal with him, and also receives a present in gratitude, an ivory tube which can be used to cure the sick and restore the dying to instant health. Pablo thanks the old man and then returns to meet his friends at the crossroads.

The three friends share their stories, and each expresses curiosity about the other's objects. Pedro opens Juan's book, where he reads that "a certain princess in a distant kingdom was very sick, and that the king her father had given orders that any person in the world who could cure his daughter should be her husband and his heir."[15] Deciding to go to that kingdom immediately, they sit on Pedro's carpet and are transported there in a flash. Pablo applies his ivory tube to the princess, who immediately revives and begins talking. The three friends explain themselves to the king, each claiming to have been the most instrumental in saving her life. The king tells them that since each has an equal share in the princess's cure, he will devise another method of choosing who shall win the hand of the princess. Pablo is successful.

The specific motifs in "Pablo and the Princess" show how the book may have first entered the Filipino versions of these three tale types. An Indic version of the same tale tells a story of how a young woman was brought back to life through the use of a magic book (motif E64.7).[16] "Three Brothers of Fortune," a Filipino tale recorded from a Pangasinan man early in the twentieth century, combines elements of both "The Four Skillful Brothers" and "The Rarest Thing in the World" yet also uses the book as a magic object to resuscitate a beautiful young woman.[17] In "Pablo and the Princess," however, an ivory tube brings the woman back to life. Other versions recorded outside the Philippines specifically describe the telescope as an "ivory telescope."[18] As the tales were transmitted into or within the Philippines, the two motifs switched places. The magic tube shifted from a soothsaying object to a device for curing sickness. The book, on the other hand, shifted from an object with healing powers to a means for perceiving the world.

It is important to notice how the book functions in "Pablo and the Princess." The old man who gave Juan the magic book told him that he had to read its text in order to obtain the necessary knowledge. Unlike other magic charms, the book required a person actively to seek the knowledge it contained. Simply owning the book is not sufficient to work its magic; it must be read. And, in fact, ownership is not essential, only possession. After the three brothers meet again, it is not Juan, the owner of the book, but Pedro, his brother, who opens it and reads the crucial information concerning the princess's whereabouts.

In a Tagalog tale, the "Legend of Prince Oswaldo," three young men, Pedro, Diego, and Juan, similarly part ways, meet old men (actually, all meet the same old man), and obtain magic objects. Pedro acquires a magic raincoat which functions in the same way as the magic carpet of "Pablo and the Princess" or, for that matter, the same way as Fortunatus's wishing cap. Diego obtains a book from its owner who tells him that it "will tell you what is going on in all parts of the world."[19] Juan acquires a bottle containing a violet liquid designed to bring the dead back to life. When the three meet back at the crossroads, Diego shows them his book, opens it, and reads what appears on the page: "The beautiful princess of Berengena is dead. Her parents, relatives, and friends grieve at her loss."[20] They wrap themselves in the raincoat, are whisked away to the kingdom, restore the princess to life, and dispute who should marry the princess when the old man (actually, the young Prince Oswaldo) shows up and marries the princess himself.

In "Three Friends and the Princess," the most recently recorded version of the tale, the book remains a prominent motif. When Antonio, the friend who receives the book from an old man, cannot understand how to use it, the old man tells him, "My young friend, it is a magic book. Looking at it, you can read and know everything that is happening at any spot in the world. You just think of the place that you have in mind and the answer will be there in front of you."[21] In other words, both reading and thinking are necessary to properly use the book. Indeed, the thinking process must precede the reading process because the friend must first imagine a place before he can read about it.

While many versions of "The Rarest Thing in the World" (AT 653A) mention a telescope which shows everything that is happening the world, "Pablo and the Princess," the "Legend of Prince Oswaldo," and "Three Friends and the Princess" eliminate the telescope in favor of the book. The earlier shift from sparrow to telescope, which had taken place in the European transmission of "The Four Skillful Brothers" (AT 653), had made the process of knowledge acquisition more direct by eliminating the intermediary source of information. The change from telescope to book reestablishes the intermediary. The book, therefore, performs the functions of both the sparrow and the telescope. Like the sparrow, it is an intermediary source of knowledge which conveys its information through language. Like the telescope, it requires its user to search actively for the knowledge it offers (he must open the book and read its text) and to use his powers of sight. Unlike the telescope, however, the reader is not seeing the event which is taking place, but only seeing words which describe the event.

As a folktale motif, the book, at first, seems scarcely adequate to its task. It lacks both the charm of a talking sparrow as well as the novelty offered by the telescope's optical powers. Furthermore, it complicates things for the brother who must use it. Reading the book requires him to use his sight yet deprives him of the opportunity to see what is going on with his own eye. Like the sparrow, the book is an intermediary source of knowledge, but, unlike the sparrow, its information cannot be received passively. Instead, it requires much more involvement on the brother's part. All in all, the book seems to combine the disadvantages of the sparrow and the disadvantages of the telescope yet offer the advantages of neither.

The shift from telescope to book parallels the earlier shift from sparrow to telescope. After the telescope had been invented, tale tellers became intrigued with its technological possibilities. The actual telescope had powers greater than many could have imagined before it was invented, but after it had been invented and had become known, people imagined powers for it greater than it possessed. Similarly, after the book was introduced into the Philippines, the people recognized its power and ascribed to it even greater powers. From a physical standpoint, the Filipinos found the book a more appropriate image than the telescope. Though the magical telescope could supposedly let its user see anything that was happening throughout the world, using it involved looking into a narrow tube and thus constricted the viewer's perspective, providing a kind of tunnel vision similar to that of the proverbial frog inside the well. The process of opening a book, on the other hand, suggests a continual broadening of perspective. After all, a book, opened flat, parallels the horizon.

Other Filipino tales emphasize the book's power. In the Bicol folktale "Three Rival Brothers," a version of "The Three Brothers" (AT 654), a father promises his estate to whichever son who can show the most skill in the profession he has chosen.[22] The three brothers leave home to seek their fortune. Cruelly abused by the two older brothers, the youngest manages to escape them and, during his travels, meets an old hermit who listens to his stories and presents him with a magic book and dagger which can furnish their possessor with whatever he desires. The three brothers eventually rejoin their father in order to prove their skills. The oldest, now a blacksmith, shoes a galloping horse. The middle brother, who has trained as a barber, trims the hair of a running man. The youngest brother, with his magic book and dagger, makes a beautiful palace appear instantly. The father decides to give his wealth to the youngest brother.

Paraphrasing the tale's conclusion, Dean Fansler remarked, "The father, somewhat unfairly, perhaps, bestows his estate on the youngest, who has really displayed no skill at all."[23] In the standard version of the tale, however, the three brothers are a blacksmith, a barber, and a swordsman. Here, the sword survives in the form of the youngest brother's magic dagger, but in combination with the magic book, the dagger can accomplish much more than the sword alone. In the standard version, the swordsman shelters himself from a heavy rainstorm by deftly wielding his sword. The youngest brother in this Bicol story goes him one better. "You want shelter?"

he asks in essence. "I'll give you shelter." Whereupon he proceeds to create an elaborate palace. No skill? Hardly. The youngest brother possesses the greatest skill of all, literacy.

"The Five Hunters," a tangentially related folktale from the Bisayas (Visayas) recorded during the first quarter of the twentieth century, tells the story of five hunters who go to the forest to hunt for wild pigs, deer, or whatever else they might happen to find.[24] Upon seeing a pretty little bird on a tree branch, Serafin, one of the hunters, wounds the bird with his blowgun, and the bird falls from the branch into a large cave. Using a stout vine, Serafin descends into the deep cave until he sees the bird alight upon the shoulder of a gray-bearded man. The old man claims the bird as his own, but Serafin shows the old man the wound on the bird's leg. "My boy," the old man replies, "I will give you this book. If you desire to get anything valuable and can't get it, just read this book, and you will see that thing you ask comes out immediately."[25] Serafin gladly accepts the book and then ascends to rejoin his companions. When he reaches the mouth of the cave, he tells them of his marvelous book. Jose, another hunter, then decides that he wants a magic book, too. He descends into the cave using the same vine Serafin had used, but the vine breaks, and Jose falls to his death. The remaining hunters learn the lesson that it is not good to envy the successful adventures of others.

As it survives, "The Five Hunters" seems to be a truncated version of a much longer tale. There are gaps in the story. It is not really clear, for example, why the old man gives Serafin the book, and three of the five hunters are not named and do not participate in the action other than as an audience to receive the moral about not envying another's success. Though it is most likely part of a longer, unrecorded tale, "The Five Hunters" remains detailed enough to provide yet another example of the book's importance within Filipino folklore. This tale seems to be related to the "Three Rival Brothers." The youngest brother in that tale acquired a book which provided anything he wanted, the same power which Serafin's book has. Just as in the other tales, this book is acquired from an old person who is met by accident. Like "Pablo and the Princess" and the "Legend of Prince Oswaldo" but unlike "Three Brothers of Fortune," the power of the book comes, not from merely possessing it but from reading it.

In the Bicol "Three Rival Brothers" and the Bisayan "The Five Hunters," the book functions differently than it does in the other tales, acting as a magic charm rather than an information-providing source. In these two tales, the book functions as a source of power. Before owning the magic book, the youngest rival brother was cruelly abused by the older two, but after acquiring the book, he out-does them and wins their father's estate. In "The Five Hunters," Serafin's book, like that of the youngest rival brother, allows him to obtain anything he desires. Unlike the rival brother, however, Serafin does not take advantage of the book's potential power.

•   •   •

To help understand these various tales, it is important to situate the book within Filipino culture, a task which involves many difficulties. Nearly all of the tales discussed so far were recorded during the early part of the twentieth century, the time of the American presence in the Philippines. With the underlying assumption that a literate and informed populace is a democratic populace, the United States vigorously reshaped the Filipino educational system. It established schools and distributed books at unprecedented rates. During the first two decades of the twentieth century, the number of students in Filipino elementary schools increased sixfold from 150,000 in 1900 to just under 1 million in 1920.[26] English was made the language of instruction, providing a way for the numerous ethnolinguistic groups to communicate with one another. Literacy increased significantly, and books became commonplace.

The American educational reforms, however, cannot account for the book's appearance in these Filipino folktales. The book may be the common motif among these tales, but its symbolic import is far from commonplace. Furthermore, while many of these tales were recorded in the early years of the twentieth century, most seem to have circulated well before America became involved in the Philippines. "Pablo and the Princess," for example, was recorded in the twentieth century from a Tagalog woman who had heard the story from her father. Filipino tales learned by children generally remain static when retold as adults.[27] These tales, therefore, extend back to the nineteenth century and perhaps even earlier.

None of the tales can be dated precisely. Since the telescope was first invented in 1608 and came into widespread use for navigation during the early years of the seventeenth century, the Ilocano "Three Brothers" in its recorded form cannot be earlier than the seventeenth century. Book-making technology was first introduced in the Philippines not long before. *Doctrina Christiana* (1593), a catechism describing the essentials of the Catholic faith in Spanish and Tagalog, was the first book printed in the Philippines.[28] Since the Filipino book industry, such as it was, and the invention of the telescope are roughly contemporaneous, they only help to establish the earliest possible dates for these tales.

To understand Filipino attitudes toward the book, it is important to consider the time before Spanish occupation. Many of the indigenous languages spoken in the Philippines were also written languages. Writing, therefore, predated the introduction of print technology in many places throughout the archipelago. The Jesuit chronicler Pedro Chirino, for example, found the Filipinos so accustomed "to writing and reading that there is scarcely a man, and much less a woman, who cannot read and write in letters proper to the island of Manila."[29] A Bicol folk legend, "The Reign of Handiong," tells the story of the people's accomplishments during the rule of the legendary hero Handiong. During this time his people invented writing, a feat which the legend calls the "crowning achievement of Handiong's reign."[30] Centuries before the Spanish came, in other words, Filipinos had a well-established tradition of and respect for literacy.

Might the books within these folktales represent the indigenous Filipino writings rather than printed books? After all, none of these tales specify *printed* books. While the longstanding tradition of literacy among many ethnolinguistic groups in the Philippines may partially account for the book as a motif, the physical descriptions within the folktales refer to the book in the familiar, modern sense. While the books may or may not be printed, the supporting details in these stories make clear that their texts are recorded in codices, that is, stitched and folded gatherings of paper divided into leaves. In "Pablo and the Princess" Pedro opens Juan's book and reads the news about the Princess. In the "Legend of Prince Oswaldo," Diego opens his book and reads what is inside. This process of opening suggests the codex. Stitched quires of paper were not introduced until the Spanish conquest; the indigenous Filipino languages were written on native materials—bark, leaves, stone, anything large enough and flat enough to take writing. Paper was only introduced to the Philippines at the same time as printing.

While many of the separate ethnolinguistic groups in the archipelago had a great respect for reading and writing during the pre-Spanish times, the ephemeral nature of their writing materials limited what they could write. The native writing was used for day-to-day communication and for writing occasional poetry, but it was not used for recording history. Furthermore, the written languages were purposefully ambiguous. One character in the Tagalog syllabary, for example, could have several different meanings. The inherent ambiguities of the language enrich the poetry, but make it less appropriate for recording history. There is no written history of the Philippines for the time before the Spanish conquest, because history was part of the oral tradition, not the written. Paradoxically, then, the time before the Spanish came to the archipelago was a time during which the people greatly respected literacy but for which no written documents survive.

While the Spanish introduced printing in the Philippines before the end of the sixteenth century and began printing books in several of the native languages, books generally were not printed for distribution to the Filipino population. Instead, they were meant to be used by the Spanish clerics who brought the Gospel to the Filipinos. At the most practical level, books were expensive to produce, and the rice paper used for these books could not withstand rough handling.[31] Besides such practical considerations, there was also a doctrinal reason the books remained in the priest's hands. The Spanish missionaries believed that the word of God was best communicated orally. While the catechism was translated into numerous Filipino languages, it remained the priest's responsibility to learn to speak the native tongues and read the religious texts to the people in their own language.[32] Books became associated with the Spanish priest and, by further association, with God and the Spanish empire.

One might expect a similar process to have taken place elsewhere in the empire. In terms of its colonial history, the Philippines is closest to Mexico and Central America. Both were conquered by the Spanish during the sixteenth century. Actually, the Philippines had closer ties to Mexico than it did to Spain. The Philippines, after all, was part of the viceroyalty of Mexico, and the Philippine trade, via the Manila galleon, went to Acapulco. One might expect the Spanish American versions of these tales to be nearest the Filipino variants, yet among the recorded and indexed variants of these three tales from Spanish America, the book is not a motif. In a Chilean version of "The Four Skillful Brothers," the youngest brother learns to tell fortunes and thus discovers the princess's plight.[33] In variants of "The Rarest Thing in the World" from Mexico to the Dominican Republic and Puerto Rico, the object which allows the brothers to learn of the princess's plight is a magic mirror or a seeing tube akin to the telescope, objects which give primacy to the act of seeing.[34] In a Mexican variant of "The Four Skillful Brothers," however, one brother learns "soothsaying by *hearing* great distances."[35] Though such extraordinary hearing powers require language, they do not require written language.

The importance of the book as a motif in the Filipino versions of these three tales becomes all the more apparent in light of other variants recorded throughout the world.[36] The book remains a vital motif in these tales because it symbolizes the importance of the written word in Filipino culture, yet it also represents the essential link between the written and the spoken word. The Spaniards gave the voice primacy over writing in the Gospel's transmission, but, lacking fluency with the native languages, they had to read aloud from the printed texts to disseminate the word of God.[37] Though the Spanish clerics introduced the book to Filipino culture, little indigenous book culture actually developed, since the book remained in the priest's hands. Indeed, the process of preaching the Gospel was an oral one in which the book merely functioned as an emblem. The book was the conduit through which the Spanish priest brought God to the Filipinos. It symbolized both the knowledge of God as well as the intrusion of Western culture. The book served as an emblem of the Catholic faith, yet it also represented the Spanish empire. Interacting with the Spanish missionaries, the Filipinos saw the book as an intermediary between themselves and God. The book, therefore, represented both supernatural knowledge as well as political power. While the priest became a sometime object of scorn in Filipino folklore,[38] the book remained an object of awe.

Filipino book culture largely remained static from the arrival of the first missionaries and the printing of the first books until the mid–nineteenth century. It was not until the second half of the nineteenth century that Spain made any concerted efforts to educate the Filipino people. It was not until the late nineteenth century that devotional books began to be printed in larger quantities for distribution to the people. These belated educational reforms and printing efforts had little impact, however. By the end of Spanish rule, only 10 percent or less of the people understood Spanish.[39]

Near the end of Spanish rule, however, more vernacular works began to be printed and distributed. One edition of an Iloko translation of Bellarmino's *Doctrina Christiana* (1895), for example, was printed in over ten thousand copies.[40] Furthermore, some modest efforts were made to publish local traditional literature. In 1890, Father Juan Navarrete published *Mga Fábula,* verse fables in the Samaro-Lytean dialect. Five years later, Father Navarrete's *Fábulas Compuestas,* a collection of Bisayan verse, appeared.[41] Once printed and distributed among the people, books such as Father Navarrete's could be read aloud and recopied by hand.[42] The late-nineteenth-century Philippines thus provides and example of how print culture could enrich the oral tradition and foster a manuscript culture.

Another folktale, also recorded during the early years of the twentieth century, specifically refers to the time of Spanish rule and may reflect Spain's failed attempts at educational reform. "The Three Wise Sons" (AT 1697) shares several motifs with "Three Brothers of Fortune" but turns out much differently. This Bisayan tale tells the story of a married couple and their sons, Juan, Marcos, and Gaspar. Much like the mothers and fathers in the other tales, these parents are anxious for their sons to be educated. They send Juan, their eldest, to an instructor who teaches him to say, "Si señor." Juan returns home triumphant, answering any question he is asked with "Si señor." The parents cannot understand him and happily conclude that he has achieved a high level of wisdom. They then send Marcos, the second son, to another teacher, who teaches him to say "Mas mejor." After completing his education, Gaspar, the third son, is able to say, "Si, si, si." With all three sons now educated, the parents are pleased.[43]

While taking a walk one day, the three brothers come upon a dead woman's body. As they gaze at the corpse, a policeman arrives and accuses them of killing the woman. They soon go on trial for murder. At the trial the judge first asks Juan if he and his brothers had killed the woman, and he replies, "Si señor." The judge next asks Marcos if he would be willing to share the punishment. Marcos answers, "Mas mejor, mas mejor." The judge finally asks Gaspar if he had really murdered the woman, and Gaspar replies, "Si, si." The brothers are convicted and sent to prison. "This was the fruit of their knowledge," the Bisayan tale teller concluded, "which they themselves could not understand."[44]

Obviously the title of this Bisayan story, "The Three Wise Sons," like the *blason populaire* "the wise men of Gotham," is ironic. The tale emphasizes the incongruity between the language of the people and the language of the establishment, the ones who enforce the laws and judge wrongdoers. The tale also mocks the parents who foolishly believe that the less they understand their boys the more educated their children have become. The boys would have been better off not knowing any Spanish than knowing the little that they did. Their incomplete education not only distances them from their parents, it also makes it more difficult for them to cope with the establishment.

While "The Three Wise Sons" belongs to a different tale type, it shares two key events with the other tales discussed here. The parents send their sons from home to be educated, and the boys locate the body of a dead woman. In a way "The Three Wise Sons" strips the other tales of their supernatural elements and tells what would really happen if three local brothers were to find a woman's dead body. They do not bring her back to life; they are not rewarded; one of them does not get to marry her. Instead, they are convicted for her murder.

Understood in relation to the history of the book in the Philippines, these various tales take on further significance as commentaries on Filipino attitudes toward reading, writing, and literacy. While the book functions differently in these tales, sometimes acting as an information-providing source and other times as a magic charm which can bring the dead back to life or provide its owner with whatever he desires, in each it represents power. In the history of the Philippines, the Spanish clerics held the books and represented both the power of the establishment and the power of God. In the folktales, the books are placed in the hands of the people, represented by the three brothers. In nearly all of these tales, the book is given to one of the brothers by an old man. The old man represents the Filipino's link to its ancient past, the time before the Spanish came, when literacy was highly valued and widely practiced. In a way, these tales function as impassioned pleas to put books into the hands of the people.

Traditional Flyleaf Rhymes

So many of the superstitions, folktales, and legends about books emphasize the importance of book ownership that perhaps it should come as no surprise that the marks of ownership which people have inscribed on the flyleaves of their books constitute a significant body of folklore. Nowadays, book owners commonly write their names inside the books they purchase. The act of autographing a book usually occurs before reading it. The signature marks the owner's property and, in case the book gets lost or stolen, helps to make sure it stays his property. In former times, however, the process of inscribing a book frequently meant more than simply autographing it. Often, the process of inscribing a book involved writing a catchy verse onto its front flyleaf. These flyleaf rhymes began well before the invention of printing and continued into the early twentieth century.[1] Surviving volumes containing such rhymes reveal much about attitudes toward book lending, book borrowing, and the circulation of knowledge, but they also provide glimpses into how book owners viewed themselves and wished others to view them. Unlike other forms of folklore, the transmission of flyleaf rhymes directly depended on the exchange of books. People borrowed books from one another, read their verse inscriptions, and copied them into books they owned, perhaps revising the verses or adapting them for themselves.

One surviving book from colonial Boston clearly shows how verse inscriptions were transmitted from one person to another. A copy of Cotton Mather's *Ecclesiastes* (Boston, 1697), a biography of Massachusetts divine Jonathan Mitchel, contains the inscription "Sarah Cotton her Book / God give her grace therein to look." The same volume is also inscribed "Joanna Cotton her Book / God give her grace therein to Look." Another kinswoman, Elizabeth Cotton, also

reused the inscription when she acquired the book.[2] As ownership of
the volume passed from one family member to the next, the new
owner read the former's inscription and liked it well enough to
recopy it, substituting her own name. The inscription thus allowed
the new book owner both to claim possession and to assert her identity within the book's covers.

A copy of another seventeenth-century book, Richard Brathwait's
Panedone, or Health from Helicon (London, 1621), similarly passed
from one family member to another, and both inscribed their own
rhymes within the volume. James Morrey wrote:

> Whose book I am if you would know,
> In letters two I will you show:
> The first is J, the most of might,
> The next is M, in all men's sight;
> Join these two letters discreetly,
> And you will know my name thereby.
>
> > Jas. Morrey.[3]

Another inscription in the same volume reads:

> Philip Morrey is my name,
> And with my pen I write the same;
> Tho' had such pen been somewhat better,
> I could have mended every letter.[4]

Philip Morrey might have copied the inscription which the previous
owner had used just as the Cotton women did. All he needed to do
was to rewrite it, substituting the letter *P* for James's *J*. Such a minor
change, however, was inadequate to the task. While the same verse
rewritten in his hand using his initials would have been enough for
Philip Morrey to show possession of the book, it did not allow
him to distinguish himself from his kinsman and to assert his own
identity. Instead, Philip used a verse he read somewhere else—probably in some other book he had borrowed from a friend—and made
it his own. This dual impulse to guarantee possession and to assert
identity is an important aspect of most flyleaf inscriptions.

The texts of different rhymes became more widely dispersed as
books were circulated among friends within a community. Ostensibly
an owner inscribed a book to make sure that it would be returned
after it had been loaned to someone else. Sometimes the inscription
could be as simple as the following couplet recorded in western
Massachusetts in the late nineteenth century: "If in this book my
name you see, / You'll know that it belongs to me."[5] Other flyleaf
rhymes were much more elaborate. The verse inscriptions frequently

detailed the activity of loaning books. Another rhyme collected from a nineteenth-century American book owner reads:

> If thou art borrowed by a friend,
> Right welcome shall he be
> To read, to study, not to lend,
> But to return to me.
> Not that imparted knowledge doth
> Diminish learning's store,
> But books, I find, if often lent,
> Return to me no more.[6]

This eight-line verse can be broken down into two parts. In the first four lines, which have been recorded independently,[7] the owner apostrophizes the book rather than speaking directly to the book borrower, who is referred to in the third person. This subtle narrative stance allows the book owner to avoid directly warning the borrower, who is most likely a good friend. The lines also reveal a kind of etiquette, even an ethics, of book borrowing. The third line makes clear that it is unacceptable for a book borrower to loan a borrowed book. Lines five through eight form what a rhetorician might call the *refutatio*. The book owner anticipates the possibility that the book borrower might lend the book to a third party and humbly explains the problem which arises when book borrowers become book lenders. He makes clear that he has nothing against disseminating knowledge; rather, he simply wants to protect his property.

In this particular case, the book owner, after inscribing the verse, appended a final sentence which, in a way, destroys the verse's subtlety. He wrote: "Read slowly, pause frequently, think seriously, keep cleanly, return duly, *with the corners of the leaves* NOT TURNED DOWN."[8] While the main purpose of this added sentence tries to make sure that the borrower will not misuse the book, it also lets the book owner provide directions about the reading process. He advises his friend to read in a way which allows time for careful thought. The inscription suggests that his status as book owner elevates him above the book borrower and thus allows him to instruct his friend about the process of knowledge acquisition. The hierarchical relationship implicit within this inscription shows one way in which the book owner is further able to assert himself. Not only did the inscription mark him as a book owner, it also established him as an expert in the process of acquiring knowledge. The inscription proved ownership; the fact of ownership, in turn, proved his personal knowledge.

William M. Beauchamp, the folklorist who recorded and published the verse during the late nineteenth century, explained that he had read it in a book during his boyhood and had copied it down for himself during his adolescence.[9] Little realizing in his youth that he would become a folklorist, Beauchamp simply did what any another adolescent interested in books and quaint verse would do, copy out the inscription for his own use. The fact that the first four lines of Beauchamp's verse have been found independently helps show how these inscriptions changed as they were transmitted from one person to another. The memory, curiosity, and creativity of the book owner determined whether the text of the inscription was shortened, kept the same, or expanded. In this instance, Beauchamp diligently copied out the whole inscription, but others may have inscribed their books from memory. A person may have read a verse inscription long before acquiring a new book, so that when he came to write his name inside his new possession he may have only remembered the first few lines of the verse he had once read.

These formulaic verse inscriptions became so popular that they began to be printed on slips of paper and sold as book labels. Beauchamp does not specify whether he copied the verse from a printed label or from an inscription. A nineteenth-century contributor to *Notes and Queries* located the same flyleaf rhyme but was equally vague as to its origins: "I enclose a copy of some doggrel verses which an old relative of mine gave me many years ago. I cannot say what the origin of them was, though I believe he told me at the time."[10] To be sure, the same verse with the cautionary sentence tacked on was also available as a printed label.[11] The printed labels indicate the popularity of the flyleaf rhymes and helped to perpetuate the circulation of holograph versions. If a book owner could not afford or could not find printed labels, then he could simply write the verse out by hand. Indeed, a handwritten verse allowed the book owner to assert his identity more effectively.

Another nineteenth-century collector located a lengthier printed version of Beauchamp's rhyme with additional stanzas. The item was printed on a slip of paper about the size of a bookplate with the sentence, "This book belongs to ———" printed at its top. Instead of the final prose sentence, this printed version contained the following two stanzas:

> Give your attention as you read,
>   And frequent pauses take;
> Think seriously; and take good heed
>   That you no *dog's-ears* make.

> Don't wet the fingers, as you turn
> The pages, one by one.
> Never *touch* prints, *observe:* and learn
> Each idle gait to shun.[12]

The tone of these two stanzas is a little too preachy, and the last two lines are a bit too neat. While Beauchamp's inscription shows that the book owner/book borrower relationship could become hierarchical, the distance between the two remains fairly close. The distance created by this printed version lacks the familiarity of the inscription. Indeed, its status as a printed label eliminates the personal touch created by a holograph inscription and thus further distances the book borrower from the owner.

Inscriptions which survive in schoolbooks also imply a close yet hierarchical relationship between book owner and book borrower. Many of these verses alternate lines of Latin with lines of English. For example, William Murray, later Lord Mansfield, inscribed the following in his copy of *Sallust* (Rotterdam, 1699):

> Will. Murray owneth me,
> Et is me jure tenet;
> And I his Book confess to be,
> Quicunque me invenit.[13]

The Latin lines are fairly basic and easy to understand, yet the question remains: Why use Latin at all? An all-English rhyme would seem to be a better theft deterrent because it would be more easily understandable. A potential thief would not have to know Latin. The bilingual lines say much about how the book owner wished to portray himself to the borrower and the book thief who was, in most cases, simply a negligent borrower. The inscription portrays the book owner as someone who found the ancient language intriguing and who had mastered it to such an extent that he could switch from English to Latin and back with ease. In other words, the bilingual verse helps define the folk group. This particular verse shows that book owner, book borrower, and, ironically, book thief belonged to the same folk group, that is, schoolboys in the process of learning and experimenting with Latin.

The attitudes toward book loaning which these inscriptions express reveal the book's unique status as a material possession. For its owner, the book's value exceeded its material worth because it represented knowledge, both in the abstract and as a reflection of the book owner's mind. However, the owner often felt a greater desire to share his books than to share other valuable possessions. Sharing books allowed the book owner to prove his knowledge to others. These rhymes often convey the owner's opposing desires to protect and yet share his books. A detailed example comes from Birmingham, England:

> Neither blemish this book, or the leaves double down,
> Nor lend it to each idle friend in the town;
> Return it when read; or if lost, please supply
> Another as good, to the mind and the eye.
> With right and with reason you need but be friends,
> And each book in my study your pleasure attends.[14]

The phrase "to the mind and the eye" specifically values the book in terms of both its intellectual and material worth. Asking the borrower either to return or to replace the book, the owner appeals to his friend's ethical and logical senses. The inscription ends with a promise, full access to his study for the careful and diligent borrower. The inscription's context suggests that it is the work of a more mature reader, that is, someone wealthy enough to own a study full of books.

While many flyleaf rhymes encourage borrowers to read the volume provided that they return it, at least one specifically warns against reading it:

> This is Joseph Johnston's book—
> You may just within it look,
> But you'd better not do more,
> For the Devil's at the door,
> And will snatch at fingering hands;
> Look behind you—There he stands![15]

While the second line seems to allow the interloper the chance to peruse the book, the remaining lines freeze him in his tracks. Pick it up, look in it, but don't dare move from this spot without replacing that book. This particular inscription echoes the legends about the inexperienced use of the black book.[16] A book borrowed and opened without the owner's permission is liable to call forth the devil.

Despite the attempts which owners made to protect their property, some books could not help getting lost. Other inscriptions encouraged anyone who might accidentally come across the book to return it. One located in both Great Britain and North America during the nineteenth and early twentieth centuries simply reads:

> If this book should chance to roam,
> Box its ears and send it home.[17]

The couplet has been located elsewhere in the United States, sometimes with the last line: "Give it a kick and send it home."[18] The alternative line, however, lacks the cleverness of the other, which puns on the idea that book's can have ears, dog-ears, that is. An inscription from Scotland similarly asks the finder to return the lost book:

> If I should chance to lose this book
> And you should chance to find it,
> Remember that my name is Rob;
> McDougall comes behind it.[19]

Neither of these lost-and-found inscriptions place blame on the person who finds the book. Instead, they simply ask the finder to return it—no questions asked.

Others, however, do place the blame on finders who do not return what they found. Consider the following eighteenth-century inscription:

> If I this lose, and you it find,
> Restore it me, be not unkind;
> For if not so you're much to blame,
> While as below you see my name.
> Thomas Higginson, his Book,
> living near Risley Chappell. 1794.[20]

Some inscriptions specifically admonish others against theft. On the flyleaf of a Bible found in Concord, Massachusetts, an eighteenth-century adolescent wrote:

> Margrett Rogers, her Book,
> gave to her by her Worthy Mamma
> the 7th day of May 1787.
> Steal not this book
> for fear of Shame
> for here You See
> the Owner['s] Name
> Peggy Rogers.[21]

A briefer inscription in a *New England Primer* (1807) uses the same admonition: "Elizabeth Capen is my name. / Steal not this book for fear of shame."[22] While these two rhymes appeal to the thief's sense of shame, another explicitly appeals to his or her moral sense:

> Steal not this book, my honest friend,
> For fear the gallows will be your end.
> The gallows is high, the rope is strong.
> To steal this book you know is wrong.[23]

This verse achieves its effect through the use of hyperbole as it suggests that the thief will hang for stealing a book. While this exaggeration may not have dissuaded the thief, the appeal to the person's sense of right and wrong in the closing line may have been more effective. A variation of this rhyme reads:

> Steal not this booke, my honest friende,
> For fear the gallows be the ende;
> For if you doe, the Lord will say,
> "Where is that booke you stole away?"[24]

This variant supplies the same essential message, but it does so without the preachy tone and without violating the camaraderie between book owner and book borrower. While the first presents the book owner speaking to the book borrower and telling him about right and wrong, the second evokes the day of judgment and lets the voice of God finish the rhyme. In the earlier version, the explicit moral judgment occurs in the book owner's voice, but this variation removes the heavy-handed judgment and substitutes humor. A variant of this rhyme from Bedford, England, during the 1850s includes two additional lines which answer the question posed in the fourth line: "And you will stand there just like a fool / And say you left it at Bedford School."[25]

The following verse also hints that the book thief will hang for his crime.

> This Book is one thing,
> Hemp is Another;
> Steal not this one thing,
> For fear of the Other.[26]

This particular inscription occurs in a copy of Richard Saunders's *Physiognomie, and Chiromancie* (London, 1653), an erudite occult work which describes how to predict a person's future according to the lines on his hands and face, the positioning of moles on his body, and his dreams. The inscription is dated 1802, a century and a half after the book was printed. The age of the book as well as its erudition and subject matter suggests that its early-nineteenth-century owner, far from being an adolescent, was an adult who took seriously the possibility of psychic predictions. This book's particular subject matter gives the inscription further impact. The person who owns this book has knowledge of the future. The person who considers stealing this book wants knowledge of the future. The first prediction that the book thief reads upon opening its cover is that he will hang.

Other inscriptions emphasize the criminality of book stealing by threatening imprisonment. Consider these two British examples:

> Steal not this book for fear of shame,
> For in it you see the owner's name—
> And if I catch you by the tail,
> You must prepare for Newgate jail.[27]

> Steal not this Book, my Friend,
> Least Tyburn be thy Latter End.[28]

Or this early-twentieth-century New York version:

> Do not steal this book of knowledge,
> Or you'll be sent to Sing-Sing College.[29]

Others emphasize the sinfulness of book theft. For example:

> Small is the wren,
> Black is the rook,
> Great is the sinner
> That steals this book.[30]

Still others evoke images of hell. The following flyleaf rhyme occurs in a seventeenth-century Psalter:

> I, John Stirling, aught this book
> the Grace of God upon me look
> And if this book be stolen or missing
> give it again for God his blessing.
> And if you doe not as I say
> Remember me on the Latter day
> and if the[e] do not as I tell,
> Remember me the paines of Hell.[31]

Another conjures up the image of the devil:

> Steal not this book for fear of shame,
> For under lies the owner's name:
> The first is JOHN, in letters bright,
> The second SMITH, to all men's sight;
> And if you dare to steal this book,
> The devil will take you with his hook.[32]

These various inscriptions suggest that people needed to be reminded that books were property and that stealing them was both a crime and a sin. While the book's status as a source of knowledge enhanced its value to the book owner, the knowledge-value, paradoxically, made it less of a crime to steal books. People who would not otherwise steal have often stolen books. Stealing other material possessions indicates an unscrupulous desire for quick and easy wealth, but stealing books reflects the loftier desire for knowledge.

An exchange of letters concerning book borrowing and book theft in the *Times* of London during the 1920s prompted several correspondents to contribute examples of flyleaf rhymes and others to defend the act of borrowing and not returning books.[33] One correspondent supplied a folktale about book borrowing:

> Your correspondence reminds me of a story which I heard when I was a child. The owner of a country house was showing some visitors over a superb library. "Do you ever lend books?" he was asked. "No," he replied promptly, "Only fools lend books." Then, waving his hand to a many-shelved section filled with handsomely bound volumes, he added, "All those books once belonged to fools."[34]

The tale emphasizes that the book borrower and the book thief are often one in the same person. The story's tone further emphasizes the laxity of the crime of book theft. The library owner is a well-to-do country gentleman who freely admits his library consists of books borrowed from friends. Though a character in a folktale, this English country gentleman has a real-life counterpart in colonial American literary history. When the library of Philadelphia bluestocking Elizabeth Graeme Ferguson was inventoried after her death, it contained over 400 volumes, 130 of which she had borrowed from friends.[35]

Perhaps more effective for preventing theft are the minatory rhymes which threaten physical violence to the book thief. Unlike the threats of the gallows or eternal damnation, threats of personal vengeance are more immediate and more certain. Sometimes only a vague threat is hinted, such as the following: "I pity the river, I pity the brook. / I pity the person who touches this book."[36] One simple couplet which allowed the book owner to include his name and link it with a threat reads: "Steal not this book, for if you do, / John Smith will be after you."[37] Others are more explicit:

> This book is one thing,
> My fist is another;
> Touch this one thing,
> You'll sure feel the other.[38]

The following inscription was recorded in central Ohio during the nineteenth century:

> Steal not this book
> For fear of life
> For the owner carries
> A butcher-knife.[39]

· · ·

While the verses admonishing others not to steal say much about the book owner's personality, another type of flyleaf inscription, the identification rhyme, makes explicit comments about personal identity. Another inscription located in central Ohio reads:

> Mansfield is my dwelling-place,
> America's my nation;
> Ira Newton is my name,
> And heaven my expectation.[40]

Here, Ira Newton, the book owner, locates himself within his community first and his nation second. The inscription ends with a hope of his ultimate home, that is, heaven. Yet this verse makes no explicit comment about the book. Ira Newton might have written it elsewhere. That he chose to inscribe the rhyme into a book suggests that the book's relative permanence made it an ideal place to preserve his name. Surviving objects from the material culture—Revolutionary War powder horns, for example—contain similar identification rhymes.[41] The identification rhymes within books reflect the owner's attitude that books were permanent objects and that they would be saved and used by future generations.

Lengthier inscriptions begin with lines akin to those of Ira Newton, yet end with references to the book and similarly confirm the owner's recognition of the book's lasting qualities. The following verse was inscribed into in a copy of *Wesleyana* (1825), a selected edition of key passages from the writings of John Wesley:

> Sarah Smeeton is my name
> and ingland is my natin
> harbrough was my dwelling place
> and christ is my salvation
> my old companions hear will be
> when I ham far away
> unless the lord doath vengeance seal
> and death steal them away
> this book my name shall ever have
> while I ham dead and in my grave
> when gready worms my body heat
> then you may read my name compleat.
> Sarah Smeeton.[42]

Clearly, Sarah Smeeton recognized the book as a permanent object. Since she believed the book would outlast her, she found it to be a fitting place to assert her existence. Her autograph, like the book's text, would survive long after its owner was dead and buried.

The following verse, also recorded in nineteenth-century England, while similar to that of Sarah Smeeton, conveys a deliberately ambiguous message:

> Christopher Johnson is my name,
> And England is my nation,
> Cold-Aston is my dwelling place,
> And Christ is my salvation.
> When I am dead and in my grave,
> And all my bones are rotten,
> Take up this book and in it look,
> When I am quite forgotten.[43]

Though the verse ends with the book owner's recognition that he will be forgotten, it begins by stating his name. Like that of Sarah Smeeton, Christopher Johnson's verse shows the owner's understanding that the book will outlast the body. An eighteenth-century copy of *Aesop's Fables* is inscribed: "The rose is red, the grass is green, / The days are spent which I have seen; / When I am dead then ring my knell, / And take my book and use him well."[44] Unlike the minatory verses which warned others against stealing, these inscriptions encourage subsequent readers to make use of the book after the book owner's death. Whoever acquires and reads the book after the death of the previous book owner will also read the name of that book owner. Book ownership, the inscription suggests, can guarantee a kind of immortality. Once the book owner is dead and buried, he will live on as long as others have the opportunity to read the book he had saved for lifetime.

Though some of the verse inscriptions quoted here were collected during the early twentieth century, the flyleaf verse largely fell into disuse by the middle of the century. Through the seventeenth century, books were relatively rare and considerably valuable, yet the only way to read a book without buying it was to borrow it from a friend. During the eighteenth and early nineteenth centuries, books became more plentiful and relatively less expensive. With the advent of circulating libraries in the mid–eighteenth century, book borrowers had other ways to obtain reading material, so friend-to-friend borrowing decreased.[45] During the nineteenth century, flyleaf rhymes were mainly used by adolescents. The unlocked desks of the schoolroom made it all too easy for books to change hands unless they were protected with inscriptions. One inscription reads:

> This book is mine
> By right divine;
> And if it go astray,

> I'll call you kind
> My desk to find
> And put it safe away.[46]

The context of this verse suggests the schoolhouse, since it specifically refers to a location where one person has easy access to the desks of others. During the late nineteenth and early twentieth centuries, the ownership of schoolbooks shifted from the individual student to the school. Before 1920, two-thirds of the United States, for example, had made provisions to supply textbooks to all students free of charge.[47]

One argument for public ownership of schoolbooks was that all students (or, more precisely, their parents) were unable to afford the necessary books. Some flyleaf rhymes captured the financial significance of schoolbooks. During the early twentieth century, one southern Michigan student inscribed her book:

> Do not steal this book, my lad,
> For fifty cents it cost my dad.[48]

Before it was resolved, the issue of private versus public ownership of schoolbooks generated much controversy. The two most often repeated arguments against distribution of free textbooks were that books furnished free would not be cared for as well as those owned by the students and that free textbooks could not be annotated for study purposes as conveniently as those the students owned. While the opponents of free textbook distribution made no mention of schoolchildren's flyleaf rhymes, they might have done so and thereby strengthened their arguments. The rhymed inscriptions which appear in surviving textbooks demonstrate both pride of ownership and the close association between the knowledge the book offered and the knowledge the book owner acquired. Quite simply, the privately owned book was an emblem of personal knowledge.

Needless to say, the champions of free textbook distribution won the argument. Books began to be supplied to students free of charge, yet students were forbidden to write in the books they temporarily possessed. While public ownership of schoolbooks sounded the death knell of the flyleaf rhyme, schoolbook folklore has continued in a different form. Early-twentieth-century proponents of free textbooks had argued that students could be taught to care for publicly owned volumes. Teachers could have their students make protective book covers, for example. Soon, making book covers from discarded grocery bags became standard practice among elementary school students. The brown paper covers gave students a place to scribble and doodle. What disappeared, however, were the messages of permanence. No longer did schoolchildren urge subsequent readers to take up their books when they were dead and gone. Students or teachers or parents simply tossed away the grocery-bag book covers at the end of the school year and, as those book covers were discarded, so too was the folklore they contained.

Conclusion

From medieval Iceland to modern New Orleans, from the Philippines to Pennsylvania, the book has become an important part of folklore. The *Volksbuch* has influenced traditional oral culture. Individual books such as *The Sixth and Seventh Books of Moses* and Johann Georg Hohman's *Long Lost Friend* have fostered many rumors and stories. As superstitious objects, books, especially schoolbooks and devotional works, have led to numerous beliefs and superstitious practices. As a motif, the book has become important to Filipino folktales, Icelandic legends, and stories of the inexperienced use of the black book recorded in Scandinavia, Great Britain, and America, to mention only some of the legends and folktales which incorporate the book. In the case of flyleaf rhymes, the book has served a dual purpose, as both a vehicle for recording traditional verse and also as the subject of that verse. The flyleaf rhyme, as I suggested in chapter 7, has fallen into disuse. Are these other forms of book-related folklore also relics of the past? After all, most of my examples come from printed collections of folklore published between the middle of the nineteenth century and the middle of the twentieth, the time before other ways of telling stories and disseminating information—television, videotape, computer, electronic mail—had evolved. Still, it was the time after the telegraph had been invented and implemented and, for the most part, after the telephone had been invented. These early communication technologies by no means eliminated book culture or its accompanying folklore.

To help situate the relationship between folklore, the book, and other forms of communication technology at the end of the twentieth century, I would like to return to the tale type "The Rarest Thing in the World" (AT 653A). "Three Friends and a Princess," the most recently recorded Filipino variant of the tale type, published in 1982, includes the book as a motif like so many other Filipino variants, but the description of the book relates it to another technological object:

> Antonio's magic book was a wonder—something that in modern parlance would be an all-seeing television set, covering the whole known world at one glance. He was glancing at it idly when he came across a sight that made him curious.
>
> Asked by his companions as to what was interesting him so much, Antonio said, "I am seeing a very beautiful princess in my magic book. She is the princess of the King of Bohol. She is pale-faced and sunken-eyed, but normally I think she is rosy-cheeked. It is clear that she is ailing, really badly sick. I can also see that she is appealing for a good physician to cure her. Let us go to her aid!"[1]

When Antonio had first received the book, the old man who gave it to him had emphasized that it could be *read* in order to learn what was happening throughout the world, but this description does not mention the reading process at all. Rather, Antonio's book seems to be a picture book. As he uses it, he describes his cognitive process as *seeing,* not reading. While the television set was added to the tale as a metaphor to help make the idea of an all-seeing book understandable, it seems to have altered the book's very nature.

I am a little unsure how much importance to attach to this particular version of the tale type. Clearly, "Three Friends and a Princess" is a literary interpretation of the tale and not the product of ethnographic fieldwork. The phrase "in modern parlance" hardly sounds like everyday speech, and, in response to Antonio's suggestion that the three friends rescue the princess, Jose, the second friend, sounds less like a native Filipino and more like Bertie Wooster: "'A capital idea!' exclaimed Jose."[2] Folklorists tend to discount such literary products, which are not authentic oral tales collected in the field, but, as Linda Dégh has recently asked, "Isn't it time we also include the study of the professional literary-artistic variants with those told by oral folk tellers?"[3] The editor of the collection *Folk Tales of the Philippines* makes no pretense that the stories contained within were gathered in the field. The book, inexpensively bound and printed on cheap paper, is a collection of tales designed not for folklorists but for the general reading public. Once disseminated among the people, the book might be read aloud or copied by hand or both. As Donn and Harriett Hart found during their field experience in the Philippines, printed texts were often copied into manuscript notebooks and used as the basis for oral tales.[4] An inexpensive printed edition like *Folk Tales of the Philippines* could thus revitalize both the oral tradition and the manuscript culture. As "Three Friends and the Princess" is recopied and retold, motif shifts may take place. Through these retellings, the television set may become the tale's all-seeing magic object, and the book may disappear from the tale in much the same way that the telescope earlier disappeared from several Filipino variants in favor of the book. The irony is that this printed version ultimately may be responsible for the book's disappearance as a motif. Indeed, the book may stop being a motif not only in Filipino versions of "The Rarest Thing in the World" but also in other tale types recorded throughout the world. Though the book may disappear from the tale, printed versions of many different stories will continue to influence the development of the orally circulated folktale.

While I begrudgingly admit the possibility that the book may stop being a folktale motif, I believe that other forms of folklore will long continue to incorporate the book. The widely known occult books remain in print, some in multiple editions. The vagaries of academic success, the fears of life-threatening illness, and the uncertainties of salvation will help guarantee that superstitions of the book will continue for as long as books continue to be used for education, healing, and worship. Furthermore, technology has made necessary new kinds of books which may lend themselves to folk treatment.

Technological innovation has often enhanced the relationship between folklore and book culture. The telephone, for instance, has prompted the need for a book listing a community's phone numbers, and the telephone directory itself has fostered a small body of folklore. We joke about its status as a book ("It has a lot of characters but not much plot"). As part of the material culture, it can be used in both practical and humorous ways to emphasize height. It may, for example, be pressed into service as a substitute high chair. Or, to cite an example from adolescence, it may be used to joke about the disparity between female and male growths rates. When my sister began dating in junior high, she was taller than most of the boys and much taller than one particular boy she dated. After he had taken her to the movies, his buddies snuck over to our house, and, anticipating his goodnight kiss, they jokingly placed a telephone book on our front porch. The telephone directory has even lent itself to a party game. A phone book is placed on the floor with two coins placed on the floor on either side of the book. Next, a couple stands atop the book facing one another. Each must then scrunch down and remove one of the coins. If they can do so without falling off, another phone book is placed atop the first, and the process is repeated.[5] Of course, phone-book lore is strictly an urban phenomenon. After all, the various folk uses of the telephone directory only make sense in places which have large phone books.

Certain folk groups which are intimately associated with books, such as special collections librarians, continue to have their own lore, and new communication technology has helped spread library folklore. The newly formed electronic discussion group, ExLibris, for example, has helped solidify rare-book librarians as a folk group. Recently, members of the discussion group traded jokes of the "an old librarian never dies" sort: "Old librarians never die; they just have a little foxing around the edges"; "Old librarians never die; they just get withdrawn from the collection"; and "Old catalogers never die; they're just shipped to remote storage." These jokes make use of the special vocabulary of rare-book collecting and make light of serious problems facing librarians today. The variety of responses contributed to the ExLibris discussion group suggests that new technology, far from making book lore obsolete, has provided new ways of reproducing, disseminating, and encouraging the folklore of the book.

Despite the many different ways in which book culture has manifested itself as part of folklore, the various folk treatments of the book share similarities. Many of the superstitions have been incorporated as part of the folktales. *The Sixth and Seventh Books of Moses,* a work which has fostered its own unique legends, has entered different versions of a standard legend type. Some of the flyleaf rhymes are reminiscent of the tales and superstitions, especially those which threaten punishment from the devil. Overall, the folklore of the book mirrors the place of the book in society. Perhaps the most important notion underlying the folklore of the book is the idea of book ownership. When first introduced to a culture, as in the case of medieval Iceland or the Philippines during the Spanish colonial period, the book remained in the hands of the privileged few, specifically the priests responsible for spreading the word of God among the people. In the tales and legends which reflect these times, the book, much like the priest who read from the book, represents great supernatural power.[6] In places where literacy became nearly universal and book ownership became widespread, a new phase of the folklore of the book evolved. The book became a source of individual power. The folk acquired the power to use the book for their own supernatural purposes. Far from eliminating superstition, book ownership actually enhanced superstition, because books gave their owners unprecedented access to knowledge.

Each folk genre discussed so far relates to one or both of these phases of book ownership. I use the word "phase" instead of "stage" to avoid implying that the first ended after the second had begun. The two phases overlap considerably. For the most part, the Filipino tales and the Icelandic legends reflect the first phase. The British versions of the legend type "Inexperienced Use of the Black Book" (*ML* 3020) suggest a transition state between the two phases. As each version of the legend begins, the master has control of the book and its magical powers, but during the course of the tale, the servant or pupil acquires the book and begins to use its powers. By the end of some versions, the master has completely lost his power to use the book. In the American versions of the same tale type, the transition between the two phases seems nearly complete. The master disappears from many American versions and the Yankee farmer and his ilk control the book's powers.

The bookish superstitions suggest that when people own books they not only read them, they also press them into service in many ways which have nothing to do with reading. These superstitions indicate the remarkable power of the printed word to evoke awe. The book has such capacity for enhancing a person's wisdom, spirituality, and well-being that merely reading its text does not come close to exhausting its potential power. The book, especially the Bible, has been made to guard against enemy gunfire, soothe headaches, stop bleeding, and predict the future, to list only some of its legendary powers treated in chapter 3. The superstitions, even those which require the book owner to deliberately deface the volume, reflect the importance people have attached to books.

The second half of the nineteenth century was a time when numerous editions of *The Sixth and Seventh Books of Moses* appeared, yet it was also a time when the flyleaf rhyme achieved its greatest popularity. These two aspects of folklore and book culture represent significantly different attitudes toward book ownership and the book's inherent powers. Before *The Sixth and Seventh Books of Moses* was printed during the mid–nineteenth century, it long had circulated in manuscript form. The rarity of manuscript copies helped their owners achieve a reputation for supernatural wisdom. After it was printed, the book became more commonplace. To safeguard their powers, owners of *The Sixth and Seventh Books of Moses* kept its contents secret. This secrecy prompted numerous legends about the book's supernatural powers and thus enhanced the book owner's status. At a time of widespread book ownership and near universal literacy, therefore, owners of *The Sixth and Seventh Books of Moses* were able to recapture attitudes toward the book analogous to those held in medieval Iceland, where books had been in the hands of the few.

While the owners of *The Sixth and Seventh Books of Moses* acquired their legendary powers by safeguarding their books, other contemporary book owners needed to share their books to assert their power. The flyleaf rhymes emphasize that the book owner's powers were intellectual, not supernatural. The need for owners to inscribe their books reflects their need to take them from home and share them with others. Simply owning books may have implied knowledge, but the manuscript flyleaf rhymes linked the owner's personality with the book's contents and made the owner's knowledge explicit.

To state the relationship between folklore and book culture as simply as possible: as long as people continue to own books, the folklore of the book will persist.

With that said, I cannot help but rescind my earlier pronouncement that the book will stop being a folktale motif. The book may very well continue to be a vital motif in story and legend. To illustrate, let me recall the phrase "black book." In Scandinavian folklore and in many of the British and American stories which follow the legend type "Inexperienced Use of the Black Book," the black book means an occult book describing black magic. The tales nearly always describe it as a big book. In late-twentieth-century America, however, the phrase "black book" is nearly always preceded by the adjective "little." The "little black book" means a book of names, phone numbers, and addresses. While anyone may possess an address book bound in black leather or vinyl, the phrase has special connotations. It means the address book of a libidinous adult man listing the names and telephone numbers of attractive, available women coded with single or multiple asterisks to indicate their level of sexual prowess.

No television show has made more imaginative use of the idea of the little black book than "Cheers," the 1980s series about daily life in a Boston bar, and, now that Linda Dégh has emphasized the importance of understanding the relationship between folklore and the mass media, I can feel comfortable taking an example from television to illustrate the ongoing relevance between folklore and book culture. For the bar's regular patrons, the sexual exploits of bartender-lothario Sam Malone are legendary, and the appearance of his little black book nearly always elicits a hushed awe from them. In one episode, Sam misplaces his little black book. As the story turns out, an adolescent boy had found the book and was telephoning the women listed, asking each to meet him for a date. Multiple women, provocatively clad, appear ready and willing to satisfy him. Unsure of what to do, the adolescent merely watches the women from afar. Sam eventually straightens the boy out and recovers the little black book. The "Cheers" episode, in other words, is yet another variant of the legend type "Inexperienced Use of the Black Book." How can the same basic story which once involved a big book of black magic now accommodate a lothario's address book?

To understand that question, it is important to compare the two books. Size is the most obvious difference. In the English tale "The Master and the Pupil," the master has a big black book which he keeps chained to a table.[7] The description of the master's book emphasizes its permanence and its stationary quality. The phrase "little black book," on the other hand, emphasizes the book's portability. The book owner can slip it into a jacket pocket and carry it with him wherever he goes. The pocket size not only indicates convenience, it also suggests that carrying the book on the person, much like carrying a Bible to guard against harm, empowers the book owner. Modern society may give little credence to the supernatural, but rumors of sexual prowess remain intimidating. The little black book not only indicates the book owner's control of women, it also represents mastery over his fellow man: "My little black book is bigger than yours."

The book owner who misplaces his little black book undergoes an appreciable loss of power. Orally circulated tales of the book often concern its loss or fear of its loss. After one person tells a story of losing his book, another may remark, "I don't know what I'd do if I lost my little black book." The legendary lothario who misplaces his little black book loses proportionately more power than the master magician who loses his book of black magic. The magician, after all, can internalize much of the occult information the book provides. The lothario may be able to memorize some phone numbers, but his power comes from the sheer number of phone numbers contained within his little black book. His power comes from the fact that he actually *needs* a book to write down his many numbers.

Perhaps the little black book's most interesting feature is the fact that it is not a printed book, but a handwritten manuscript. As printed books have become ubiquitous in modern society, a manuscript book, curiously enough, has assumed the legendary status once held by such printed books as *The Sixth and Seventh Books of Moses* and *Albertus Magnus*. While those two books remain in print, they do not seem as powerful nowadays as they seem in the recorded tales and legends about them because, after all, anyone can go to a bookstore and purchase a copy. A newly purchased address book, however, is blank. The volume may be little and it may be black (though it does not have to be), but it will take years before an address book becomes a little black book. At a time when information can be replicated electronically and disseminated to millions of readers or viewers at the speed of light, and when a printed book can be reproduced as many times as there are people who wish to read it, the book which becomes the stuff of legend is one written in the book owner's hand which reflects years of personal experience and which cannot be replicated, a unique manuscript book.

Stories of little black books suggest that where print is ubiquitous, manuscript books can take on great power. Far from eliminating manuscript culture, print culture actually can enhance and privilege the manuscript book. Just as print culture has not eliminated manuscript culture, the electronic media will not eliminate print. In a world filled with electronic media, the printed book itself may take on an even greater aura of power. Though television is often cited as the cause for decreasing interest in books, and though advances in data storage and transmission have led some to fear that the end of the book as a physical object is quickly approaching, the fact that television episodes tell stories about legendary books and that librarians use a worldwide computer network to tell jokes about rare books show that electronic media has not diminished the book's symbolic importance. Even in places with near-universal literacy, where books can be purchased at every grocery store, the book has not lost its mystery or its ability to evoke awe. It remains a powerful mythic symbol, and those who possess it can share its power.

Notes

Abbreviations

AT	Aarne, Antti, and Stith Thompson. *The Types of the Folktale: A Classification and Bibliography . . . Second Revision.* Helsinki: Suomalainen Tiedeakatemia Academia Scientarum Fennica, 1961.
BLC	*British Library General Catalogue of Printed Books to 1975.* 360 vols. London: Clive Bingley, 1979.
Brown (North Carolina)	Brown, Frank C. *The Frank C. Brown Collection of North Carolina Folklore.* Ed. Newman Ivey White et al. 7 vols. Durham, N.C.: Duke Univ. Press, 1952–64.
Cannon (Utah)	Cannon, Anthon S. *Popular Beliefs and Superstitions from Utah.* Ed. Wayland D. Hand and Jeannine E. Talley. Salt Lake City: Univ. of Utah Press, 1984.
Hyatt (Illinois)	Hyatt, Harry Middleton. *Folk-Lore from Adams County Illinois.* Rev. ed. Hannibal, Mo.: Alma Egan Hyatt Foundation, 1965.
ML	Christiansen, Reidar Th. *The Migratory Legends.* 1958. Rpt., New York: Arno Press, 1977.
NUC	*National Union Catalog: Pre-1956 Imprints.* 754 vols. London: Mansell, 1968–81.
OCLC	Online Computer Library Center
Puckett (Ohio)	Puckett, Newbell Niles. *Popular Beliefs and Superstitions: A Compendium of American Folklore from the Ohio Collection of Newbell Niles Puckett.* Ed. Wayland D. Hand, Anna Casetta, and Sondra B. Thiederman. 3 vols. Boston: G. K. Hall, 1981.
RLIN	Research Libraries Information Network
Shaw and Shoemaker	Shaw, Ralph R., and Richard H. Shoemaker. *American Bibliography: A Preliminary Checklist for 1801 [–1819].* New York: Scarecrow Press, 1958–63.

Thomas and Thomas (Kentucky)	Thomas, Daniel Lindsey and Lucy Blayney Thomas. *Kentucky Superstitions*. Princeton, N.J.: Princeton Univ. Press, 1920.
Thompson, *Motif-Index*	Thompson, Stith. *Motif-Index of Folk-Literature: A Classification of Narrative Elements in Folktales, Ballads, Myths, Fables, Mediaeval Romances, Exempla, Fabliaux, Jest-Books, and Local Legends*. Rev. ed. 6 vols. Bloomington: Indiana Univ. Press, 1955–58. Motifs specifically pertaining to books and reading are cited parenthetically within the text.

Introduction

1. Georgia Writers' Project, Savannah Unit, Works Progress Administration, *Drums and Shadows: Survival Studies among the Georgia Coastal Negroes* (Athens: Univ. of Georgia Press, 1940), 15. I have not been able to locate a copy of the twelfth edition, so I have taken my information about the book's contents from the 1904 edition.

2. Georgia Writers' Project, *Drums and Shadows*, 15.

3. Georgia Writers' Project, *Drums and Shadows*, 16.

4. Georgia Writers' Project, *Drums and Shadows*, 13.

5. Mary Granger, introduction to *Drums and Shadows: Survival Studies among the Georgia Coastal Negroes* (Athens: Univ. of Georgia Press, 1940), xix.

6. Harry Middleton Hyatt, *Hoodoo-Conjuration-Witchcraft-Rootwork* (Hannibal, Mo.: Western Publishing, 1970–), 4:3589.

7. Albrecht Classen, *The German Volksbuch: A Critical History of a Late-Medieval Genre* (Lewiston, N.Y.: Edwin Mellen Press, 1995); John L. Flood, "Fortunatus in London," in *Reisen und Welterfahrung in der deutschen Literatur des Mittelalters*, ed. Dietrich Huschenbett and John Margetts (Würzburg: Könighausen und Neumann, 1991), 240–63; Bodo Gotzkowsky, *"Volksbücher." Prosaromane, Renaissancenovellen, Versdichtungen und Schwankbücher. Bibliographie der deutshen Drucke* (Baden-Baden: Hoerner, 1991).

8. Robert Mandrou, *De la culture populaire aux 17e et 18e siecles: La Bibliothèque bleue de Troyes* (1964; rpt., Paris: Editions Imago, 1985); Roger Chartier, *The Cultural Uses of Print in Early Modern France*, trans. Lydia G. Cochrane (Princeton, N.J.: Princeton Univ. Press, 1987), see esp. chaps. 7 and 8.

9. Margaret Spufford, *Small Books and Pleasant Histories: Popular Fiction and Its Readership in Seventeenth-Century England* (Athens: Univ. of Georgia Press, 1981); Tessa Watt, *Cheap Print and Popular Piety, 1550–1640* (New York: Cambridge Univ. Press, 1991); Victor Neuburg, "Chapbooks in America: Reconstructing the Popular Reading of Early America," in *Reading in America: Literature and Social History*, ed. Cathy N. Davidson (Baltimore: Johns Hopkins Univ. Press, 1989), 81–113.

10. Hubert Seelow, *Die isländischen Übersetzungen der deutschen Volks-*

bücher: Handschriftenstudien zur Rezeption und Überlieferung ausländis-cher unterhaltender Literatur in Island in der Zeit zwischen Reformation und Aufklärung (Reykjavik: Stofnun Árna Magnússonar, 1989); Joaquin Marco, *Literatura popular en Espana en los siglos XVIII y XIX: Una aprox-imacion a los pliegos de cordel* (Madrid: Taurus, 1977); Candace Slater, *Stories on a String: The Brazilian Literatura de Cordel* (Berkeley and Los Angeles: Univ. of California Press, 1982).

11. Chartier, *Cultural Uses of Print in Early Modern France,* 256, 260.

12. Paul Heitz and François Ritter, *Versuch einer Zusammenstellung der deutschen Volksbücher des 15. and 16. Jahrhunderts nebst deren spateren Ausgaben und Literatur* (Strasbourg: J. H. E. Heitz, 1924). For a brief over-view of the issue, see John L. Flood, "The Bibliography of German 'Volks-bücher': A Review Article," review of *"Volksbücher." Prosaromane, Renais-sancenovellen, Versdichtungen und Schwankbücher,* by Bodo Gotzkowsky, *Modern Language Review* 88 (1993): 894–95. For the most detailed recent treatment, see Jan-Dirk Müller, "Volksbuch/Prosaroman im 15./16. Jahr-hundert.—Perspektiven der Forschung," *Internationales Archiv für Sozial-geschichte der deutschen Literatur* 1 (1985): 1–128.

13. Holbrook Jackson, *The Anatomy of Bibliomania,* 2 vols. (London: Soncino Press, 1930–31); Don Yoder, "Hohman and Romanus: Origins and Diffusion of the Pennsylvania German Powwow Manual," in *American Folk Medicine: A Symposium,* ed. Wayland D. Hand (Berkeley and Los Angeles: Univ. of California Press, 1976), 235–48; David Cressy, "Books as Totems in Seventeenth-Century England and New England," *Journal of Library History* 21 (1986): 92–106; Carlo Ginzburg, *The Cheese and the Worms: The Cosmos of a Sixteenth-Century Miller,* trans. John and Anne Tedeschi (Baltimore: Johns Hopkins Univ. Press, 1980); David S. Shields, "The Manuscript in the British American World of Print," *Proceedings of the American Antiquarian Society* 102 (1992): 403–16.

14. Hermann Bausinger, *Folk Culture in a World of Technology,* trans. Elke Dettmer (Bloomington: Indiana Univ. Press, 1990); Linda Dégh, *Amer-ican Folklore and the Mass Media* (Bloomington: Indiana Univ. Press, 1994); Alan Dundes and Carl R. Pagter, *Urban Folklore from the Paperwork Empire* (Austin: American Folklore Society, 1975); Alan Dundes and Carl R. Pagter, *When You're Up to Your Ass in Alligators* (Detroit: Wayne State Univ. Press, 1987) and *Never Try to Teach a Pig to Sing: Still More Urban Folklore from the Paperwork Empire* (Detroit: Wayne State Univ. Press, 1991).

15. Dégh, *American Folklore and the Mass Media,* 2, 17.

16. Balliolensis, "Inscriptions in Books," *Notes and Queries,* 1st ser., vol. 7 (5 Feb. 1853): 127.

17. Fanny D. Bergen, "Fly Leaf Rhymes and Decorations," *New England Magazine* 23 (1900): 505–11.

18. *Funk & Wagnalls Standard Dictionary of Folklore, Mythology and Legend,* ed. Maria Leach and Jerome Fried (San Francisco: Harper & Row, 1984), 157.

19. Alan Dundes, *Folklore Matters* (Knoxville: Univ. of Tennessee Press, 1989), 1–2.

20. Norman D. Stevens, review of *Urban Folklore from the Paperwork Empire,* by Alan Dundes and Carl R. Pagter, *Journal of Academic Librarianship* 2 (May 1976): 90.

21. Dundes and Pagter, *Urban Folklore from the Paperwork Empire,* xix.

Chapter 1. *Volksbuch* and Proverb in Early America

1. Donald Wing, *Short-Title Catalogue of Books Printed in England, Scotland, Ireland, Wales, and British America and of English Books Printed in Other Countries, 1641–1700,* 2d ed. (New York: Index Committee of the Modern Language Association of America, 1972–88), nos. D1783–D1786A, D1786C–D1787; *BLC* 84:522.

2. James Granger, *A Biographical History of England from Egbert the Great to the Revolution,* 2d ed. (London: For T. Davies, J. Robson, G. Robinson, T. Becket, T. Cadell, and T. Evans, 1775), 1:370–71.

3. Treating the period before *Dod's Sayings* was first published, Tessa Watt, *Cheap Print and Popular Piety, 1550–1640* (New York: Cambridge Univ. Press, 1991), 131–253, provides an excellent discussion showing how printed broadside pictures were used similarly.

4. Roger Chartier, *The Cultural Uses of Print in Early Modern France,* trans. Lydia G. Cochrane (Princeton, N.J.: Princeton Univ. Press, 1987), 243–46.

5. *Old Mr. Dod's Sayings, Composed in Verse* (London: A. P. and T. H. for T. Passinger, 1678).

6. For more on *The History of the Holy Jesus,* see Kevin J. Hayes, *A Colonial Woman's Bookshelf* (Knoxville: Univ. of Tennessee Press, 1996), 34–35.

7. *Old Mr. Dod's Sayings, Composed in Verse,* 1, 16.

8. Samuel Sewall, *The Diary of Samuel Sewall, 1674–1729,* ed. M. Halsey Thomas (New York: Farrar, Straus and Giroux, 1973), 1:33.

9. Sewall, *Diary* 1:454; Bartlett Jere Whiting, *Early American Proverbs and Proverbial Phrases* (Cambridge: Belknap Press, Harvard Univ. Press, 1977), no. A43.

10. Morris Palmer Tilley, *A Dictionary of the Proverbs in England in the Sixteenth and Seventeenth Centuries: A Collection of the Proverbs Found in English Literature and the Dictionaries of the Period* (Ann Arbor: Univ. of Michigan Press, 1950), no. A53.

11. Studies which have treated the relationship between the *Volksbuch* and the proverb have generally treated the opposite phenomenon, that is, how proverbs influenced the *Volksbuch* rather than how the *Volksbuch* influenced the proverb. See, for example, O. R. Reuter, *Proverbs, Proverbial Sentences and Phrases in Thomas Deloney's Works* (Helsinki: Societas Scientiarum Fennica, 1986). For other references, see Wolfgang Mieder, *International Proverb Scholarship: An Annotated Bibliography* (New York: Gar-

land, 1982), nos. 471, 947, 1072, and 1145; and Mieder, *International Proverb Scholarship: An Annotated Bibliography, Supplement 1 (1800–1981)* (New York: Garland, 1990), nos. 2290, 2383, and 2813.

12. Margaret Spufford, *Small Books and Pleasant Histories: Popular Fiction and Its Readership in Seventeenth-Century England* (Athens: Univ. of Georgia Press, 1981), 48–49.

13. Dr. Alexander Hamilton, *The History of the Ancient and Honorable Tuesday Club,* ed. Robert Micklus (Chapel Hill: Univ. of North Carolina Press, 1990), 1:22–23.

14. "Books in Colonial Virginia," *Virginia Magazine of History and Biography* 10 (1903): 402.

15. Joseph Towne Wheeler, "Books Owned by Marylanders, 1700–1776," *Maryland Historical Magazine* 35 (1940): 349.

16. Elizabeth Cometti, "Some Early Best Sellers in Piedmont North Carolina," *Journal of Southern History* 16 (1950): 324–37, located several documents concerning the mercantile activities of William Johnston and Richard Bennehan, proprietors of the Little River Store in the rural community of Snow Hill, North Carolina, during the last third of the eighteenth century. Not recognizing that "histories" meant chapbooks in the store inventories, Cometti emphasized the backcountry North Carolinians apparent distaste for fiction and concluded, "The people of Orange County would not be corrupted by profane literature." Many of the "histories," however, may have been fictional histories. Another book title listed in the inventories is "Aristotle," a title which refers to one of the numerous pseudo-Aristotelian midwifery chapbooks which were frequently read by men as pornography. In other words, the people who Cometti claims "would not be corrupted by profane literature" had been reading the "Aristotle" chapbooks as pornography for years.

17. Joseph Towne Wheeler, "Booksellers and Circulating Libraries in Colonial Maryland," *Maryland Historical Magazine* 34 (1939): 130, 133–34.

18. Worthington Chauncey Ford, *The Boston Book Market, 1679–1700* (Boston: Club of Odd Volumes, 1917); Roger Thompson, "Worthington Chauncey Ford's *Boston Book Market, 1679–1700*: Some Corrections and Additions," *Proceedings Massachusetts Historical Society* 86 (1974): 67.

19. In a diary entry written in the autumn of 1713, Cotton Mather wrote, "I am informed, that the Minds and Manners of many People about the Countrey are much corrupted, by foolish Songs and Ballads, which the Hawkers and Pedlars carry into all parts of the Countrey. By way of Antidote, I would procure poetical Composures full of Piety, and such as may have a Tendency to advance Truth and Goodness, to be published, and scattered into all Corners of the Land"; *Diary of Cotton Mather,* ed. Worthington Chauncey Ford (1911; rpt., New York: Frederick Ungar, 1957), 242. According to Isaiah Thomas, *The History of Printing in America,* ed. Marcus A. McCorison (New York: Weathervane Books, 1970), 146, 132–33, Boston printers Zechariah Fowle and Samuel Draper issued "a variety of

pamphlets, chapmen's small books, and ballads" during the 1750s and "kept a great supply of ballads, and small pamphlets for book pedlers, of whom there were many at that time." Ezekiel Russell, also according to Thomas, "printed and sold ballads, and published whole and half sheet pamphlets for peddlers" (153–54). Thomas further wrote that besides his newspaper, Connecticut printer John Trumbull's confined his printing efforts to "small articles with which he supplied country chapmen" (303).

20. Ford, *Boston Book Market,* 104; William Bradford, *William Bradford, Printer, Bookseller, and Stationer, at His Store Adjoining the London Coffee-House: Has Imported a Collection of Books* [Philadelphia: William Bradford, 1760?]. The conjectural date comes from Robert B. Winans, *A Descriptive Checklist of Book Catalogues Separately Printed in America 1693–1800* (Worcester, Mass.: American Antiquarian Society, 1981). Philadelphia bookseller Andrew Steuart advertised the work for sale in 1763. See Victor Neuburg, "Chapbooks in America: Reconstructing the Popular Reading of Early America," in *Reading in America: Literature and Social History,* ed. Cathy N. Davidson (Baltimore: Johns Hopkins Univ. Press, 1989), 89. The fullest treatment of the literary reception of *Guy of Warwick* remains Ronald S. Crane, "The Vogue of *Guy of Warwick* from the Close of the Middle Ages to the Romantic Revival," *PMLA* 30 (1915): 125–94.

21. Hamilton, *History of the Ancient and Honorable Tuesday Club* 2:8, 3:313; *NUC,* nos. L0128622–L0128631.

22. Charles Evans, *American Bibliography* (Chicago, 1903–34), no. 35716; Shaw and Shoemaker, nos. 29319 and 38037.

23. Tilley, *Dictionary of the Proverbs,* no. L91; *Oxford Dictionary of English Proverbs,* 3d ed., revised by F. P. Wilson (Oxford: Clarendon Press, 1970), 444.

24. Hamilton, *History of the Ancient and Honorable Tuesday Club* 3:313–14.

25. Charles Welsh and William H. Tillinghast, *Catalogue of English and American Chapbooks and Broadside Ballads in Harvard College Library* (1905; rpt., Detroit: Singing Tree Press, 1968), nos. 501–12, 584–92, 2030–35, 1856–67.

26. Hamilton, *History of the Ancient and Honorable Tuesday Club* 1:22.

27. Hamilton, *History of the Ancient and Honorable Tuesday Club* 3:312.

28. John Wise, *The Churches Quarrel Espoused* (1713; rpt., Gainesville, Fla.: Scholars' Facsimiles & Reprints, 1966), 90; Whiting, *Early American Proverbs,* no. H232.

29. B. J. Whiting, Francis W. Bradley, Richard Jente, Archer Taylor, and M. P. Tilley, "The Study of Proverbs," *Modern Language Forum* 24 (1939): 69–70, use "Hobson's Choice" as an example of a proverbial phrase using a proper name which deserves further study. The following discussion resolves some of their queries.

30. A. W. Pollard, G. R. Redgrave, et al., *A Short-Title Catalogue of Books Printed in England, Scotland, and Ireland and of English Books*

Printed Abroad, 1475–1640, 2d. ed. (London: Bibliographical Society, 1976–83), nos. 14688–14689.7; Wing, *Short-Title Catalogue,* no. J809A.

31. Thomas Morton, *New English Canaan,* ed. C. F. Adams Jr. (Boston: Prince Society, 1883), 281.

32. Ford, *Boston Book Market,* 105, 170. In Philadelphia Andrew Steuart advertised the work in 1763; Neuburg, "Chapbooks in America," 90. Providence, Rhode Island, printer and bookseller John Carter also advertised the work; see *Just Imported from London* [Providence, R.I.: John Carter, 1783]; Winans, *Descriptive Checklist of Book Catalogues,* no. 100.

33. *Oxford Dictionary of English Proverbs,* 281; Whiting, *Early American Proverbs,* no. F268.

34. Thomas Jefferson to Wilson Miles Cary, 12 Aug. 1787, *The Papers of Thomas Jefferson,* ed. Julian P. Boyd et al. (Princeton, N.J.: Princeton Univ. Press, 1950–), 12:23.

35. Jefferson to Maria Cosway, 24 Dec. 1786, *Papers of Thomas Jefferson* 10:627.

36. Evans, *American Bibliography,* no. 8534; Clifford K. Shipton and James E. Mooney, *National Index of American Imprints through 1800: The Short-Title Evans* (Worcester, Mass.: American Antiquarian Society and Barre Publishers, 1969), no. 41192.

37. Esther Edwards Burr, *The Journal of Esther Edwards Burr, 1754–1757,* ed. Carol F. Karlsen and Laurie Crumpacker (New Haven, Conn.: Yale Univ. Press, 1984), 101–2. As I showed in *A Colonial Woman's Bookshelf,* 117, the editors mistranscribed "Ansor" for "Anson" and consequently did not identify the reference. In *A Colonial Woman's Bookshelf,* I used Burr's reference to Anson as evidence that she had read *Anson's Voyages.* While I am still reasonably certain she had read the extremely popular work, I see now that her reference is a proverbial comparison (not in Whiting, *Early American Proverbs*).

38. Neuburg, "Chapbooks in America," 102.

39. For a discussion of the Rowlandson revival in the 1770s, see Hayes, *A Colonial Woman's Bookshelf,* 121–22.

40. Shipton and Mooney, *National Index of American Imprints,* no. 47207.

41. Jeremy Belknap to Ebenezer Hazard, 25 Oct. 1786, "The Belknap Papers," *Collections of the Massachusetts Historical Society,* 5th ser., vol. 2 (1877): 444; Whiting, *Early American Proverbs,* no. M260.

42. Though the standard proverb dictionaries do not list the work, Jan Harold Brunvand, *The Study of American Folklore: An Introduction,* 2d ed. (New York: Norton, 1978), 55, uses "as bare as Mother Hubbard's cupboard" as an example of a proverbial comparison.

43. John Dod, *Moral Reflections* (Exeter, N.H.: J. Lamson and T. Odionre, 1793); Shipton and Mooney, *National Index of American Imprints,* no. 46735; *Old Mr. Dod's Sayings* (Suffield, 1803), Shaw and Shoemaker, no. 4792.

44. Benjamin Franklin, *The Autobiography of Benjamin Franklin: A*

Genetic Text, ed. J. A. Leo Lemay and P. M. Zall (Knoxville: Univ. of Tennessee Press, 1981), 94.

45. The best bibliographical overview of *The Way to Wealth* is the headnote to "Poor Richard Improved, 1758," in *The Papers of Benjamin Franklin,* ed. Leonard W. Labaree et al. (New Haven, Conn.: Yale Univ. Press, 1959–), 7:326–40. There has never been a thorough attempt to catalog all editions. For the most complete listing, see *NUC,* nos. F0339527–F0339857. For the finest appreciation of *The Way to Wealth,* see J. A. Leo Lemay, "Benjamin Franklin," in *Major Writers of Early American Literature,* ed. Everett Emerson (Madison: Univ. of Wisconsin Press, 1972), 214–17. Lemay reprints the work in *An Early American Reader* (Washington, D.C.: United States Information Agency, 1988), 28–38, where he makes the important comment that Franklin did not refer to earlier almanacs to write the essay but, rather, he wrote it from memory. There have been numerous other treatments of Franklin's *Way to Wealth,* but most have emphasized the work's sources or its literary value and have ignored its cultural impact. See Cameron C. Nickels, "Franklin's Poor Richard's Almanacs: 'The Humblest of his Labors,'" in *The Oldest Revolutionary: Essays on Benjamin Franklin,* ed. J. A. Leo Lemay (Philadelphia: Univ. of Pennsylvania Press, 1976), 77–89; Stuart A. Gallacher, "Franklin's *Way to Wealth*: A Florilegium of Proverbs and Wise Sayings," *Journal of English and Germanic Philology* 49 (1949): 229–51; Edward J. Gallagher, "The Rhetorical Strategy of Franklin's 'Way to Wealth,'" *Eighteenth-Century Studies* 6 (1973): 475–85; Charles W. Meister, "Franklin as a Proverb Stylist," *American Literature* 24 (1952): 157–66; Wolfgang Mieder, *American Proverbs: A Study of Texts and Contexts* (Bern: Peter Lang, 1989), 129–42; Patrick Sullivan, "Benjamin Franklin, the Inveterate (and Crafty) Public Instructor: Instruction on Two Levels in 'The Way to Wealth,'" *Early American Literature* 21 (1986/7): 248–59; and Harry B. Weiss, "The Way to Wealth and Other Franklin Chapbooks," *American Book Collector* (May–June 1935): 193–95. For the cultural history of one particular Franklinian proverb, see Mieder, "'Early to Bed and Early to Rise': From Proverb to Benjamin Franklin and Back," in his *Proverbs Are Never Out of Season: Popular Wisdom in the Modern Age* (New York: Oxford Univ. Press, 1993), 98–134. To be sure, other Franklinian proverbs are worthy of the kind of exhaustive treatment Mieder's essay exemplifies.

46. *Father Abraham's Speech* (Dedham, Mass.: H. Mann, for Wm. Tileston Clapp, Boston, 1807).

47. *NUC,* no. F0339622.

48. Benjamin Franklin, *The Way to Wealth* (New Ipswich, N.H.: Simeon Ide, 1816), 35–36.

49. d'Alté A. Welch, *A Bibliography of American Children's Books Printed Prior to 1821* (Worcester, Mass.: American Antiquarian Society and Barre Publishers, 1972), nos. 421.1–424.3; A. S. W. Rosenbach, *Early American Children's Books* (1933; rpt., New York: Kraus, 1966), no. 488.

50. Franklin, *Autobiography,* 94.

51. Herman Melville, *Israel Potter: His Fifty Years of Exile,* ed. Harrison Hayford, Hershel Parker, and G. Thomas Tanselle (Evanston: Northwestern Univ. Press and the Newberry Library, 1982), 61.

52. E. A. Wallis Budge, *Amulets and Talismans* (New Hyde Park, N.Y.: Univ. Books, 1961), 52–53.

Chapter 2. *The Sixth and Seventh Books of Moses*

1. Zora Neale Hurston, "Hoodoo in America," *Journal of American Folklore* 44 (Oct.–Dec. 1931): 414.

2. Zora Neale Hurston, "The Fire and the Cloud," in *Zora Neale Hurston: Novels and Stories,* ed. Cheryl A. Wall (New York: Library of America, 1995), 997–1000.

3. Zora Neale Hurston, *Mules and Men* and *Tell My Horse,* in *Zora Neale Hurston: Folklore, Memoirs, and Other Writings,* ed. Cheryl A. Wall (New York: Library of America, 1995), 177, 378.

4. For good appreciations of *Moses: Man of the Mountain,* see Blyden Jackson, "Some Negroes in the Land of Goshen," *Tennessee Folklore Society Bulletin* 19 (Dec. 1953): 103–7; Robert E. Hemenway, *Zora Neale Hurston: A Literary Biography* (Urbana: Univ. of Illinois Press, 1977), 256–72; Deborah E. McDowell, "Lines of Descent/Dissenting Lines," in *Zora Neale Hurston: Critical Perspectives Past and Present,* ed. Henry Louis Gates Jr. and K. A. Appiah (New York: Amistad, 1993), 230–40. See also Blyden Jackson's introduction to the 1984 reprint of the work, which since has been reprinted as "*Moses, Man of the Mountain:* A Study of Power," in *Zora Neale Hurston: Modern Critical Views,* ed. Harold Bloom (New York: Chelsea House, 1986), 151–55.

5. Hurston, *Moses: Man of the Mountain,* in *Zora Neale Hurston: Novels and Stories,* ed. Cheryl A. Wall (New York: Library of America, 1995), 443.

6. Hurston, *Moses: Man of the Mountain,* 448.

7. Hurston, *Moses: Man of the Mountain,* 448.

8. Harry Middleton Hyatt, *Hoodoo-Conjuration-Witchcraft-Rootwork* (Hannibal, Mo.: Western Publishing, 1970–), 2:1758. Theophus H. Smith compares Hurston's attitude toward Moses with that of Hyatt's "Hoodoo Book Man" in *Conjuring Culture: Biblical Formations of Black America* (New York: Oxford Univ. Press, 1994), 34.

9. Georgia Writers' Project, Savannah Unit, Works Progress Administration, *Drums and Shadows: Survival Studies among the Georgia Coastal Negroes* (Athens: Univ. of Georgia Press, 1940), 28.

10. For a brilliant explanation as to how such a process occurs, see Carlo Ginzburg, *The Cheese and the Worms: The Cosmos of a Sixteenth-Century Miller,* trans. John and Anne Tedeschi (Baltimore: Johns Hopkins Univ. Press, 1980).

11. Hurston, *Tell My Horse,* 378.

12. Hurston, *Moses: Man of the Mountain,* 337.

13. John G. Gager, *Moses in Greco-Roman Paganism* (Nashville: Abingdon Press, 1972), 137–38.

14. Gager, *Moses in Greco-Roman Paganism,* 160.

15. Hurston, *Mules and Men,* 263.

16. Gager, *Moses in Greco-Roman Paganism,* 146.

17. Hans Sebald, *Witchcraft: The Heritage of a Heresy* (New York: Elsevier, 1978), 91. For the German background, see Hans Bächtold-Stäubli, *Handwörterbuch des Deutschen Aberglaubens* (Berlin and Leipzig: Walter De Gruyter, 1935), 6:583–94.

18. David C. Henning, *Tales of the Blue Mountains,* vol. 3 of *Publications of the Historical Society of Schuylkill County* (Pottsville, Pa.: Daily Republican Book Rooms, 1911), 49, tells the story of Paul Heim, whose activities predate the earliest known published edition of the work.

19. *NUC,* nos. S0372757–S0372762, S0372766–S0372768. Describing his copy of the work, E. Grumbine, "Folk-Lore of Lebanon County [Pennsylvania]," *Papers of the Lebanon County Historical Society* 3 (1905): 271, notes: "This is a curious volume, a copy of which came into the writer's possession at the public sale of a library belonging to an old medical practitioner, who, in the first half of the nineteenth century, enjoyed a large practice in the townships of North and South Annville. The volume contains over one hundred and fifty pages and was printed in Stuttgart, in Germany."

20. *NUC,* nos. S0372759–S0372762, S0589613–S0589625.

21. OCLC, nos. 7814999, 6796338, 1845359, 27259038, 15074446.

22. "Concerning Negro Sorcery in the United States," *Journal of American Folklore* 3 (1890): 283, reprints an account from the *Philadelphia Press,* 4 Aug. 1885, which states that the "Obeah Man" of the West Indies "has his cabalistic book (albeit he can seldom read), full of strange characters, crude figures, and roughly traced diagrams and devices, which he pretends to consult in the exercise of his calling." The author does not identify the book, but the description makes *The Sixth and Seventh Books of Moses* the likeliest possibility.

23. Qtd. in Carleton F. Brown, "The Long Hidden Friend," *Journal of American Folklore* 17 (1904): 91.

24. RLIN, no. CSX8870608-B.

25. Arthur H. Lewis, *Hex* (New York: Trident Press, 1969), 42–43.

26. Newbell Niles Puckett, *Folk Beliefs of the Southern Negro* (Chapel Hill: Univ. of North Carolina Press, 1926), 579.

27. RLIN, nos. CSFX8870608-B, UTBG87-B34639.

28. Hurston, *Moses: Man of the Mountain,* 337–38.

29. Lewis Untermeyer, review of *Moses: Man of the Mountain,* by Zora Neale Hurston, *Saturday Review,* 11 Nov. 1939, rpt. in *Zora Neale Hurston: Critical Perspectives Past and Present,* ed. Henry Louis Gates Jr. and K. A. Appiah (New York: Amistad, 1993), 26–27.

30. Hyatt, *Hoodoo-Conjuration-Witchcraft-Rootwork* 1:276, 288; 2:1758–59.

31. "Six and Seven Books of Moses," a song written by F. Hibbert, a.k.a.

"Toots," was recorded by the Vikings in 1963 and rereleased on *More Intensified! Vol. 2: Original Ska, 1963–1967,* Mango, 1980. Hibbert's group, renamed Toots and the Maytals, rerecorded the song, retitled "Six and Seven Books," on the album *Reggae Got Soul,* Mango, 1976.

32. OCLC, nos. 12111680, 13140557.

33. *Books in Print: 1994–1995* (New Providence, N.J.: R. R. Bowker, 1994), 7:5208, 8:6870.

34. *The Sixth and Seventh Books of Moses* (Cedar Knolls, N.J.: Wehman Bros., n.d.), 2.

35. *The New Revised Sixth and Seventh Books of Moses and the Magical Uses of the Psalms,* ed. Migene González-Wippler, 2d ed. (New York: Original Publications, 1991).

36. Sebald, *Witchcraft,* 92.

37. *New Revised Sixth and Seventh Books of Moses,* 197.

38. Hyatt, *Hoodoo-Conjuration-Witchcraft-Rootwork* 1:288.

39. Don Yoder, "Hohman and Romanus: Origins and Diffusion of the Pennsylvania German Powwow Manual," in *American Folk Medicine: A Symposium,* ed. Wayland D. Hand (Berkeley and Los Angeles: Univ. of California Press, 1976), 242, shows that the Pennsylvania German work, Johann Georg Hohman's *Long Hidden Friend,* was occasionally used the same way and was sometimes even printed with such a purpose in mind. Yoder located parts of the book "printed on separate sheets of paper, one charm per page and on only one side of the sheet" and conjectures that the individual pages were used as amulets.

40. "Witch Doctors to Be Banished," *Philadelphia Public Ledger,* 14 May 1904, p. 13.

41. See chap. 3.

42. Lewis, *Hex,* 230.

43. Puckett (Ohio), no. 25601.

44. Alvin W. Schillinger, "Hell's Bells and Panther Tracks: Lore of Western Sullivan County," *New York Folklore Quarterly* 9 (1953): 36.

45. Puckett (Ohio), nos. 25600, 25602, 25603.

46. In their pop reggae song, "Six and Seven Books," Toots and the Maytals associate *The Sixth and Seventh Books of Moses* with other books in the Bible.

47. Hyatt, *Hoodoo-Conjuration-Witchcraft-Rootwork* 2:1759.

48. Puckett (Ohio), no. 25776.

49. Jacqueline Simpson, ed. and trans., *Icelandic Folktales and Legends* (Berkeley and Los Angeles: Univ. of California Press, 1972) 149; Charlotte S. Burne, "Reminiscences of Lancashire and Cheshire When George IV. Was King," *Folk-Lore* 20 (1909): 205. A nineteenth-century contributor to *Notes and Queries* suggests that reading the Lord's Prayer backward to call forth the devil was a commonplace school superstition; A. C., "School Superstitions," *Notes and Queries,* 1st ser., vol. 1 (26 July 1851): 53. See also Vincent Stuckey Lean, *Lean's Collectanea* (Bristol: J. W. Arrowsmith, 1902–4), 2:430.

50. Puckett (Ohio), no. 25600.

51. Puckett (Ohio), no. 25601.

52. George R. Nielson, "Folklore of the German-Wends in Texas," in *Singers and Storytellers,* ed. Mody C. Boatright, Wilson M. Hudson, and Allen Maxwell, vol. 30 of the *Publications of the Texas Folklore Society* (Dallas: Southern Methodist Univ. Press, 1961), 255–56; Schillinger, "Hell's Bells," 36–37.

53. Henning, *Tales of the Blue Mountains,* 49.

54. Robert H. Byington, "Powwowing in Pennsylvania," *Keystone Folklore Quarterly* 9 (Fall 1964): 111.

55. Puckett (Ohio), no. 7981. For more on blood stopping, see chap. 3.

56. Schillinger, "Hell's Bells," 36; Helen Creighton, *Bluenose Magic: Popular Beliefs and Superstitions in Nova Scotia* (Toronto: Ryerson Press, 1968), 19, records a belief that "if a person reads a witchcraft book they can make something wrong with the cow."

57. Puckett (Ohio), no. 29343.

58. Puckett (Ohio), no. 25602.

59. Schillinger, "Hell's Bells," 36.

60. Hyatt (Illinois), no. 15875.

61. *The New Revised Sixth and Seventh Books of Moses,* 80.

62. S. P. Bayard, "Witchcraft and Spirits on the Border of Pennsylvania and West Virginia," *Journal of American Folklore* 51 (1938): 48. Bayard's informant does not specifically identify the book, but the tale's setting—eastern Pennsylvania during the late nineteenth century—makes *The Sixth and Seventh Books of Moses* the likeliest book.

63. Schillinger, "Hell's Bells," 36.

64. Hyatt (Illinois), no. 15877.

65. Jacqueline Simpson, *Scandinavian Folktales* (New York: Penguin, 1988), 135. Evald Tang Kristensen, the foremost Danish folklorist, collected several handwritten copies of the *Cyprianus* which are now kept at the Danish Folklore Archives. See Joan Rockwell, *Evald Tang Kristensen: A Lifelong Adventure in Folklore* (Aalborg, Denmark: Aalborg Univ. Press and the Danish Folklore Society, 1982), xi, 167, 208.

66. Hyatt (Illinois), no. 15876. For a similar belief, see Ray B. Browne, *Popular Beliefs and Practices from Alabama* (Berkeley and Los Angeles: Univ. of California Press, 1958), no. 3302.

67. Karl John Richard Arndt, Reimer C. Eck, Gerd-J. Bötte, Werner Tannof, and Annelies Müller, *The First Century of German Language Printing in the United States of America: A Bibliography Based on the Studies of Oswald Seidensticker and Wilbur H. Oda,* no. 22 of *Publications the Pennsylvania German Society* (Göttingen, 1989), nos. 2462, 2470, 2779, 2919, and 3000; Carol Rinderknecht and Scott Bruntjen, *A Checklist of Imprints for 1843* (Metuchen, N.J.: Scarecrow, 1993), no. 43-2499.

68. *The Long Hidden Friend* was reprinted in the *Journal of American Folklore* 17 (Apr.–June 1904): 89–152, with an introduction by Carleton F. Brown. For the numerous reprintings through 1956, see *NUC,* nos.

H0450852–H0450874. For subsequent reprintings, see RLIN and OCLC. The best overview of the work is Yoder, "Hohman and Romanus," 235–48.

69. Grumbine, "Folk-Lore of Lebanon County," 270.

70. Lewis ably retells the story in *Hex.*

71. Loudell F. Snow, *Walkin' Over Medicine* (Boulder, Colo.: Westview Press, 1993), 64 n. 7. For a treatment of the medical uses of the almanac in early America, see Kevin J. Hayes, *A Colonial Woman's Bookshelf* (Knoxville: Univ. of Tennessee Press, 1996), 88–91.

72. Johann Georg Hohman, *Pow-Wows; or, Long Lost Friend: A Collection of Mysterious and Invaluable Arts and Remedies for Man as Well as Animal* (State College, Pa.: Yardbird Books, 1992).

73. *BLC* 86:492, 499; Albert L. Caillet, *Manuel bibliographique des sciences psychiques ou occultes* (Paris: Lucien Dorbon, 1912), no. 3237; *NUC,* nos. D0363869–D0363873; Charles Nisard, *Histoire des livres populaires,* 2d ed. (Paris: E. Dentu, 1864), 141–42; RLIN, no. UKBXM88051823-B. During the 1860s, the work was attacked by a novel also titled *Le Dragon Rouge.*

74. Richard M. Dorson, *Bloodstoppers & Bearwalkers: Folk Traditions of the Upper Peninsula* (Cambridge: Harvard Univ. Press, 1952), 82, records this anecdote, but does not identify the "Red Dragon."

75. Puckett (Ohio), no. 25603.

76. Caillet, *Manuel bibliographique,* nos. 131–35; *Catalogue général de livres imprimés de la Bibliothèque Nationale* (Paris: Paul Catin, 1924), 1:500; *NUC,* nos. A0141064–A0141090.

77. *BLC* 4:329; Caillet, *Manuel bibliographique,* nos. 137–42; *Catalogue général de livres imprimés de la Bibliothèque Nationale* 1:501; *NUC,* nos. A0141311–A0141327.

78. Judith Devlin, *The Superstitious Mind: French Peasants and the Supernatural in the Nineteenth Century* (New Haven, Conn.: Yale Univ. Press, 1987), 166; George W. Cable, *The Grandissimes* (1880; rpt., New York: Charles Scribner's Sons, 1912), 136; Robert E. Park, "Magic, Mentality, and City Life," *Publications of the American Sociological Society* 18 (1924): 111.

79. RLIN, no. UKBXM90028316-B.

80. The earliest dated German edition listed in *NUC* is dated 1834. The text of the work, however, contains a reference which helps date the work more specifically. The "Remedy for the Hydrophobia" begins "The 'Swabian Mercury,' a German daily, printed at Stuttgart, Germany, contains in No. 181, Monday September 10, 1810 the following article, with regard to hydrophobia, which deserves to be reproduced and embodied into this book"; *Albertus Magnus* (Cedar Knolls, N.J.: Wehman Bros., n.d.), 46.

81. *Albertus Magnus,* iv.

82. *Albertus Magnus,* 17.

83. *NUC,* nos. A0141199–A0141212. Puckett, *Folk Beliefs of the Southern Negro,* 579, mentions the "Secrets of Albertus Magnus" but does not precisely identify the work. Park, "Magic, Mentality, and City Life," 111,

locates a copy in Trinidad and, though he too does not identify the work, his description makes clear that this is the book: "A book of magic ritual published in Chicago, which pretended to be . . . translated originally from the writings of Albertus Magnus."

84. *NUC,* no. A0141216.

85. *NUC,* no. A0141205.

86. Hurston, "Hoodoo in America," 414.

Chapter 3. Superstition and the Book

1. Cannon (Utah), nos. 817, 820. The maternity hospitals in R. A. Dague's utopian work, *Henry Ashton: A Thrilling Story and How the Famous Co-operative Commonwealth Was Established in Zanland* (Alameda, Calif.: By the author, 1903), 204–5, contain libraries "well supplied with books, magazines and other publications, from various parts of the world," so that the expectant mothers "can read good books" and therefore help guarantee "that their children come into the world endowed with robust constitutions, cheerful, happy dispositions and bright minds."

2. Hyatt (Illinois), no. 3513; Puckett (Ohio), no. 3633.

3. Puckett (Ohio), no. 1966.

4. Brown (North Carolina), no. 209; Hyatt (Illinois), no. 3514; Puckett (Ohio), no. 3634.

5. Thomas and Thomas (Kentucky), no. 3702.

6. Hyatt (Illinois), no. 3515.

7. Vance Randolph, *Ozark Superstitions* (New York: Columbia Univ. Press, 1947), 336.

8. Hyatt (Illinois), no. 3518; King James Version, Psalms 109:10; Revelations 3:3. Uses of the Bible for divination purposes will be discussed in greater detail below.

9. Thomas and Thomas (Kentucky), no. 3702.

10. Margaret Cannell, *Signs, Omens, and Portents in Nebraska Folklore,* University of Nebraska Studies in Language, Literature, and Criticism, no. 13 (Lincoln, Nebr., 1933), 48; T. J. Farr, "Riddles and Superstitions of Middle Tennessee," *Journal of American Folklore* 48 (1935): 330; T. J. Farr, "Tennessee Folk Beliefs Concerning Children," *Journal of American Folklore* 52 (1939), nos. 14–15; Hyatt (Illinois), nos. 3522, 3524, 3527–29, 3531–33; Ethel Todd Norlin, "Present-Day Superstitions at La Harpe, Ill., Survivals in a Community of English Origin," *Journal of American Folklore* 31 (1918): 211; Puckett (Ohio), nos. 3644–48; Randolph, *Ozark Superstitions,* 207; Thomas and Thomas (Kentucky), no. 42.

11. Puckett (Ohio), no. 3650. Hyatt (Illinois), no. 3533, also stipulates that by touching the pile of dirt, the child signified an early death.

12. Hyatt (Illinois), nos. 3526–28.

13. Hyatt (Illinois), no. 3531.

14. Puckett (Ohio), nos. 3644, 3648.

15. Puckett (Ohio), no. 3647.

16. Puckett (Ohio), no. 3648.

17. Cannon (Utah), no. 1316; Hyatt (Illinois), no. 3529–30; Puckett (Ohio), no. 3651.

18. Hyatt (Illinois), no. 3532.

19. Lelah Allison, "Folk Beliefs in Southeastern Illinois," *Journal of American Folklore* 63 (1950): 317; Brown (North Carolina), nos. 438, 439; Margaret M. Bryant, "Folklore from Edgefield County, South Carolina," *Southern Folklore Quarterly* 12 (1948): 147; Cannon (Utah), no. 1284; Farr, "Tennessee Folk Beliefs," no. 9; E. Grumbine, "Folk-Lore of Lebanon County [Pennsylvania]," *Papers of the Lebanon County Historical Society* 3 (1905): 284; Puckett (Ohio), nos. 3510, 3525; Earl J. Stout, *Folklore from Iowa* (New York: American Folk-Lore Society, 1936), no. 1311.

20. Puckett (Ohio), nos. 3514, 3522.

21. Puckett (Ohio), nos. 3513, 3523, 3524; Stout, *Folklore from Iowa*, no. 1225.

22. Allison, "Folk Beliefs Collected in Southeastern Illinois," 324; Fanny D. Bergen, *Current Superstitions Collected from the Oral Tradition of English Speaking Folk* (Boston: For the American Folk-Lore Society by Houghton Mifflin, 1896), no. 1275 (Maryland); Bryant, "Folklore from Edgefield County, South Carolina," 147; Arthur Palmer Hudson, *Specimens of Mississippi Folk-Lore* (Ann Arbor: Edwards Brothers, 1928), 149; Hilda Roberts, "Louisiana Superstitions," *Journal of American Folklore* 40 (1927): 152.

23. Brown (North Carolina), no. 435; Farr, "Riddles and Superstitions of Middle Tennessee," 329; Farr, "Tennessee Folk Beliefs Concerning Children," no. 8; Puckett (Ohio), no. 3507; Newbell Niles Puckett, *Folk Beliefs of the Southern Negro* (Chapel Hill: Univ. of North Carolina Press, 1926), 463; Annie Weston Whitney and Caroline Canfield Bullock, *Folklore from Maryland* (New York: American Folk-Lore Society, 1925), no. 1395.

24. Bergen, *Current Superstitions*, no. 1276 (Alabama); Brown (North Carolina), nos. 432–34; Cannon (Utah), no. 1262; Hannibal Gerald Duncan and Winnie Leach Duncan, "Superstitions and Sayings among the Southern Highlanders," *Journal of American Folklore* 42 (1929): 236.

25. Puckett (Ohio), no. 24812.

26. Cannon (Utah), no. 9954.

27. Puckett (Ohio), nos. 24818–24820.

28. Puckett (Ohio), nos. 16333, 16342, 17003, 17039–17040, 17061–17063; Whitney and Bullock, *Folk-Lore from Maryland*, nos. 1468, 1469, 1469A.

29. Whitney and Bullock, *Folk-Lore from Maryland*, no. 1067.

30. Puckett (Ohio), nos. 24809–24810; Hyatt (Illinois), no. 13148.

31. Brown (North Carolina), no. 3486; Helen Creighton, *Bluenose Magic: Popular Beliefs and Superstitions in Nova Scotia* (Toronto: Ryerson Press, 1968), 167; Puckett (Ohio), nos. 24808–24810.

32. Puckett (Ohio), no. 24809.

33. Grumbine, "Folk-Lore of Lebanon County," 270.

34. Cannon (Utah), no. 9950.

35. Hyatt (Illinois), no. 13149.

36. G. F. Abbott, *Macedonian Folklore* (Cambridge: Cambridge Univ. Press, 1903), 227.

37. Puckett (Ohio), no. 24823; cf. Cannon (Utah), no. 9951.

38. Puckett (Ohio), no. 5269.

39. Brown (North Carolina), nos. 3487, 5705–5706; Creighton, *Bluenose Magic,* 38; Hyatt (Illinois), no. 7248; Puckett (Ohio), no. 25875; Thomas and Thomas (Kentucky), no. 3826.

40. Hyatt (Illinois), no. 5934.

41. Hyatt (Illinois), no. 5939.

42. Brown (North Carolina), no. 5708; Hyatt (Illinois), no. 5950.

43. Grumbine, "Folk-Lore of Lebanon County," 268.

44. Puckett (Ohio), no. 5269–5270.

45. Hyatt (Illinois), no. 5909.

46. John Hawkins, "An Old Mauma's Folk-Lore," *Journal of American Folklore* 9 (1896): 129–30.

47. Charlotte S. Burne, "Reminiscences of Lancashire and Cheshire When George IV. Was King," *Folk-Lore* 20 (1909): 205.

48. Hyatt (Illinois), no. 13147; Puckett, *Folk Beliefs of the Southern Negro,* 165.

49. A. S. W. Rosenbach, *Books and Bidders: The Adventures of a Bibliophile* (Boston: Little, Brown, 1927), 239.

50. Puckett (Ohio), no. 20723.

51. Puckett (Ohio), no. 20726.

52. Margaret T. Hills, *The English Bible in America: A Bibliography of Editions of the Bible & the New Testament Published in America 1777–1957* (New York: American Bible Society and the New York Public Library, 1961), nos. 2232–2233, 2237–2238, 2244–2247, 2399–2400, 2405–2409, 2414; Harold R. Willoughby, *Soldiers' Bibles through Three Centuries* (Chicago: Univ. of Chicago Press, 1944), 33–40.

53. Puckett (Ohio), no. 20725.

54. Puckett (Ohio), no. 7153.

55. Puckett (Ohio), no. 8404.

56. Puckett (Ohio), no. 12553.

57. Cannon (Utah), no. 3744.

58. Harriet Ne, *Tales of Molokai: The Voice of Harriet Ne,* ed. Gloria L. Cronin (Laie, Hawaii: Institute for Polynesian Studies, 1992), 138.

59. Mark Twain, *Adventures of Huckleberry Finn,* ed. Walter Blair and Victor Fischer (Berkeley and Los Angeles: Univ. of California Press, 1985), 187.

60. Puckett (Ohio), no. 28676.

61. Puckett (Ohio), no. 9981. An alternate version recorded in Michigan says to open the Bible to the Twenty-third psalm and place it under the mattress to cure a headache; Loudell F. Snow, *Walkin' Over Medicine* (Boulder, Colo.: Westview Press, 1993), 28.

62. Brown (North Carolina), nos. 879–80, 1624; Puckett (Ohio), nos. 7982–7983, 7990, 10719; F. W. Waugh, "Canadian Folk-Lore from Ontario," *Journal of American Folklore* 31 (1918): 21; Frost Woodhull, "Ranch Remedios," in *Man, Bird and Beast,* ed. J. Frank Dobie, vol. 8 of the Publications of the Texas Folklore Society (1930; rpt., Dallas: Southern Methodist Univ. Press, 1965), 31.

63. Carl Carmer, *Stars Fell on Alabama* (New York: Farrar & Rinehart, 1934), 282.

64. Richard M. Dorson, *Bloodstoppers & Bearwalkers: Folk Traditions of the Upper Peninsula* (Cambridge: Harvard Univ. Press, 1952), 150–65; Walter R. Smith, "Northwestern Oklahoma Folk Cures," in *Man, Bird, and Beast,* ed. J. Frank Dobie, vol. 8 of the Publications of the Texas Folklore Society (1930; rpt., Dallas: Southern Methodist Univ. Press, 1965), 79, locates the blood-stopping superstition in Oklahoma, but admits, "It is difficult to get any information on how blood is stopped."

65. Brown (North Carolina), no. 879.

66. Brown (North Carolina), no. 880; Puckett (Ohio), no. 7991.

67. Randolph, *Ozark Superstitions,* 122.

68. John Q. Anderson, "Special Powers in Folk Cures and Remedies," in *Tire Shrinker to Dragster,* ed. Wilson M. Hudson, vol. 34 of the Publications of the Texas Folklore Society (Austin: Encino Press, 1968), 166; Carmer, *Stars Fell on Alabama,* 282; Randolph, *Ozark Superstitions,* 122.

69. Anderson, "Special Powers," 166; Paul G. Brewster, "Folk Cures and Preventives from Southern Indiana," *Southern Folklore Quarterly* 3 (1939): 43; Brown (North Carolina), nos. 881–82, 1907; J. Hampden Porter, "Notes on the Folk-Lore of the Mountain Whites of the Alleghanies," *Journal of American Folklore* 7 (1894): 111; Sadie F. Price, "Kentucky Folk-Lore," *Journal of American Folk-Lore* 14 (1901): 30–38; Puckett (Ohio), nos. 7984–7986, 10721; Randolph, *Ozark Superstitions,* 123; Paul W. Schedler, "Folk Medicine in Denton County Today: Or, Can Dermatology Displace Dishrags?" in *Hunters & Healers: Folklore Types and Topics,* ed. Wilson M. Hudson, vol. 35 of the Publications of the Texas Folklore Society (Austin: Encino Press, 1971), 15; Snow, *Walkin' Over Medicine,* 55 (Arizona); Thomas B. Stroup, "A Charm for Stopping Blood," *Southern Folklore Quarterly* 1 (Mar. 1937): 19 (Florida); Thomas and Thomas (Kentucky), no. 1078.

70. François Rabelais, *The Complete Works of François Rabelais,* trans. Donald M. Frame (Berkeley and Los Angeles: Univ. of California Press, 1991), 284.

71. Rabelais, *Complete Works,* 289–92.

72. Philip Sidney, "An Apology for Poetry," in *English Critical Essays (Sixteenth, Seventeenth and Eighteenth Centuries),* ed. Edmund D. Jones (New York: Oxford Univ. Press, 1922), 5.

73. John Aubrey, *Remaines of Gentilisme and Judaisme,* ed. James Britten (London: For the Folk-Lore Society by W. Satchell, Peyton, 1881), 90–91.

74. *The Novels and Tales of Robert Louis Stevenson: The Wrong Box & The Ebb Tide* (New York: Charles Scribner's Sons, 1895), 225; Herman Melville, *The Confidence-Man: A Norton Critical Edition,* ed. Hershel Parker (New York: Norton, 1971), 22. The practice of seeking *sortes* has continued into the twentieth century, even among the highbrow. One English book reviewer, faced with the daunting task of reading Henry James's *American Scene* (1907), attempted what he calls the "Sortes Jacobeanae," and, randomly opening the leaves of the work, he noted a few sentences, "each more astounding than the last"; Y. Y., "The American Scene," *Bookman* (London) 31 (Mar. 1907): 265–66; rpt. in Kevin J. Hayes, *Henry James: The Contemporary Reviews* (New York: Cambridge Univ. Press, 1996), 451.

75. Elizabeth L. Eisenstein, *The Printing Press as an Agent of Change: Communications and Cultural Transformations in Early-Modern Europe,* 2 vols. (New York: Cambridge Univ. Press, 1979), 1:330–34; Lawrence Stone, "Literacy and Education in England, 1640–1900," *Past and Present* 42 (Feb. 1969): 78–79.

76. Brown (North Carolina), no. 3490; Hyatt (Illinois), no. 8697; Puckett (Ohio), no. 24827; Puckett, *Folk Beliefs of the Southern Negro,* 567; Thomas and Thomas (Kentucky), no. 195.

77. Ray B. Browne, *Popular Beliefs and Practices from Alabama* (Berkeley and Los Angeles: Univ. of California Press, 1958), no. 3365; Randolph, *Ozark Superstitions,* 336; Whitney and Bullock, *Folklore from Maryland,* no. 1509.

78. Hyatt (Illinois), no. 13151.

79. Cannell, *Signs, Omens, and Portents in Nebraska Folklore,* 48.

80. Puckett (Ohio), no. 24829.

81. Puckett (Ohio), no. 24831.

82. Brown (North Carolina), no. 3489; Puckett (Ohio), nos. 24832–24833; R. J. S., "Bible Divination in Suffolk," *Notes and Queries,* 1st ser., vol. 4 (30 Aug. 1851): 148; Stout, *Folklore from Iowa,* no. 1125; A. R. Wright, *British Calendar Customs: England, Vol. II: Fixed Festivals, January–May, Inclusive,* ed. T. E. Jones (London: For the Folk-Lore Society, 1938), 39–41.

83. H. Y. N., "Superstition in Shropshire," *Notes and Queries,* 5th ser., vol. 11 (25 Jan. 1879): 74.

84. S. L., "New Year's Day," *Notes and Queries,* 2d ser., vol. 12 (19 Oct. 1861): 303.

85. M. Banks, "Gleanings from Magazines," *Folk-Lore* 54 (1943): 309; "Bible Divination," *Folk-Lore Journal* 1 (1883): 333; "Bible Divination," *Folk-Lore Journal* 2 (1884): 380–81; D. Barron Brightwell, "Superstition in Shropshire," *Notes and Queries,* 5th ser., vol. 11 (18 Jan. 1879): 45; Robert Brown, "Bible and Key," *Folk-Lore Journal* 2 (1884): 156–57; Margaret M. Bryant, "Folklore from Edgefield County, South Carolina, II," *Southern Folklore Quarterly* 13 (1949): 287; E. C., "Divination by Bible and Key," *Notes and Queries,* 1st ser., vol. 2 (8 June 1850): 19; Cannell,

Signs, Omens, and Portents in Nebraska Folklore, 18; Jonathan Ceredig Davies, *Folk-Lore of West and Mid-Wales* (Aberystwyth, Wales: Welsh Gazette, 1911), 13; Claude R. Flory, "A Hazard of Good Fortunes," *Journal of American Folklore* 82 (1969): 71–72; Emelyn Elizabeth Gardner, *Folklore from the Schoharie Hills, New York* (Ann Arbor: Univ. of Michigan Press, 1937), 278; Wilfred Hargarve, "Turning the Key and the Bible," *Notes and Queries,* 6th ser., vol. 7 (10 Mar. 1883): 189; William Hone, *The Year Book of Daily Recreation and Information,* ed. Leslie Shepard (1831–32; rpt., Detroit: Gale, 1967), 254–55; Harry Middleton Hyatt, *Hoodoo-Conjuration-Witchcraft-Rootwork* (Hannibal, Mo.: Western Publishing, 1970–), nos. 8882–8889; Georgina F. Jackson, *Shropshire Folk-Lore: A Sheaf of Gleanings,* ed. Charlotte Sophia Burne (London: Trübner, 1883), 172–74; T. Gwynn Jones, *Welsh Folklore and Folk-Custom* (London: Methuen, 1930), 138; George Lyman Kittredge, *Witchcraft in Old and New England* (Cambridge: Harvard Univ. Press, 1929), 196–98; Edward Marshall, "Turning the Key and the Bible," *Notes and Queries,* 6th ser., vol. 7 (23 June 1883): 495; Elias Owen, *Welsh Folk-Lore: A Collection of the Folk-Tales and Legends of North Wales,* rev. ed. (Oswestry, England: Woodall, Minshall, 1896), 288–89; Puckett (Ohio), no. 24826; John Ewart Simpkins, *County Folk-Lore, Vol. VII: Examples of Printed Folk-Lore Concerning Fife with Some Notes on Clackmannan and Kinross-Shires* (London: For the Folk-Lore Society, 1914), 115–17; David Stevens, "Divination by the Bible and Key," *Notes and Queries,* 1st ser., vol. 1 (27 Apr. 1850): 413; T. W., "Bible and Key," *Notes and Queries,* 1st ser., vol. 2 (1 June 1850): 5; F. W. Weaver, "Turning the Key and the Bible," *Notes and Queries,* 6th ser., vol. 8 (18 Aug. 1883): 130; W. J. Wintemberg and Katherine H. Wintemberg, "Folk-Lore from Grey County, Ontario," *Journal of American Folklore* 31 (1918): 96–97.

86. Georgina F. Jackson, *Shropshire Folk-Lore,* 172.

87. M. Deansley, "Vernacular Books in England in the Fourteenth and Fifteenth Centuries," *Modern Language Review* 15 (Oct. 1920): 352. For more on Rolle's *English Psalter,* see Nicholas Watson, *Richard Rolle and the Invention of Authority* (New York: Cambridge Univ. Press, 1991), 242–49.

Chapter 4. The Book in Icelandic Magicians' Legends

1. Kirsten Hastrup, *Culture and History in Medieval Iceland: An Anthropological Analysis of Structure and Change* (Oxford: Clarendon Press, 1985), 179–86; Darryl Wieland, "The Idea of Mystical Power in Modern Iceland," in *The Anthropology of Iceland,* ed. E. Paul Durrenberger and Gísli Pálsson (Iowa City: Univ. of Iowa Press, 1989), 26; Kirsten Hastrup, *Nature and Policy in Iceland: An Anthropological Analysis of History and Mentality* (Oxford: Clarendon Press, 1990), 199–200.

2. Hastrup, *Nature and Policy in Iceland,* 200.

3. Halldór Hermannsson, *Sæmund Sigfússon and the Oddaverjar,* vol. 22 of *Islandica* (Ithaca, N.Y.: Cornell Univ. Press, 1932), 5; Jon Hnefill Aðal-

steinsson, "Saemundr *Fróði*: A Medieval Master of Magic," trans. Terry Gunnell, *Arv: Nordic Yearbook of Folklore* 50 (1994): 119–26.

4. Hermannsson, *Sæmund Sigfússon,* 33–35.

5. Benedikt S. Benedikz, "The Master Magician in Icelandic Folk-Legend," *Durham University Journal,* n.s., 26 (1964): 25.

6. Halldór Hermannsson, *Jón Guðmundsson and His Natural History of Iceland,* vol. 15 of *Islandica* (Ithaca, N.Y.: Cornell Univ. Press, 1924), v, xi.

7. Benedikz, "Master Magician," 26–28.

8. Reidar Th. Christiansen, *Folktales of Norway,* trans. Pat Shaw Iversen (London: Routledge and Kegan Paul, 1964), xxv; *ML,* 18–20.

9. Jacqueline Simpson, trans., *Legends of Icelandic Magicians* (Totowa, N.J.: Rowman and Littlefield, 1975), 19, rpt. in Simpson, *Scandinavian Folktales* (New York: Penguin, 1988), 129.

10. Reimund Kvideland and Henning K. Sehmsdorf, eds., *Scandinavian Folk Belief and Legend* (Minneapolis: Univ. of Minnesota Press, 1988), 286.

11. Alan Boucher, trans., "The Witch-Ride: An Icelandic Tale," *Atlantica and Iceland Review* 16 (1978): 34.

12. William A. Craigie, *Scandinavian Folk-Lore: Illustrations of the Traditional Beliefs of the Northern Peoples* (Paisley, Scotland: Alexander Gardner, 1896), 153.

13. Simpson, *Legends of Icelandic Magicians,* 24.

14. Simpson, *Legends of Icelandic Magicians,* 23, includes a Sæmundur story, "Old Nick Mucks out the Cowhouse," and notes a variant of the same legend with Hálfdán as hero.

15. Simpson, *Legends of Icelandic Magicians,* 42–43.

16. See chap. 3.

17. Simpson, *Legends of Icelandic Magicians,* 22–23.

18. Simpson, *Legends of Icelandic Magicians,* 53–55, rpt. in Simpson, *Scandinavian Folktales,* 136–37.

19. Simpson, *Legends of Icelandic Magicians,* 53.

20. Simpson, *Legends of Icelandic Magicians,* 53.

21. Simpson, *Legends of Icelandic Magicians,* 103, notes: "The old man's devotion to his cow in the present tale is to be seen as an indication of heathenism, for the pre-Christian Scandinavians were believed by their descendants, quite erroneously, to have worshipped cattle as idols."

22. Hastrup, *Nature and Policy in Iceland,* 205; Simpson, *Legends of Icelandic Magicians,* 103.

23. Simpson, *Legends of Icelandic Magicians,* 55.

24. Simpson, *Legends of Icelandic Magicians,* 55–56. This legend is type *ML* 3020, "Inexperienced Use of the Black Book," though the use of the book as a test is atypical. For more on the type, see chap. 5.

25. Simpson, *Legends of Icelandic Magicians,* 62–66.

26. Benedikt S. Benedikz, *The Spread of Printing: Western Hemisphere: Iceland* (Amsterdam: Vangendt, 1969), 17. Benedikz further suggests that the tombs of many a dead bishop could help solve several longstanding mysteries about Iceland's early history of printing.

27. Simpson, *Legends of Icelandic Magicians*, 72. A similar story is told of Sæmundur; see Hermannsson, *Sæmund Sigfússon*, 48.

28. Simpson, *Legends of Icelandic Magicians*, 73.

29. Simpson, *Legends of Icelandic Magicians*, 75.

30. Simpson, *Legends of Icelandic Magicians*, 77.

31. Qtd. in Halldór Hermannsson, introduction to *The Hólar Cato: An Icelandic Schoolbook of the Seventeenth Century*, ed. Halldór Hermannsson, vol. 39 of *Islandica* (Ithaca, N.Y.: Cornell Univ. Press, 1958), x.

34. Qtd. in Hermannsson, "Introduction," xi.

33. Qtd. in Hermannsson, "Introduction," xi.

34. Hermannsson, "Introduction," xvii.

35. Hermannsson, "Introduction," xviii.

36. Halldór Hermannsson, *Icelandic Books of the Sixteenth Century (1534–1600)*, vol. 9 of *Islandica* (Ithaca, N.Y.: Cornell Univ. Press, 1916), ii–iii.

37. Halldór Hermannsson, *Icelandic Books of the Seventeenth Century, 1601–1700*, vol. 14 of *Islandica* (Ithaca, N.Y.: Cornell Univ. Press, 1922), viii.

38. Hermannsson, *Icelandic Books of the Seventeenth Century*, viii–ix.

39. Hubert Seelow, *Die isländischen Übersetzungen der deutschen Volksbücher: Handschriftstudien zur Rezeption und Überlieferung ausländischer unterhaltender Literatur in Island in der Zeit zwischen Reformation und Aufklärung* (Reykjavik: Stofnun Árna Magnússonar, 1989), 1–57, passim.

40. Richard F. Tomasson, *Iceland: The First New Society* (Minneapolis: Univ. of Minnesota Press, 1980), 118–24.

41. Qtd. in Tomasson, *Iceland*, 121.

42. Tomasson, *Iceland*, 119; Harvey J. Graff, *The Legacies of Literacy: Continuities and Contradictions in Western Culture and Society* (Bloomington: Indiana Univ. Press, 1987), 230.

43. Qtd. in "Iceland," *Library Journal* 5 (1880): 229.

44. Archer Taylor, *English Riddles from Oral Tradition* (Berkeley and Los Angeles: Univ. of California Press, 1951), 764.

45. Tomasson, *Iceland*, 123.

Chapter 5. Inexperienced Use of the Black Book in Great Britain and America

1. *ML*, no. 3020. For English translations of Scandinavian versions of the legend type, see Reidar Th. Christiansen, ed., *Folktales of Norway*, trans. Pat Shaw Iversen (London: Routledge and Kegan Paul, 1964), no. 15; and Reimund Kvideland and Henning K. Sehmsdorf, eds., *Scandinavian Folk Belief and Legend* (Minneapolis: Univ. of Minnesota Press, 1988), 285.

2. Joseph Jacobs, *English Fairy Tales* (New York: G. P. Putnam's Sons, 1902), 74–77; Katharine M. Briggs, *A Dictionary of British Folk-Tales in the English Language* (Bloomington: Indiana Univ. Press, 1970), 1:411–12.

3. Frederick A. Bearman, Nati H. Krivatsky, and J. Franklin Mowery, *Fine and Historic Bookbindings from the Folger Shakespeare Library* (Washington, D.C.: Folger Shakespeare Library, 1992), 161.

4. William Blades, *Books in Chains and Other Bibliographical Papers* (1892; rpt., Detroit: Gale, 1968), 3–81; Bearman, Krivatsky, and Mowery, *Fine and Historic Bookbindings*, 30; John Glenn and David Walsh, *Catalogue of the Francis Trigge Chained Library, St. Wulfram's Church, Grantham* (Cambridge, England: D. S. Brewer, 1988).

5. Blades, *Books in Chains,* 27, retells the legend, and it is worth quoting in full: "In the church of St. Wallberg, at Zutphen, in Holland, there is a large collection of books, originally unchained, but which, being all of a religious tendency, excited the animosity of the Devil, who, on several occasions, gained admittance and stole the best of them. The evidence was indisputable, for the marks of his cloven feet upon the flagstones showed plainly, not only the personality of the thief, but the very course he had taken in his sacrilegious visits. The matter was serious, for no one could tell where the depredations would stop; so a consultation was held, and the determination taken to secure the whole of the residue with chains sprinkled with holy water, after which his Satanic Majesty discreetly kept at a distance."

6. John Lindow, *Swedish Legends and Folktales* (Berkeley and Los Angeles: Univ. of California Press, 1978), 45.

7. Hans Sebald, *Witchcraft: The Heritage of a Heresy* (New York: Elsevier, 1978), 89.

8. See chap. 2.

9. Puckett (Ohio), no. 3639.

10. Sean O'Sullivan, *A Handbook of Irish Folklore* (1942; rpt., Detroit: Singing Tree Press, 1970), 521; Sean O'Sullivan, *Folktales of Ireland* (Chicago: Univ. of Chicago Press, 1966), 236–40, 283–84.

11. Henry Glassie, ed., *Irish Folktales* (New York: Pantheon, 1985), 213.

12. Richard M. Dorson, "Collecting in County Kerry," *Journal of American Folklore* 66 (1953): 34–35. Seán Ó Súilleabháin, "Oliver Cromwell in Irish Oral Tradition," in *Folklore Today: A Festschrift for Richard M. Dorson,* ed. Linda Dégh, Henry Glassie, and Felix J. Oinas (Bloomington: Research Center for Language and Semiotic Studies, Indiana Univ., 1976), 479–81, reprints a different version yet asserts that it is the only recorded version. In *Irish Folktales* (1985), 214–15, Henry Glassie reprints the story from Ó Súilleabháin.

13. Dorson, "Collecting in County Kerry," 35.

14. Dorson, "Collecting in County Kerry," 35.

15. Zacharie Boyd, *The Last Battell of the Soule in Death* (Edinburgh: Heires of Andro Hart, 1629), 656.

16. Ó Súilleabháin, "Oliver Cromwell," 479.

17. Miss Dempster, "The Folk-Lore of Sutherlandshire," *Folk-Lore Journal* 6 (1888): 153–54.

18. T. A. Davies, "Folklore of Gwent," *Folk-Lore* 48 (1937): 50.

19. Mrs. Murray-Aynsley, "Scraps of English Folklore, XVI: Hereford-shire," *Folk-Lore* 39 (1928): 383.

20. Charlotte S. Burne, "Reminiscences of Lancashire and Cheshire When George IV. Was King," *Folk-Lore* 20 (1909): 205.

21. Richard M. Dorson, *Jonathan Draws the Long Bow* (Cambridge: Harvard Univ. Press, 1946), 214–18.

22. D. P. Thompson, *Gaut Gurley; The Trappers of Umbagog. A Tale of Border Life* (Boston: John P. Jewett, 1857), 109.

23. *Pennsylvania Gazette,* 21 May 1741, qtd. in Edwin Wolf II, *The Book Culture of a Colonial American City: Philadelphia Books, Bookmen, and Booksellers* (Oxford: Clarendon Press, 1988), 152.

24. Louis C. Jones, "The Devil in York State," *New York Folklore Quarterly* 8 (1952): 10–11.

25. Emelyn Elizabeth Gardner, *Folklore from the Schoharie Hills, New York* (Ann Arbor: Univ. of Michigan Press, 1937), 77.

26. George R. Nielson, "Folklore of the German-Wends in Texas," in *Singers and Storytellers,* ed. Mody C. Boatright, Wilson M. Hudson, and Allen Maxwell, vol. 30 of the Publications of the Texas Folklore Society (Dallas: Southern Methodist Univ. Press, 1961), 255–56.

27. Alvin W. Schillinger, "Hell's Bells and Panther Tracks: Lore of Western Sullivan County," *New York Folklore Quarterly* 9 (1953): 36–37.

Chapter 6. Three Brothers in the Philippines

1. Damiana L. Eugenio, ed., *Philippine Folk Literature: The Proverbs* (Quezon City: U.P. Folklorists, 1992), 50, 148–49, 405; Donn V. Hart, *Riddles in Filipino Folklore: An Anthropological Analysis* (Syracuse: Syracuse Univ. Press, 1964), 209–11.

2. I make no claims to have read or located all recorded versions of these three tales. My statement concerning the importance which the Filipino versions of these tales give the book as a motif is based on an exhaustive reading of Thompson, *Motif-Index,* and a reasonably full (though by no means exhaustive) reading of versions of the three tales which have been recorded and published since the *Motif-Index* or are listed in AT or the numerous other tale-type indexes based on the Aarne-Thompson classification system. For a partial list of English translations of these three tales, see D. L. Ashliman, *A Guide to Folktales in the English Language* (Westport, Conn.: Greenwood Press, 1987), 135–36. For the most thorough listing of the recorded versions of tale type AT 653A, see Stephen S. Jones, "'The Rarest Thing in the World': Indo-European or African?" in *African Folklore in the New World,* ed. Daniel J. Crowley (Austin: Univ. of Texas Press, 1977), 54–64.

3. For theories of the tale's literary origins, see W. A. Clouston, *Popular Tales and Fictions: Their Migrations and Transformations* (1887; rpt., Detroit: Singing Tree Press, 1968), 1:285–86; and Stith Thompson, *The Folktale* (1946; rpt., Berkeley and Los Angeles: Univ. of California Press, 1977), 81. Jones, "Rarest Thing," however, challenges the efforts of Clous-

ton and others to trace AT 653 and, more specifically, AT 653A to literary works.

4. Clouston, *Popular Tales and Fictions* 1:285–86.

5. *The Pentamerone of Giambattista Basile,* trans. Benedetto Croce, ed. N. M. Penzer (New York: E. P. Dutton, 1932), 2:141.

6. Hermann Bausinger, *Folk Culture in a World of Technology,* trans. Elke Dettmer (Bloomington: Indiana Univ. Press, 1990), 12.

7. For an extended analysis of one version of this tale type, see Daniel J. Crowley, "'The Greatest Thing in the World' Type 653A, in Trinidad," in *Folklore Today: A Festschrift for Richard M. Dorson,* ed. Linda Dégh, Henry Glassie, and Felix J. Oinas (Bloomington: Indiana Univ., 1976), 93–100. Jones, "Rarest Thing," suggests the tale originated in the African oral tradition.

8. In *The Folktale* (1946), 82, Thompson states that "The Three Brothers" does not seem to have traveled beyond the European continent, but he records Caribbean versions of it in the subsequently published *Types of the Folktale . . . Second Revision* (1961).

9. Dean S. Fansler, *Filipino Popular Tales,* vol. 12 of *Memoirs of the American Folk-Lore Society* (Lancaster, Pa.: American Folklore Society, 1921), 12:116–18. The tales Fansler supplies were recorded between 1908 and 1914. This tale is reprinted in Damiana L. Eugenio, ed., *Philippine Folk Literature: The Folktales* (Quezon City: U.P. Folklorists, 1989), 200–202. Eugenio lists another version of the tale which survives as part of the Fansler manuscript collection of Philippine folktales.

10. Fansler, *Filipino Popular Tales,* 117.

11. "The Four Skillful Brothers" (no. 129), in *The Complete Fairy Tales of the Brother Grimm,* ed. and trans. Jack Zipes (New York: Bantam Books, 1992), 458.

12. Fansler, *Filipino Popular Tales,* 120–22.

13. Fansler, *Filipino Popular Tales,* 120.

14. Fansler, *Filipino Popular Tales,* 120.

15. Fansler, *Filipino Popular Tales,* 121.

16. *The Katha Sarit Sagara: Or Ocean of the Streams of Story,* trans. C. H. Tawney (1880; rpt., Delhi: Munshiram Manoharlal, 1968), 2:242–45.

17. Fansler, *Filipino Popular Tales,* 118–19.

18. Clouston, *Popular Tales and Fictions* 1:284.

19. Fansler, *Filipino Popular Tales,* 123.

20. Fansler, *Filipino Popular Tales,* 123.

21. M. Mariano, *Folk Tales of the Philippines* (New Delhi: Sterling Publishers, 1982), 34–35.

22. Fansler, *Filipino Popular Tales,* 127. Unlike the other tales in this section of Fansler's work, he simply paraphrases the original. Since Fansler does not title this tale, I have assigned it the title "Three Rival Brothers."

23. Fansler, *Filipino Popular Tales,* 127.

24. Milagros Gonzalez-Tabujara, *Visayan Folklore,* ed. Ernesto Constantino (Diliman, Quezon City: Folklore Studies Program, College of Social Sci-

ences and Philosophy, Univ. of the Philippines and the U.P. Folklorists, 1985), 67–68. Gonzalez-Tabujara's collection of tales was originally completed in 1925 as an undergraduate project under Professor Fansler.

25. Gonzalez-Tabujara, *Visayan Folklore,* 67–68.

26. David Joel Steinberg, *The Philippines: A Singular and a Plural Place,* 3d ed. (Boulder, Colo.: Westview Press, 1994), 50.

27. Fansler, *Filipino Popular Tales,* 116, 120. For a fine treatment of the transmission of folktales from one generation to the next, see Donn V. Hart and Harriett C. Hart, "Cinderella in the Eastern Bisayas with a Summary of the Philippine Folktale," *Journal of American Folklore* 79 (1966): 317–20.

28. The work has been reprinted as *Doctrina Christiana: The First Book Printed in the Philippines,* ed. Edwin Wolf II (Washington, D.C.: Library of Congress, 1947). It is also reprinted in *Encyclopedia of the Philippines,* 3d ed., ed. Zoilo M. Galang (Manila: Exequel Floro, 1950), 1:226–301.

29. *Relacion de las Islas Filipinas,* trans. Ramón Echevarria (Manila: Historical Conservation Society, 1969), 280.

30. Damiana L. Eugenio, ed., *Philippine Folk Literature: The Legends* (Quezon City: U.P. Folklorists, 1987), 6.

31. John Leddy Phelan, *The Hispanization of the Philippines: Spanish Arms and Filipino Responses, 1565–1700* (Madison: Univ. of Wisconsin Press, 1959), 58.

32. Vicente L. Rafael, *Contracting Colonialism: Translation and Christian Conversion in Tagalog Society under Early Spanish Rule* (Ithaca, N.Y.: Cornell Univ. Press, 1988), 31–33.

33. Yolando Pino-Saacedra, ed., *Folktales of Chile,* trans. Rockwell Gray (Chicago: Univ. of Chicago Press, 1967), 136.

34. Terrence Leslie Hansen, *The Types of the Folktale in Cuba, Puerto Rico, the Dominican Republic, and Spanish South America* (Berkeley and Los Angeles: Univ. of California Press, 1957), 77. Hansen lists the tales under tale type 653, "The Four Skillful Brothers," but it is important to note that his study appeared before the second revision of Aarne-Thompson, which differentiated "The Rarest Thing in the World" (AT 653A). See also, Helen L. Flowers, *A Classification of the Folktale of the West Indies by Types and Motifs* (New York: Arno Press, 1980), 218–21; Stanley L. Robe, *Index of Mexican Folktales Including Narrative Texts from Mexico, Central America, and the Hispanic United States* (Berkeley and Los Angeles: Univ. of California Press, 1973), 112.

35. Robe, *Index of Mexican Folktales,* 112 (my emphasis). Versions recorded in Albania and in the East African cattle area also attribute to the brother the power of hearing at great distances. See Clouston, *Popular Tales and Fictions* 1:279, and May Augusta Klipple, *African Folktales with Foreign Analogues* (New York: Garland, 1992), 221.

36. Recorded and indexed Asian variants of the three tales do not mention the book. See Hiroko Ikeda, *A Type and Motif Index of Japanese Folk-Literature,* no. 209 of *FF Communications* (Helsinki: Suomalainen

Tiedeakatemia Academia Scientarum Fennica, 1971), 159–60; and Nai-Tung Ting, *A Type Index of Chinese Folktales in the Oral Tradition and Major Works on Non-Religious Classical Literature*, no. 223 of *FF Communications* (Helsinki: Suomalainen Tiedeakatemia Academia Scientarum Fennica, 1978), 114–15.

37. Rafael, *Contracting Colonialism*, 39.

38. Donn V. Hart and Harriett C. Hart, "The Images of the Catholic Priest in Bisayan Filipino Folklore," *Southern Folklore Quarterly* 40 (1976): 308.

39. Rafael, *Contracting Colonialism*, 56, suggests that even after the Spanish liberals instituted educational reforms in 1863 only 10 percent of the indigenous population could understand Spanish. Steinberg, *Philippines*, 51, suggests that at the time of the American takeover, less than 5 percent of the Filipino people could speak Spanish.

40. *NUC*, no. B0283865.

41. *NUC*, nos. N0078961, N0078962.

42. Hart and Hart, "Cinderella," 310–11.

43. Gonzalez-Tabujara, *Visayan Folklore*, 56–57.

44. Gonzalez-Tabujara, *Visayan Folklore*, 56–58.

Chapter 7. Traditional Flyleaf Rhymes

1. H. S. Bennett, *England from Chaucer to Caxton* (1928; rpt., London: Methuen, 1952), 160–62, cites several examples from fifteenth-century manuscripts. W. Wallace, "To the Editor of the Times," *Times* (London), 3 Mar. 1928, p. 13, cites an example from a fourteenth-century manuscript. Adam Gacek, "The Use of '*kabikaj*' in Arabic Manuscripts," *Manuscripts of the Middle East* 1 (1986): 49–53, describes several surviving medieval Arabic manuscripts with inscriptions to protect them from destruction by insects.

2. Thomas James Holmes, *Cotton Mather: A Bibliography of His Works* (1940; rpt., Newton, Mass.: Crofton, 1974), no. 103-A. Thomas James Holmes, *Increase Mather: A Bibliography of His Works* (Cleveland: For William Gwinn Mather by the Harvard Univ. Press, 1931), no. 83, locates a surviving copy of Increase Mather's *Now or Never is the Time for Men to Make Sure of Their Eternal Salvation* (Boston, 1713) with the inscription, "Susanah Morgan Her Book / god give her grace there in to Look [17]22." An English observer, known only by the pseudonym Balliolensis, "Inscriptions in Books," *Notes and Queries*, 1st ser., vol. 7 (5 Feb. 1853): 128, locates the same inscription. Holmes, *Increase Mather*, no. 13, locates a surviving copy of Increase Mather's *The Blessed Hope, and the Glorious Appearing of the Great God Our Saviour, Jesus Christ* (Boston, 1701) inscribed: "ledy Smith her book / God give her grace thire into / look that She may rone [i.e., run] her / blessed race that heaven / may be her resting place." Similar inscriptions have been located in seventeenth- and early-eighteenth-century books. A 1608 Bible is inscribed: "John Petty his book, /

God give him grace therein to Looke: / And when thee Bell doth begin to toole, / Lord Jesus Christ Receive his Soule"; Esligh, "Inscription on Fly-Leaf of a Breeches Bible, 1608," *Notes and Queries,* 2d ser., vol. 9 (24 Mar. 1860): 218. Another inscription, dated 1704, reads: "John Ellis his Book. / God give him grace in it to looke, / and when the bell for him doth toull / the Lord of heaven Receive his Soulle"; J. Eliot Hodgkin, "MS. Notes of Possession in Books," *Notes and Queries,* 7th ser., vol. 3 (12 Mar. 1887): 206.

3. Cestriensis, "Inscriptions in Books," *Notes and Queries,* 1st ser., vol. 8 (17 Dec. 1853): 591. W. C. B., "Book Inscriptions," *Notes and Queries,* 4th ser., vol. 2 (18 July 1868): 53–54, locates a similar example dated 1671. Boileau, "Sixteenth Century Book Inscription," *Notes and Queries,* 5th ser., vol. 9 (15 June 1878): 466, also locates a similar example. Michael Aislabie Denham, *The Denham Tracts: A Collection of Folklore by Michael Aislabie Denham, and Reprinted from the Original Tracts and Pamphlets Printed by Mr. Denham Between 1846 and 1859,* ed. James Hardy (1892–1986; rpt., Nendeln/Liechtenstein: Kraus, 1967), 2:339, locates a similar inscription, dated 1708, in Sir James Calder's copy of John Skene's *Regiam Majestatem* (Edinburgh, 1609).

4. Cestriensis, "Inscriptions in Books," 591. W. R. Tate, "Conclusion of Verses Sought," *Notes and Queries,* 8th ser., vol. 6 (13 Oct. 1894): 294, locates a similar verse dated 1642. Ronald D. Whittenbury-Kaye, "Book Inscriptions," *Notes and Queries,* 12th ser., vol. 11 (8 July 1922): 27, locates another dated 1664.

5. Fanny D. Bergen, "Fly Leaf Rhymes and Decorations," *New England Magazine* 23 (1900): 510.

6. W. M. Beauchamp, "Note Written on the Fly-Leaf of a Book," *Journal of American Folklore* 3 (1890): 244. F. A. Legge, "To the Editor of the Times," *Times* (London), 28 Feb. 1928, p. 17, cites the same verse with the alternative seventh line, "But this I know, that books once lent."

7. Sidney Oldall Addy, *Household Tales with Other Traditional Remains Collected in the Counties of York, Lincoln, Derby, and Nottingham* (London: David Nutt, 1895), 145; Thomas Ollive Mabbott, "Book Borrowers," *Notes and Queries* 149 (11 July 1925): 33.

8. Beauchamp, "Note Written on the Fly-Leaf," 244. These verses combined with the concluding prose sentence have been separately recorded. See John T. Page, "A Rhyming Warning to Book-Borrowers," *Notes and Queries,* 9th ser., vol. 1 (25 June 1898): 512.

9. Beauchamp, "Note Written on the Fly-Leaf," 244. Beauchamp was born in 1830 (*Dictionary of American Biography,* ed. Allen Johnson [1927; rpt., New York: Charles Scribner's Sons, 1964], 1:103), so this inscription was probably recorded sometime during the early 1840s.

10. John Murray, "A Rhyming Warning to Book-Borrowers," *Notes and Queries,* 9th ser., vol. 1 (25 June 1898): 512.

11. W. J. Hardy, *Book-Plates* (London: Kegan Paul, Trench, Trübner, 1893), 128–29; Brian North Lee, *British Bookplates: A Pictorial History* (London: David & Charles, 1979), no. 250.

12. Balliolensis, "Inscriptions in Books," 128.

13. Edward Marshall, "Ex-Libris: Lord Mansfield," *Notes and Queries,* 6th ser., vol. 4 (27 Aug. 1881): 166.

14. O. P., "Inscriptions in Books," *Notes and Queries,* 1st ser., vol. 7 (2 Apr. 1853): 337.

15. Sm. De., "A Book Inscription," *Notes and Queries,* 3d ser., vol. 2 (16 Aug. 1862): 125. The original contributor used a blank for the book owner's name. I have supplied the fictional name "Joseph Johnston" to make the verse readable.

16. See chap. 5.

17. Bergen, "Fly Leaf Rhymes," 510; Brown (North Carolina), 1:200; Jan Harold Brunvand, *The Study of American Folklore: An Introduction,* 2d ed. (New York: Norton, 1978), 90. Thomas Ollive Mabbott, "Book Borrowers," *Notes and Queries* 149 (3 Oct. 1925): 250, locates a similar example.

18. Bergen, "Fly Leaf Rhymes," 510.

19. Bergen, "Fly Leaf Rhymes," 511.

20. M. D., "Notes on Fly-Leaves," *Notes and Queries,* 4th ser., vol. 8 (16 Dec. 1871): 514.

21. Bergen, "Fly Leaf Rhymes," 510. For another example see W. J. Wintemberg and Katherine H. Wintemberg, "Folk-Lore from Grey County, Ontario," *Journal of American Folklore* 31 (1918): 120.

22. Mabbott, "Book Borrowers," *Notes and Queries* 149 (11 July 1925): 33.

23. Bergen, "Fly Leaf Rhymes," 511.

24. J. C., "Inscriptions in Books," *Notes and Queries,* 1st ser., vol. 7 (2 Apr. 1853): 337. Henry Attwell, "A Rhyming Warning to Book-Borrowers," *Notes and Queries,* 9th ser., vol. 1 (7 May 1898): 366, locates a similar version: "Steal not this book for fear of shame, / For in it is the owner's name, / And when you die the Lord will say, / Where is that book you stole away?" See also Brunvand, *Study of American Folklore,* 90.

25. F. Whitmore Smith, "To the Editor of the Times," *Times* (London), 6 Mar. 1928, p. 17.

26. J. P. B., "Book Inscription," *Notes and Queries,* 4th ser., vol. 6 (9 July 1870): 26. This inscription is a variation on a much earlier verse, probably from the sixteenth century or earlier: "Thys boke is one and GODES kors [i.e., curse] ys anoder: / They that take the on[e]; GOD gefe them the toder"; John Timbs and Alexander Gunn, *Abbeys, Castles and Ancient Halls of England and Wales: Their Legendary Lore and Popular History* (London: Frederick Warne, n.d.), 2:375. David Pearson, *Provenance Research in Book History: A Handbook* (London: British Library, 1994), 16, supplies another flyleaf rhyme which threatens hanging: "John Barcllay This booke ise mine he that steles this book frome me he shaal be hanged on a trie."

27. G. F. Northall, *English Folk-Rhymes: A Collection of Traditional Verses Relating to Places and Persons, Customs, Superstitions, Etc* (London: Kegan Paul, Trench, Trübner, 1892), 102.

28. W. R. H., "Book-Stealing: Degrees of Blackness," *Notes and Queries,* 10th ser., vol. 7 (16 Mar. 1907): 212.

29. Mabbott, "Book Borrowers," *Notes and Queries* 149 (11 July 1925): 33.

30. W. W., "Inscriptions in Books," *Notes and Queries,* 1st ser., vol. 7 (30 Apr. 1853): 438. Thomas Ratcliffe, "Book-Stealing: Degrees of Blackness," *Notes and Queries,* 10th ser., vol. 6 (20 Oct. 1906): 305, locates a similar example: "Black is the raven, / Black is the rook, / Blacker is the one / that steals this book." Ratcliffe suggested that the rhyme was new, but follow-up studies by S. O. Addy and T. N. Postlethwaite dated it at least as early as the mid-nineteenth century; *Notes and Queries,* 10th ser., vol. 6 (3 Nov. 1906): 353. John T. Page, "Book-Stealing: Degrees of Blackness," *Notes and Queries,* 10th ser., vol. 7 (16 Mar. 1907): 212, locates a similar example.

31. T. O. Mabbott, "John Stirling Autograph," *Notes and Queries* 153 (2 July 1927): 8.

32. Honoré DeMarville, "Inscriptions in Books," *Notes and Queries,* 1st ser., vol. 7 (4 June 1853): 554.

33. "Book Borrowing," *Times* (London), 7 Mar. 1928, p. 17; M. Gilbert, "Book-Borrowers' Conscience," *Times* (London), 9 Mar. 1928, p. 10.

34. Frank Hird, "To the Editor of the Times," *Times* (London), 7 Mar. 1928, p. 17.

35. Edwin Wolf II, "Report of the Librarian," *Annual Report of the Library Company of Philadelphia for 1962* (Philadelphia: Library Company of Philadelphia, 1963), 43; Kevin J. Hayes, *A Colonial Woman's Bookshelf* (Knoxville: Univ. of Tennessee Press, 1996), 22.

36. Mabbott, "Book Borrowers," *Notes and Queries* 149 (11 July 1925): 33.

37. Bergen, "Fly Leaf Rhymes," 510, also lists variants for the second line: "My wrath will surely follow you," "You'll feel the leather of my shoe," and "The devil will be after you."

38. Russell Gole, "Inscriptions in Books," *Notes and Queries,* 1st ser., vol. 7 (2 Apr. 1853): 337.

39. Bergen, "Fly Leaf Rhymes," 511. Wintemberg and Wintemberg, "Folk-Lore from Grey County, Ontario," 119, cite a similar example: "Don't steal this book for fear of strife, / For here you see my butcher-knife."

40. Bergen, "Fly Leaf Rhymes," 511. For another example, see *Funk & Wagnalls Standard Dictionary of Folklore, Mythology and Legend,* ed. Maria Leach and Jerome Fried (San Francisco: Harper & Row, 1984), 157. Alan Dundes briefly discusses these identification rhymes in *Folklore Matters* (Knoxville: Univ. of Tennessee Press, 1989), 1–2.

41. W. M. Beauchamp, "Rhymes from Old Powder-Horns," *Journal of American Folklore* 2 (1889): 117–22.

42. Charles A. Federer, "Doggerel Book-Inscriptions," *Notes and Queries,* 10th ser., vol. 6 (18 Aug. 1906): 128.

43. Addy, *Household Tales*, 145. For similar examples, see W. M. Beauchamp, "Lines from the Cover of an Old Bible," *Journal of American Folklore* 2 (1889): 311; F. M. M., "Inscriptions in Books," *Notes and Queries*, 1st ser., vol. 7 (26 Feb. 1853): 221; Northall, *English Folk-Rhymes*, 102; Arthur O. Norton, "Harvard Text-Books and Reference Books of the Seventeenth Century." *Proceedings of the Colonial Society of Massachusetts* (Apr. 1933): 394–95; and Wintemberg and Wintemberg, "Folk-Lore from Grey County, Ontario," 119.

44. W. E. Buckley, "Inscriptions in Books," *Notes and Queries*, 6th ser., vol. 6 (15 July 1882): 46.

45. For the most thorough treatment of the circulating library, see David Kaser, *A Book for a Sixpence: The Circulating Library in America* (Pittsburgh: Beta Phi Mu, 1980).

46. Gole, "Inscriptions in Books," 337.

47. Alfred Lawrence Hall-Quest, *The Textbook: How to Use and Judge It* (New York: Macmillan, 1918), 48–49.

48. Reported by Carole Hayes, who remembered reading it in an old schoolbook of her mother's (c. 1910). Brunvand, *Study of American Folklore*, 90, cites a similar example.

Conclusion

1. M. Mariano, *Folk Tales of the Philippines* (New Delhi: Sterling Publishers, 1982), 35.

2. Mariano, *Folk Tales of the Philippines*, 35.

3. Linda Dégh, *American Folklore and the Mass Media* (Bloomington: Indiana Univ. Press, 1994), 18.

4. Donn V. Hart and Harriett C. Hart, "Cinderella in the Eastern Bisayas with a Summary of the Philippine Folktale," *Journal of American Folklore* 79 (1966): 311.

5. Reported by James Wall, Oklahoma City, 9 July 1995. Personal interview.

6. Hermann Bausinger, *Folk Culture in a World of Technology*, trans. Elke Dettmer (Bloomington: Indiana Univ. Press, 1990), 12.

7. See chap. 5.

Sources

Aarne, Antti, and Stith Thompson. *The Types of the Folktale: A Classification and Bibliography . . . Second Revision.* Helsinki: Suomalainen Tiedeakatemia Academia Scientarum Fennica, 1961.

Abbott, G. F. *Macedonian Folklore.* Cambridge: Cambridge Univ. Press, 1903.

Aðalsteinsson, Jon Hnefill. "Saemundr *Fróði*: A Medieval Master of Magic." Trans. Terry Gunnell. *Arv: Nordic Yearbook of Folklore* 50 (1994): 117–32.

Addy, Sidney Oldall. "Book-Stealing: Degrees of Blackness." *Notes and Queries,* 10th ser., vol. 6 (3 Nov. 1906): 353.

————. *Household Tales with Other Traditional Remains Collected in the Counties of York, Lincoln, Derby, and Nottingham.* London: David Nutt, 1895.

Albertus Magnus: Being the Approved, Verified, Sympathetic and Natural Egyptian Secrets or White and Black Art for Man and Beast. Cedar Knolls, N.J.: Wehman Bros., n.d.

Allison, Lelah. "Folk Beliefs in Southeastern Illinois." *Journal of American Folklore* 63 (1950): 309–24.

Anderson, John Q. "Special Powers in Folk Cures and Remedies." In *Tire Shrinker to Dragster,* ed. Wilson M. Hudson, 163–74. Vol. 34 of the Publications of the Texas Folklore Society. Austin: Encino Press, 1968.

Arndt, Karl John Richard, Reimer C. Eck, Gerd-J. Bötte, Werner Tannof, and Annelies Müller. *The First Century of German Language Printing in the United States of America: A Bibliography Based on the Studies of Oswald Seidensticker and Wilbur H. Oda.* No. 22 of *Publications the Pennsylvania German Society.* Göttingen, 1989.

Ashliman, D. L. *A Guide to Folktales in the English Language.* Westport, Conn.: Greenwood Press, 1987.

Attwell, Henry. "A Rhyming Warning to Book-Borrowers." *Notes and Queries,* 9th ser., vol. 1 (7 May 1898): 366.

Aubrey, John. *Remaines of Gentilisme and Judaisme.* Ed. James Britten. London: For the Folk-Lore Society by W. Satchell, Peyton, 1881.

Axon, William E. A. "Divination by Books." *Manchester Quarterly* 26 (1907): 26–35.

B., J. P. "Book Inscription." *Notes and Queries,* 4th ser., vol. 6 (9 July 1870): 26.

B., W. C. "Book Inscriptions." *Notes and Queries,* 4th ser., vol. 2 (18 July 1868): 53–54.

Bächtold-Stäubli, Hanns. *Handwörterbuch des Deutschen Aberglaubens.* Vol. 6. Berlin: Walter De Gruyter, 1935.

Balliolensis. "Inscriptions in Books." *Notes and Queries,* 1st ser., vol. 7 (5 Feb. 1853): 127–28.

Banks, M. M. "Gleanings from Magazines." *Folk-Lore* 54 (1943): 309–10.

Basile, Giambattista. *The Pentamerone of Giambattista Basile.* Trans. Benedetto Croce. Ed. N. M. Penzer. 2 vols. New York: E. P. Dutton, 1932.

Baughman, Ernest W. *Type and Motif-Index of the Folktales of England and North America.* No. 20 of the Indiana Univ. Folklore Series. The Hague: Mouton, 1966.

Bausinger, Hermann. *Folk Culture in a World of Technology.* Trans. Elke Dettmer. Bloomington: Indiana Univ. Press, 1990.

Bayard, S. P. "Witchcraft and Spirits on the Border of Pennsylvania and West Virginia." *Journal of American Folklore* 51 (1938): 47–59.

Bearman, Frederick A., Nati H. Krivatsky, and J. Franklin Mowery. *Fine and Historic Bookbindings from the Folger Shakespeare Library.* Washington, D.C.: Folger Shakespeare Library, 1992.

Beauchamp, W. M. "Lines from the Cover of an Old Bible." *Journal of American Folklore* 2 (1889): 310–11.

———. "Note Written on the Fly-Leaf of a Book." *Journal of American Folklore* 3 (1890): 244.

———. "Rhymes from Old Powder-Horns." *Journal of American Folklore* 2 (1889): 117–22.

Belknap, Jeremy. "The Belknap Papers." *Collections of the Massachusetts Historical Society,* 5th ser., vol. 2 (1877): 1–500.

Benedikz, Benedikt S. "The Master Magician in Icelandic Folk-Legend." *Durham University Journal,* n.s., 26 (1964): 22–34.

———. *The Spread of Printing: Western Hemisphere: Iceland.* Amsterdam: Vangendt, 1969.

Bennett, H. S. *England from Chaucer to Caxton.* 1928. Rpt. London: Methuen, 1952.

Bergen, Fanny D. *Current Superstitions Collected from the Oral Tradition of English Speaking Folk.* Boston: For the American Folk-Lore Society by Houghton Mifflin, 1896.

———. "Fly Leaf Rhymes and Decorations." *New England Magazine* 23 (1900): 505–11.

———. "On the Eastern Shore." *Journal of American Folklore* 2 (1889): 295–300.

"Bible Divination." *Folk-Lore Journal* 1 (1883): 333.

"Bible Divination." *Folk-Lore Journal* 2 (1884): 380–81.

Blades, William. *Books in Chains and Other Bibliographical Papers.* 1892. Rpt. Detroit: Gale, 1968.

Boggs, Ralph S. *Index of Spanish Folktales.* No. 90 of *FF Communications.* Helsinki: Suomalainen Tiedeakatemia Academia Scientarum Fennica, 1930.

Boileau. "Sixteenth Century Book Inscription." *Notes and Queries,* 5th ser., vol. 9 (15 June 1878): 466.

"Book Borrowing." *Times* (London), 7 Mar. 1928, p. 17.

"Books in Colonial Virginia." *Virginia Magazine of History and Biography* 10 (1903): 389–405.

Books in Print: 1994–1995. Vols. 7 and 8. New Providence, N.J.: R. R. Bowker, 1994.

Boucher, Alan, trans. "The Witch-Ride: An Icelandic Tale." *Atlantica and Iceland Review* 16 (1978): 34–35.

Boyd, Zacharie. *The Last Battell of the Soule in Death.* Edinburgh: Heires of Andro Hart, 1629.

Bradford, William. *William Bradford, Printer, Bookseller, and Stationer, at His Store Adjoining the London Coffee-House: Has Imported a Collection of Books.* [Philadelphia: William Bradford, 1760?]

Brewster, Paul G. "Folk Cures and Preventives from Southern Indiana." *Southern Folklore Quarterly* 3 (1939): 33–43.

Briggs, Katharine M. *A Dictionary of British Folk-Tales in the English Language.* 2 vols. in 4. Bloomington: Indiana Univ. Press, 1970.

Brightwell, D. Barron. "Superstition in Shropshire." *Notes and Queries,* 5th ser., vol. 11 (18 Jan. 1879): 45.

British Library General Catalogue of Printed Books to 1975. 360 vols. London: Clive Bingley, 1979.

Brown, Carleton F. "The Long Hidden Friend." *Journal of American Folklore* 17 (1904): 89–152.

Brown, Frank C. *The Frank C. Brown Collection of North Carolina Folklore.* Ed. Newman Ivey White. 7 vols. Durham, N.C.: Duke Univ. Press, 1952–64.

Brown, Robert. "Bible and Key." *Folk-Lore Journal* 2 (1884): 156–57.

Browne, Ray B. *Popular Beliefs and Practices from Alabama.* Berkeley and Los Angeles: Univ. of California Press, 1958.

Brunvand, Jan Harold. *The Study of American Folklore: An Introduction.* 2d ed. New York: Norton, 1978.

Bryant, Margaret M. "Folklore from Edgefield County, South Carolina." *Southern Folklore Quarterly* 12 (1948): 136–48.

———. "Folklore from Edgefield County, South Carolina, II." *Southern Folklore Quarterly* 13 (1949): 279–91.

Buckley, W. E. "Inscriptions in Books." *Notes and Queries,* 6th ser., vol. 6 (15 July 1882): 45–46.

Budge, E. A. Wallis. *Amulets and Talismans.* New Hyde Park, N.Y.: Univ. Books, 1961.

Burne, Charlotte S. "Reminiscences of Lancashire and Cheshire When George IV. Was King." *Folk-Lore* 20 (1909): 203–7.

Burr, Esther Edwards. *The Journal of Esther Edwards Burr, 1754–1757.* Ed. Carol F. Karlsen and Laurie Crumpacker. New Haven, Conn.: Yale Univ. Press, 1984.

Byington, Robert H. "Powwowing in Pennsylvania." *Keystone Folklore Quarterly* 9 (1964): 111–17.

C., A. "School Superstitions." *Notes and Queries,* 1st ser., vol. 1 (26 July 1851): 53.

C., E. "Divination by Bible and Key." *Notes and Queries,* 1st ser., vol. 2 (8 June 1850): 19.

C., J. "Inscriptions in Books." *Notes and Queries,* 1st ser., vol. 7 (2 Apr. 1853): 337.

Cable, George W. *The Grandissimes.* 1880. Rpt. New York: Charles Scribner's Sons, 1912.

Caillet, Albert L. *Manuel bibliographique des sciences psychiques ou occultes.* Vol. 1. Paris: Lucien Dorbon, 1912.

Campbell, J. F. *Popular Tales of the West Highlands.* New ed. Vol. 2. London: Alexander Gardner, 1890.

Cannell, Margaret. *Signs, Omens, and Portents in Nebraska Folklore.* University of Nebraska Studies in Language, Literature, and Criticism, no. 13. Lincoln, Nebr., 1933.

Cannon, Anthon S. *Popular Beliefs and Superstitions from Utah.* Ed. Wayland D. Hand and Jeannine E. Talley. Salt Lake City: Univ. of Utah Press, 1984.

Carmer, Carl. *Stars Fell on Alabama.* New York: Farrar & Rinehart, 1934.

Carter, Landon. *The Diary of Colonel Landon Cater of Sabine Hall, 1752–1778.* Ed. Jack P. Greene. Richmond: Virginia Historical Society, 1987.

Catalogue général de livres imprimés de la Bibliothèque Nationale. Vol. 1. Paris: Paul Catin, 1924.

Cestriensis. "Inscriptions in Books." *Notes and Queries,* 1st ser., vol. 8 (17 Dec. 1853): 591.

Chartier, Roger. *The Cultural Uses of Print in Early Modern France.* Trans. Lydia G. Cochrane. Princeton, N.J.: Princeton Univ. Press, 1987.

Child, Francis James, ed. *The English and Scottish Popular Ballads.* 5 vols. in 3. 1882–98. Rpt. New York: Folklore Press and Pageant Book, 1956.

Chirino, Pedro. *Relacion de las Islas Filipinas.* Trans. Ramón Echevarria. Manila: Historical Conservation Society, 1969.

Christiansen, Reidar Th., ed. *Folktales of Norway.* Trans. Pat Shaw Iversen. London: Routledge and Kegan Paul, 1964.

———. *The Migratory Legends.* 1958. Rpt. New York: Arno Press, 1977.

Classen, Albrecht. *The German Volksbuch: A Critical History of a Late-Medieval Genre.* Lewiston, N.Y.: Edwin Mellen Press, 1995.

Clouston, W. A. *Popular Tales and Fictions: Their Migrations and Transformations.* 1887. Rpt. Detroit: Singing Tree Press, 1968.

Cometti, Elizabeth. "Some Early Best Sellers in Piedmont North Carolina." *Journal of Southern History* 16 (1950): 324–37.

"Concerning Negro Sorcery in the United States." *Journal of American Folklore* 3 (1890): 281–87.

Courtney, M. A. "Cornish Folk-Lore." *Folk-Lore Journal* 5 (1887): 14–61, 85–112, 177–220.

Craigie, William A. *Scandinavian Folk-Lore: Illustrations of the Traditional Beliefs of the Northern Peoples.* Paisley, Scotland: Alexander Gardner, 1896.

Crane, Ronald S. "The Vogue of *Guy of Warwick* from the Close of the Middle Ages to the Romantic Revival." *PMLA* 30 (1915): 125–94.

Creighton, Helen. *Bluenose Magic: Popular Beliefs and Superstitions in Nova Scotia.* Toronto: Ryerson Press, 1968.

Cressy, David. "Books as Totems in Seventeenth-Century England and New England." *Journal of Library History* 21 (1986): 92–106.

Crowley, Daniel J. "'The Greatest Thing in the World' Type 653A, in Trinidad." In *Folklore Today: A Festschrift for Richard M. Dorson,* ed. Linda Dégh, Henry Glassie, and Felix J. Oinas, 93–100. Bloomington: Research Center for Language and Semiotic Studies, Indiana Univ., 1976.

D., M. "Notes on Fly-Leaves." *Notes and Queries,* 4th ser., vol. 8 (16 Dec. 1871): 514.

Dague, R. A. *Henry Ashton: A Thrilling Story and How the Famous Co-operative Commonwealth Was Established in Zanland.* Alameda, Calif.: By the author, 1903.

Davies, Jonathan Ceredig. *Folk-Lore of West and Mid-Wales.* Aberystwyth, Wales: Welsh Gazette, 1911.

Davies, T. A. "Folklore of Gwent." *Folk-Lore* 48 (1937): 41–59.

De., Sm. "A Book Inscription." *Notes and Queries,* 3d ser., vol. 2 (16 Aug. 1862): 125.

Deansley, M. "Vernacular Books in England in the Fourteenth and Fifteenth Centuries." *Modern Language Review* 15 (1920): 349–58.

Dégh, Linda. *American Folklore and the Mass Media.* Bloomington: Indiana Univ. Press, 1994.

DeMarville, Honoré. "Inscriptions in Books." *Notes and Queries,* 1st ser., vol. 7 (4 June 1853): 554.

Dempster, Miss. "The Folk-Lore of Sutherlandshire." *Folk-Lore Journal* 6 (1888): 149–89, 215–52.

Denham, Michael Aislabie. *The Denham Tracts: A Collection of Folklore by Michael Aislabie Denham, and Reprinted from the Original Tracts and Pamphlets Printed by Mr. Denham Between 1846 and 1859.* Ed. James Hardy. 2 vols. 1892–95. Rpt. Nendeln/Liechtenstein: Kraus, 1967.

Devlin, Judith. *The Superstitious Mind: French Peasants and the Supernatural in the Nineteenth Century.* New Haven, Conn.: Yale Univ. Press, 1987.

Dictionary of American Biography. Ed. Allen Johnson. Vol. 1. 1927. Rpt. New York: Charles Scribner's Sons, 1964.

Doctrina Christiana: The First Book Printed in the Philippines. Ed. Edwin Wolf II. Washington, D.C.: Library of Congress, 1947.

Dorson, Richard M. *Bloodstoppers & Bearwalkers: Folk Traditions of the Upper Peninsula.* Cambridge: Harvard Univ. Press, 1952.

———. "Collecting in County Kerry." *Journal of American Folklore* 66 (1953): 19–42.

———. *Jonathan Draws the Long Bow.* Cambridge: Harvard Univ. Press, 1946.

Duncan, Hannibal Gerald, and Winnie Leach Duncan. "Superstitions and Sayings among the Southern Highlanders." *Journal of American Folklore* 42 (1929): 233–37.

Dundes, Alan. *Folklore Matters.* Knoxville: Univ. of Tennessee Press, 1989.

———. *Interpreting Folklore.* Bloomington: Indiana Univ. Press, 1980.

Dundes, Alan, and Carl R. Pagter. *Never Try to Teach a Pig to Sing: Still More Urban Folklore from the Paperwork Empire.* Detroit: Wayne State Univ. Press, 1991.

———. *Urban Folklore from the Paperwork Empire.* Austin: American Folklore Society, 1975.

———. *When You're Up to Your Ass in Alligators.* Detroit: Wayne State Univ. Press, 1987.

Eisenstein, Elizabeth L. *The Printing Press as an Agent of Change: Communications and Cultural Transformations in Early-Modern Europe.* 2 vols. New York: Cambridge Univ. Press, 1979.

Encyclopedia of the Philippines. 3d ed. Ed. Zoilo M. Galang. Vol. 1. Manila: Exequel Floro, 1950.

Esligh. "Inscription on Fly-Leaf of a Breeches Bible, 1608." *Notes and Queries,* 2d ser., vol. 9 (24 Mar. 1860): 218.

Eugenio, Damiana L., ed. *Philippine Folk Literature: The Folktales*. Quezon City: U.P. Folklorists, 1989.

———. *Philippine Folk Literature: The Legends*. Quezon City: U.P. Folklorists, 1987.

———. *Philippine Folk Literature: The Proverbs*. Quezon City: U.P. Folklorists, 1992.

Evans, Charles. *American Bibliography*. 12 vols. Chicago: for the author, 1903–34.

Eyre, Margaret. "Folk-Lore of the Wye Valley." *Folk-Lore* 16 (1905): 162–79.

Fansler, Dean S. *Filipino Popular Tales*. Vol. 12 of *Memoirs of the American Folk-Lore Society*. Lancaster, Pa.: American Folklore Society, 1921.

Farr, T. J. "Riddles and Superstitions of Middle Tennessee." *Journal of American Folklore* 48 (1935): 318–36.

———. "Tennessee Folk Beliefs Concerning Children." *Journal of American Folklore* 52 (1939): 112–16.

Federer, Charles A. "Doggerel Book-Inscriptions." *Notes and Queries*, 10th ser., vol. 6 (18 Aug. 1906): 128.

Flood, John L. "The Bibliography of German 'Volksbücher': A Review Article." Review of *"Volksbücher." Prosaromane, Renaissancenovellen, Versdichtungen und Schwankbücher*, by Bodo Gotzkowsky. *Modern Language Review* 88 (1993): 894–904.

———. "Fortunatus in London." In *Reisen und Welterfahrung in der deutschen Literatur des Mittelalters*, ed. Dietrich Huschenbett and John Margetts. 240–63. Würzburg: Königshausen und Neumann, 1991.

Flory, Claude R. "A Hazard of Good Fortunes." *Journal of American Folklore* 82 (1969): 71–72.

Flowers, Helen L. *A Classification of the Folktale of the West Indies by Types and Motifs*. New York: Arno Press, 1980.

Ford, Worthington Chauncey. *The Boston Book Market, 1679–1700*. Boston: Club of Odd Volumes, 1917.

Franklin, Benjamin. *The Autobiography of Benjamin Franklin: A Genetic Text*. Ed. J. A. Leo Lemay and P. M. Zall. Knoxville: Univ. of Tennessee Press, 1981.

———. *The Papers of Benjamin Franklin*. Ed. Leonard W. Labaree, Ralph L. Ketchan, Helen C. Boatfield, and Helene H. Fineman. Vol. 7. New Haven, Conn.: Yale Univ. Press, 1963.

Funk & Wagnalls Standard Dictionary of Folklore, Mythology and Legend. Ed. Maria Leach and Jerome Fried. San Francisco: Harper & Row, 1984.

Gacek, Adam. "The Use of 'kabikaj' in Arabic Manuscripts." *Manuscripts of the Middle East* 1 (1986): 49–53.

Gager, John G. *Moses in Greco-Roman Paganism*. Nashville: Abingdon Press, 1972.

Gallacher, Stuart A. "Franklin's *Way to Wealth*: A Florilegium of Proverbs and Wise Sayings." *Journal of English and Germanic Philology* 49 (1949): 229–51.

Gallagher, Edward J. "The Rhetorical Strategy of Franklin's 'Way to Wealth.'" *Eighteenth-Century Studies* 6 (1973): 475–85.

Gardner, Emelyn Elizabeth. *Folklore from the Schoharie Hills, New York*. Ann Arbor: Univ. of Michigan Press, 1937.

Gaunt, J. L. "Popular Fiction and the Ballad Market in the Second Half of the Seventeenth Century." *Papers of the Bibliographical Society of America* 72 (1978): 1–13.

Georgia Writers' Project, Savannah Unit, Works Progress Administration. *Drums and Shadows: Survival Studies among the Georgia Coastal Negroes*. Athens: Univ. of Georgia Press, 1940.

Gilbert, M. "Book-Borrowers' Conscience." *Times* (London), 9 Mar. 1928, p. 10.

Ginzburg, Carlo. *The Cheese and the Worms: The Cosmos of a Sixteenth-Century Miller*. Trans. John Tedeschi and Anne Tedeschi. Baltimore: Johns Hopkins Univ. Press, 1980.

Glassie, Henry, ed. *Irish Folktales*. New York: Pantheon, 1985.

Glenn, John, and David Walsh. *Catalogue of the Francis Trigge Chained Library, St. Wulfram's Church, Grantham*. Cambridge, England: D. S. Brewer, 1988.

Gole, Russell. "Inscriptions in Books." *Notes and Queries*, 1st ser., vol. 7 (2 Apr. 1853): 337.

Gonzalez-Tabujara, Milagros. *Visayan Folklore*. Ed. Ernesto Constantino. Diliman, Quezon City: Folklore Studies Program, College of Social Sciences and Philosophy, Univ. of the Philippines and U. P. Folklorists, 1985.

Gotzkowsky, Bodo. *"Volksbücher." Prosaromane, Renaissancenovellen, Versdichtungen und Schwankbücher. Bibliographie der deutshen Drucke*. Baden-Baden: Hoerner, 1991.

Graff, Harvey J. *The Legacies of Literacy: Continuities and Contradictions in Western Culture and Society*. Bloomington: Indiana Univ. Press, 1987.

Granger, James. *A Biographical History of England, from Egbert the Great to the Revolution*. 2d ed. Vol. 1. London: For T. Davies, J. Robson, G. Robinson, T. Becket, T. Cadell, and T. Evans, 1775.

Granger, Mary. Introduction to *Drums and Shadows: Survival Studies among the Georgia Coastal Negroes*, by Georgia Writers' Project. Athens: Univ. of Georgia Press, 1940.

Grimm, Jacob, and Wilhelm Grimm. *The Complete Fairy Tales of the Brothers Grimm*. Ed. and trans. Jack Zipes. New York: Bantam Books, 1992.

Grumbine, E. "Folk-Lore of Lebanon County." *Papers of the Lebanon County Historical Society* 3 (1905): 254–94.

H., W. R. "Book-Stealing: Degrees of Blackness." *Notes and Queries,* 10th ser., vol. 7 (16 Mar. 1907): 212.

Hall-Quest, Alfred Lawrence. *The Textbook: How to Use and Judge It.* New York: Macmillan, 1918.

Hamilton, Dr. Alexander. *The History of the Ancient and Honorable Tuesday Club.* Ed. Robert Micklus. 3 vols. Chapel Hill: Univ. of North Carolina Press, 1990.

Hansen, Terrence Leslie. *The Types of the Folktale in Cuba, Puerto Rico, the Dominican Republic, and Spanish South America.* Berkeley and Los Angeles: Univ. of California Press, 1957.

Hardy, W. J. *Book-Plates.* London: Kegan Paul, Trench, Trübner, 1893.

Hargarve, Wilfred. "Turning the Key and the Bible." *Notes and Queries,* 6th ser., vol. 7 (10 Mar. 1883): 189.

Hart, Donn V. *Riddles in Filipino Folklore: An Anthropological Analysis.* Syracuse: Syracuse Univ. Press, 1964.

Hart, Donn V., and Harriett C. Hart. "Cinderella in the Eastern Bisayas with a Summary of the Philippine Folktale." *Journal of American Folklore* 79 (1966): 307–37.

———. "The Images of the Catholic Priest in Bisayan Filipino Folklore." *Southern Folklore Quarterly* 40 (1976): 307–41.

Hastrup, Kirsten. *Culture and History in Medieval Iceland: An Anthropological Analysis of Structure and Change.* Oxford: Clarendon Press, 1985.

———. *Nature and Policy in Iceland: An Anthropological Analysis of History and Mentality.* Oxford: Clarendon Press, 1990.

Hawkins, John. "An Old Mauma's Folk-Lore." *Journal of American Folklore* 9 (1896): 129–31.

Hayes, Kevin J. *A Colonial Woman's Bookshelf.* Knoxville: Univ. of Tennessee Press, 1996.

———. *Henry James: The Contemporary Reviews.* New York: Cambridge Univ. Press, 1996.

Hayward, L. H. "Shropshire Folklore of Yesterday and Today." *Folk-Lore* 49 (1938): 223–43.

Heitz, Paul, and François Ritter. *Versuch einer Zusammenstellung der deutschen Volksbücher des 15. and 16. Jahrhunderts nebst deren spateren Ausgaben und Literatur.* Strasbourg: J. H. E. Heitz, 1924.

Hemenway, Robert E. *Zora Neale Hurston: A Literary Biography.* Urbana: Univ. of Illinois Press, 1977.

Henderson, William. *Notes of the Folk-Lore of the Northern Counties of England and the Borders.* London: For the Folk-Lore Society by W. Satchell, Peyton, 1879.

Henning, David C. *Tales of the Blue Mountains.* Vol. 3 of *Publications of the Historical Society of Schuylkill County.* Pottsville, Pa.: Daily Republican Book Rooms, 1911.

Hermannsson, Halldór. *Icelandic Books of the Seventeenth Century, 1601–1700.* Vol. 14 of *Islandica.* Ithaca, N.Y.: Cornell Univ. Press, 1922.

———. *Icelandic Books of the Sixteenth Century (1534–1600).* Vol. 9 of *Islandica.* Ithaca, N.Y.: Cornell Univ. Press, 1916.

———. Introduction to *The Hólar Cato: An Icelandic Schoolbook of the Seventeenth Century,* ed. Halldór Hermannsson. Vol. 39 of *Islandica.* Ithaca, N.Y.: Cornell Univ. Press, 1958.

———. *Jón Guðmundsson and His Natural History of Iceland.* Vol. 15 of *Islandica.* Ithaca, N.Y.: Cornell Univ. Press, 1924.

———. *Sæmund Sigfússon and the Oddaverjar.* Vol. 22 of *Islandica.* Ithaca, N.Y.: Cornell Univ. Press, 1932.

Hills, Margaret T. *The English Bible in America: A Bibliography of Editions of the Bible & the New Testament Published in America, 1777–1957.* New York: American Bible Society and the New York Public Library, 1961.

Hird, Frank. "To the Editor of the Times." *Times* (London), 7 Mar. 1928, p. 17.

Hodgkin, J. Eliot. "MS. Notes of Possession in Books." *Notes and Queries,* 7th ser., vol. 3 (12 Mar. 1887): 206.

Hoffman, W. J. "Folk-Lore of the Pennsylvania Germans." *Journal of American Folklore* 2 (1889): 23–35.

Hohman, Johann Georg. *Pow-Wows; or, Long Lost Friend: A Collection of Mysterious and Invaluable Arts and Remedies for Man as Well as Animal.* State College, Pa.: Yardbird Books, 1992.

Holmes, Thomas James. *Cotton Mather: A Bibliography of His Works.* 3 vols. 1940. Rpt. Newton, Mass.: Crofton, 1974.

———. *Increase Mather: A Bibliography of His Works.* 2 vols. Cleveland: For William Gwinn Mather by Harvard Univ. Press, 1931.

Hone, William. *The Year Book of Daily Recreation and Information.* Ed. Leslie Shepard. 1831–32. Rpt. Detroit: Gale, 1967.

Hudson, Arthur Palmer. *Specimens of Mississippi Folk-Lore.* Ann Arbor: Edwards Brothers, 1928.

Hurston, Zora Neale. "The Fire and the Cloud." In *Zora Neale Hurston: Novels and Stories,* ed. Cheryl A. Wall, 997–1,000. New York: Library of America, 1995.

———. "Hoodoo in America." *Journal of American Folklore* 44 (1931): 317–417.

———. *Moses: Man of the Mountain.* In *Zora Neale Hurston: Novels and Stories,* ed. Cheryl A. Wall. New York: Library of America, 1995.

————. *Mules and Men.* In *Zora Neale Hurston: Folklore, Memoirs, and Other Writings,* ed. Cheryl A. Wall. New York: Library of America, 1995.

————. *Tell My Horse.* In *Zora Neale Hurston: Folklore, Memoirs, and Other Writings,* ed. Cheryl A. Wall. New York: Library of America, 1995.

Hyatt, Harry Middleton. *Folk-Lore from Adams County Illinois.* Rev. ed. Hannibal, Mo.: Alma Egan Hyatt Foundation, 1965.

————. *Hoodoo-Conjuration-Witchcraft-Rootwork.* 5 vols. Hannibal, Mo.: Western Publishing, 1970–.

"Iceland." *Library Journal* 5 (1880): 229.

Ikeda, Hiroko. *A Type and Motif Index of Japanese Folk-Literature.* No. 209 of *FF Communications.* Helsinki: Suomalainen Tiedeakatemia Academia Scientarum Fennica, 1971.

Jackson, Blyden. "*Moses, Man of the Mountain:* A Study of Power." In *Zora Neale Hurston: Modern Critical Views,* ed. Harold Bloom, 151–55. New York: Chelsea House, 1986.

————. "Some Negroes in the Land of Goshen." *Tennessee Folklore Society Bulletin* 19 (1953): 103–7.

Jackson, Georgina F. *Shropshire Folk-Lore: A Sheaf of Gleanings.* Ed. Charlotte Sophia Burne. London: Trübner, 1883.

Jackson, Holbrook. *The Anatomy of Bibliomania.* 2 vols. London: Soncino Press, 1930–31.

Jacobs, Joseph. *English Fairy Tales.* New York: G. P. Putnam's Sons, 1902.

Jefferson, Thomas. *The Papers of Thomas Jefferson.* Ed. Julian P. Boyd, Mina R. Bryan, and Frederick Amdahl. Vols. 10 and 12. Princeton, N.J.: Princeton Univ. Press, 1954–55.

Johnson, Thomas H. "Jonathan Edwards and the 'Young Folks' Bible.'" *New England Quarterly* 5 (1932): 37–54.

Jones, Louis C. "The Devil in York State." *New York Folklore Quarterly* 8 (1952): 5–19.

Jones, Stephen S. "'The Rarest Thing in the World': Indo-European or African?" In *African Folklore in the New World,* ed. Daniel J. Crowley, 54–64. Austin: Univ. of Texas Press, 1977.

Jones, T. Gwynn. *Welsh Folklore and Folk-Custom.* London: Methuen, 1930.

Kaser, David. *A Book for a Sixpence: The Circulating Library in America.* Pittsburgh: Beta Phi Mu, 1980.

Katha Sarit Sagara: Or Ocean of the Streams of Story. Trans. C. H. Tawney. 2 vols. 1880. Rpt. Delhi: Munshiram Manoharlal, 1968.

Keisling, William. Introduction to *Pow-Wows; or, Long Lost Friend: A Collection of Mysterious and Invaluable Arts and Remedies for Man as Well as Animal,* by Johann Georg Hohman. State College, Pa.: Yardbird Books, 1992.

Kittredge, George Lyman. *Witchcraft in Old and New England.* Cambridge: Harvard Univ. Press, 1929.

Klipple, May Augusta. *African Folktales with Foreign Analogues.* New York: Garland, 1992.

Kvideland, Reimund, and Henning K. Sehmsdorf, eds. *Scandinavian Folk Belief and Legend.* Minneapolis: Univ. of Minnesota Press, 1988.

L., S. "New Year's Day." *Notes and Queries,* 2d ser., vol. 12 (19 Oct. 1861): 303.

Lean, Vincent Stuckey. *Lean's Collectanea.* 4 vols. Bristol: J. W. Arrowsmith, 1902–4.

Lee, Brian North. *British Bookplates: A Pictorial History.* London: David & Charles, 1979.

Legge, F. A. "To the Editor of the Times." *Times* (London), 28 Feb. 1928, p. 17.

Lemay, J. A. Leo. "Benjamin Franklin." In *Major Writers of Early American Literature,* ed. Everett Emerson, 205–43. Madison: Univ. of Wisconsin Press, 1972.

———, ed. *An Early American Reader.* Washington, D.C.: United States Information Agency, 1988.

Lewis, Arthur H. *Hex.* New York: Trident Press, 1969.

Lighter, J. E., J. Ball, and J. O'Connor, eds. *Random House Historical Dictionary of American Slang: Volume 1, A–G.* New York: Random House, 1994.

Lindow, John. *Swedish Legends and Folktales.* Berkeley and Los Angeles: Univ. of California Press, 1978.

M., F. M. "Inscriptions in Books." *Notes and Queries,* 1st ser., vol. 7 (26 Feb. 1853): 221.

Mabbott, Thomas Ollive. "Book Borrowers." *Notes and Queries* 149 (11 July 1925): 33.

———. "Book Borrowers." *Notes and Queries* 149 (3 Oct. 1925): 250.

———. "John Stirling Autograph." *Notes and Queries* 153 (2 July 1927): 8.

McDonogh, Gary W., ed. *The Florida Negro: A Federal Writers' Project Legacy.* Jackson: Univ. Press of Mississippi, 1993.

McDowell, Deborah E. "Lines of Descent/Dissenting Lines." In *Zora Neale Hurston: Critical Perspectives Past and Present,* ed. Henry Louis Gates Jr. and K. A. Appiah, 230–40. New York: Amistad, 1993.

Mandrou, Robert. *De la culture populaire aux 17e et 18e siecles: la Bibliothèque bleue de Troyes.* 1964. Rpt. Paris: Editions Imago, 1985.

Marco, Joaquin. *Literatura popular en Espana en los siglos XVIII y XIX: Una aproximacion a los pliegos de cordel.* Madrid: Taurus, 1977.

Mariano, M. *Folk Tales of the Philippines*. New Delhi: Sterling, 1982.

Marshall, Edward. "Ex-Libris: Lord Mansfield." *Notes and Queries,* 6th ser., vol. 4 (27 Aug. 1881): 165–66.

———. "Turning the Key and the Bible." *Notes and Queries,* 6th ser., vol. 7 (23 June 1883): 495.

Mather, Cotton. *Diary of Cotton Mather.* Ed. Worthington Chauncey Ford. 1911. Rpt. New York: Frederick Ungar, [1957].

Meister, Charles W. "Franklin as a Proverb Stylist." *American Literature* 24 (1952): 157–66.

Melville, Herman. *The Confidence-Man: A Norton Critical Edition.* Ed. Hershel Parker. New York: Norton, 1971.

———. *Israel Potter: His Fifty Years of Exile.* Ed. Harrison Hayford, Hershel Parker, and G. Thomas Tanselle. Evanston and Chicago: Northwestern Univ. Press and the Newberry Library, 1982.

Mieder, Wolfgang. *American Proverbs: A Study of Texts and Contexts.* Bern: Peter Lang, 1989.

———. *International Proverb Scholarship: An Annotated Bibliography.* New York: Garland, 1982.

———. *International Proverb Scholarship: An Annotated Bibliography, Supplement 1 (1800–1981).* New York: Garland, 1990.

———. *Proverbs Are Never Out of Season: Popular Wisdom in the Modern Age.* New York: Oxford Univ. Press, 1993.

Morton, Thomas. *New English Canaan.* Ed. C. F. Adams Jr. Boston: Prince Society, 1883.

Müller, Jan-Dirk. "Volksbuch/Prosaroman im 15./16. Jahrhundert.—Perspektiven der Forschung." *Internationales Archiv für Sozialgeschichte der deutschen Literatur* 1 (1985): 1–128.

Murray, John. "A Rhyming Warning to Book-Borrowers." *Notes and Queries,* 9th ser., vol. 1 (25 June 1898): 512.

Murray-Aynsley, Mrs. "Scraps of English Folklore, XVI: Herefordshire." *Folk-Lore* 39 (1928): 381–92.

N., H. Y. "Superstition in Shropshire." *Notes and Queries,* 5th ser., vol. 11 (25 Jan. 1879): 74.

National Union Catalog: Pre-1956 Imprints. 754 vols. London: Mansell, 1968–81.

Ne, Harriet. *Tales of Molokai: The Voice of Harriet Ne.* Ed. Gloria L. Cronin. Laie, Hawaii: Institute for Polynesian Studies, 1992.

Neuburg, Victor. "Chapbooks in America: Reconstructing the Popular Reading of Early America." In *Reading in America: Literature and Social History,* ed. Cathy N. Davidson, 81–113. Baltimore: Johns Hopkins Univ. Press, 1989.

New (The) Revised Sixth and Seventh Books of Moses and the Magical Uses of the Psalms. Ed. Migene González-Wippler. 2d ed. New York: Original Publications, 1991.

Nickels, Cameron C. "Franklin's Poor Richard's Almanacs: 'The Humblest of his Labors.'" In *The Oldest Revolutionary: Essays on Benjamin Franklin,* ed. J. A. Leo Lemay, 77–89. Philadelphia: Univ. of Pennsylvania Press, 1976.

Nielson, George R. "Folklore of the German-Wends in Texas." In *Singers and Storytellers,* ed. Mody C. Boatright, Wilson M. Hudson, and Allen Maxwell, 244–59. Vol. 30 of the *Publications of the Texas Folklore Society.* Dallas: Southern Methodist Univ. Press, 1961.

Nisard, Charles. *Histoire des livres populaires.* 2d ed. 2 vols. Paris: E. Dentu, 1864.

Norlin, Ethel Todd. "Present-Day Superstitions at La Harpe, Ill., Survivals in a Community of English Origin." *Journal of American Folklore* 31 (1918): 202–15.

Northall, G. F. *English Folk-Rhymes: A Collection of Traditional Verses Relating to Places and Persons, Customs, Superstitions, Etc.* London: Kegan Paul, Trench, Trübner, 1892.

Norton, Arthur O. "Harvard Text-Books and Reference Books of the Seventeenth Century." *Proceedings of the Colonial Society of Massachusetts* (Apr. 1933): 361–438.

Opie, Iona, and Moira Tatem, eds. *A Dictionary of Superstitions.* New York: Oxford Univ. Press, 1989.

O'Sullivan, Sean. *Folktales of Ireland.* Chicago: Univ. of Chicago Press, 1966.

———. *A Handbook of Irish Folklore.* 1942. Rpt. Detroit: Singing Tree Press, 1970.

———. "Oliver Cromwell in Irish Oral Tradition." In *Folklore Today: A Festschrift for Richard M. Dorson,* ed. Linda Dégh, Henry Glassie, and Felix J. Oinas, 473–83. Bloomington: Research Center for Language and Semiotic Studies, Indiana Univ., 1976.

Owen, Elias. *Welsh Folk-Lore: A Collection of the Folk-Tales and Legends of North Wales.* Rev. ed. Oswestry, England: Woodall, Minshall, 1896.

Oxford Dictionary of English Proverbs. 3d ed. Revised by F. P. Wilson. Oxford: Clarendon Press, 1970.

P., O. "Inscriptions in Books." *Notes and Queries,* 1st ser., vol. 7 (2 Apr. 1853): 337.

Page, John T. "Book-Stealing: Degrees of Blackness." *Notes and Queries,* 10th ser., vol. 7 (16 Mar. 1907): 212.

———. "A Rhyming Warning to Book-Borrowers." *Notes and Queries,* 9th ser., vol. 1 (25 June 1898): 512–13.

Paine, Thomas. *Collected Writings.* Ed. Eric Foner. New York: Library of America, 1995.

Park, Robert E. "Magic, Mentality, and City Life." *Publications of the American Sociological Society* 18 (1924): 102–15.

Pearson, David. *Provenance Research in Book History: A Handbook.* London: British Library, 1994.

Phelan, John Leddy. *The Hispanization of the Philippines: Spanish Arms and Filipino Responses, 1565–1700.* Madison: Univ. of Wisconsin Press, 1959.

Pino-Saacedra, Yolando, ed. *Folktales of Chile.* Trans. Rockwell Gray. Chicago: Univ. of Chicago Press, 1967.

Pollard, A. W., G. R. Redgrave, W. A. Jackson, F. S. Ferguson, and Katharine F. Pantzer. *A Short-Title Catalogue of Books Printed in England, Scotland, and Ireland and of English Books Printed Abroad, 1475–1640.* 2d. ed. 3 vols. London: Bibliographical Society, 1976–91.

Porter, J. Hampden. "Notes on the Folk-Lore of the Mountain Whites of the Alleghanies." *Journal of American Folklore* 7 (1894): 105–17.

Postlethwaite, T. N. "Book-Stealing: Degrees of Blackness." *Notes and Queries,* 10th ser., vol. 6 (3 Nov. 1906): 353.

Price, Sadie F. "Kentucky Folk-Lore." *Journal of American Folk-Lore* 14 (1901): 30–38.

Puckett, Newbell Niles. *Folk Beliefs of the Southern Negro.* Chapel Hill: Univ. of North Carolina Press, 1926.

———. *Popular Beliefs and Superstitions: A Compendium of American Folklore from the Ohio Collection of Newbell Niles Puckett.* Ed. Wayland D. Hand, Anna Casetta, and Sondra B. Thiederman. 3 vols. Boston: G. K. Hall, 1981.

Rabelais, François. *The Complete Works of François Rabelais.* Trans. Donald M. Frame. Berkeley and Los Angeles: Univ. of California Press, 1991.

Rafael, Vicente L. *Contracting Colonialism: Translation and Christian Conversion in Tagalog Society under Early Spanish Rule.* Ithaca, N.Y.: Cornell Univ. Press, 1988.

Randolph, Vance. *Ozark Superstitions.* New York: Columbia Univ. Press, 1947.

Ratcliffe, Thomas. "Book-Stealing: Degrees of Blackness." *Notes and Queries,* 10th ser., vol. 6 (20 Oct. 1906): 305.

Reuter, O. R. *Proverbs, Proverbial Sentences and Phrases in Thomas Deloney's Works.* Helsinki: Societas Scientiarum Fennica, 1986.

Rinderknecht, Carol, and Scott Bruntjen. *A Checklist of Imprints for 1843.* Metuchen, N.J.: Scarecrow, 1993.

Robe, Stanley L. *Index of Mexican Folktales Including Narrative Texts from Mexico, Central America, and the Hispanic United States.* Berkeley and Los Angeles: Univ. of California Press, 1973.

Roberts, Hilda. "Louisiana Superstitions." *Journal of American Folklore* 40 (1927): 144–208.

Rockwell, Joan. *Evald Tang Kristensen: A Lifelong Adventure in Folklore.* Aalborg, Denmark: Aalborg Univ. Press and the Danish Folklore Society, 1982.

Rosenbach, A. S. W. *Books and Bidders: The Adventures of a Bibliophile.* Boston: Little, Brown, 1927.

———. *Early American Children's Books.* 1933. Rpt. New York: Kraus, 1966.

S., R. J. "Bible Divination in Suffolk." *Notes and Queries,* 1st ser., vol. 4 (30 Aug. 1851): 148.

Schedler, Paul W. "Folk Medicine in Denton County Today: Or, Can Dermatology Displace Dishrags?" In *Hunters & Healers: Folklore Types and Topics,* ed. Wilson M. Hudson, 11–17. Vol. 35 of the Publications of the Texas Folklore Society. Austin: Encino Press, 1971.

Schillinger, Alvin W. "Hell's Bells and Panther Tracks: Lore of Western Sullivan County." *New York Folklore Quarterly* 9 (1953): 28–39.

Sebald, Hans. *Witchcraft: The Heritage of a Heresy.* New York: Elsevier, 1978.

Seelow, Hubert. *Die isländischen Übersetzungen der deutschen Volksbücher: Handschriftenstudien zur Rezeption und Überlieferung ausländischer unterhaltender Literatur in Island in der Zeit zwischen Reformation und Aufklärung.* Reykjavik: Stofnun Árna Magnússonar, 1989.

Sewall, Samuel. *The Diary of Samuel Sewall, 1674–1729.* Ed. M. Halsey Thomas. 2 vols. New York: Farrar, Straus and Giroux, 1973.

Shields, David S. "The Manuscript in the British American World of Print." *Proceedings of the American Antiquarian Society* 102 (1992): 403–16.

Shipton, Clifford K., and James E. Mooney. *National Index of American Imprints through 1800: The Short-Title Evans.* Worcester, Mass.: American Antiquarian Society and Barre Publishers, 1969.

Sidney, Philip. "An Apology for Poetry." In *English Critical Essays (Sixteenth, Seventeenth and Eighteenth Centuries),* ed. Edmund D. Jones, 1–54. New York: Oxford Univ. Press, 1922.

Simpkins, John Ewart. *County Folk-Lore, Vol. VII: Examples of Printed Folk-Lore Concerning Fife with Some Notes on Clackmannan and Kinross-Shires.* London: For the Folk-Lore Society, 1914.

Simpson, Jacqueline, trans. *Legends of Icelandic Magicians.* Totowa, N.J.: Rowman and Littlefield, 1975.

———, ed. and trans. *Scandinavian Folktales.* New York: Penguin, 1988.

Sixth (The) and Seventh Books of Moses: Or, Moses' Magical Spirit Art. New ed. Cedar Knolls, N.J.: Wehman Bros., n.d.

Slater, Candace. *Stories on a String: The Brazilian Literatura de Cordel.* Berkeley and Los Angeles: Univ. of California Press, 1982.

Smith, F. Whitmore. "To the Editor of the Times." *Times* (London), 6 Mar. 1928, p. 17.

Smith, M. Linton. "Spells." *Folk-Lore* 51 (1940): 295–98.

Smith, Theophus H. *Conjuring Culture: Biblical Formations of Black America.* New York: Oxford Univ. Press, 1994.

Smith, Walter R. "Northwestern Oklahoma Folk Cures." In *Man, Bird, and Beast,* ed. J. Frank Dobie, 74–85. Vol. 8 of the Publications of the Texas Folklore Society. 1930. Rpt. Dallas: Southern Methodist Univ. Press, 1965.

Snow, Loudell F. *Walkin' Over Medicine.* Boulder, Colo.: Westview Press, 1993.

Spence, Lewis. *The Fairy Tradition in Britain.* New York: Rider, 1948.

Spufford, Margaret. *Small Books and Pleasant Histories: Popular Fiction and Its Readership in Seventeenth-Century England.* Athens: Univ. of Georgia Press, 1981.

Steinberg, David Joel. *The Philippines: A Singular and a Plural Place.* 3d ed. Boulder, Colo.: Westview Press, 1994.

Stevens, David. "Divination by the Bible and Key." *Notes and Queries,* 1st ser., vol. 1 (27 Apr. 1850): 413.

Stevens, Norman D. Review of *Urban Folklore from the Paperwork Empire,* by Alan Dundes and Carl R. Pagter. *Journal of Academic Librarianship* 2 (1976): 90.

Stevenson, Robert Louis. *The Ebb Tide.* In *The Novels and Tales of Robert Louis Stevenson: The Wrong Box & The Ebb Tide.* New York: Charles Scribner's Sons, 1895.

Stokes, Whitley, ed. and trans. *Lives of Saints from the Book of Lismore.* Oxford: Clarendon Press, 1890.

Stone, Lawrence. "Literacy and Education in England 1640–1900." *Past and Present* 42 (Feb. 1969): 69–139.

Stout, Earl J. *Folklore from Iowa.* New York: American Folk-Lore Society, 1936.

Stroup, Thomas B. "A Charm for Stopping Blood." *Southern Folklore Quarterly* 1 (Mar. 1937): 19–20.

Sullivan, Patrick. "Benjamin Franklin, the Inveterate (and Crafty) Public Instructor: Instruction on Two Levels in 'The Way to Wealth.'" *Early American Literature* 21 (1986/7): 248–59.

Tate, W. R. "Conclusion of Verses Sought." *Notes and Queries,* 8th ser., vol. 6 (13 Oct. 1894): 294.

Taylor, Archer. *English Riddles from Oral Tradition.* Berkeley and Los Angeles: Univ. of California Press, 1951.

Taylor, Archer, and Bartlett Jere Whiting. *A Dictionary of American Proverbs and Proverbial Phrases, 1820–1880.* Cambridge: Belknap Press, Harvard Univ. Press, 1958.

Thomas, Daniel Lindsey, and Lucy Blayney Thomas. *Kentucky Superstitions.* Princeton, N.J.: Princeton Univ. Press, 1920.

Thomas, Isaiah. *The History of Printing in America.* Ed. Marcus A. McCorison. New York: Weathervane Books, 1970.

Thomas, R. E. "Book Borrowers." *Notes and Queries* 150 (2 Jan. 1926): 16.

Thompson, D. P. *Gaut Gurley; The Trappers of Umbagog. A Tale of Border Life.* Boston: John P. Jewett, 1857.

Thompson, Roger. "Worthington Chauncey Ford's *Boston Book Market, 1679–1700*: Some Corrections and Additions." *Proceedings Massachusetts Historical Society* 86 (1974): 67–78.

Thompson, Stith. *The Folktale.* 1946. Rpt. Berkeley and Los Angeles: Univ. of California Press, 1977.

———. *Motif-Index of Folk-Literature: A Classification of Narrative Elements in Folktales, Ballads, Myths, Fables, Mediaeval Romances, Exempla, Fabliaux, Jest-Books, and Local Legends.* Rev. ed. 6 vols. Bloomington: Indiana Univ. Press, 1955–58.

Thompson, Stith, and Jonas Balys. *The Oral Tales of India.* Bloomington: Indiana Univ. Press, 1958.

Tilley, Morris Palmer. *A Dictionary of the Proverbs in England in the Sixteenth and Seventeenth Centuries: A Collection of the Proverbs Found in English Literature and the Dictionaries of the Period.* Ann Arbor: Univ. of Michigan Press, 1950.

Timbs, John, and Alexander Gunn. *Abbeys, Castles and Ancient Halls of England and Wales: Their Legendary Lore and Popular History.* 3 vols. London: Frederick Warne, n.d.

Ting, Nai-Tung. *A Type Index of Chinese Folktales in the Oral Tradition and Major Works on Non-Religious Classical Literature.* No. 223 of *FF Communications.* Helsinki: Suomalainen Tiedeakatemia Academia Scientarum Fennica, 1978.

Tomasson, Richard F. *Iceland: The First New Society.* Minneapolis: Univ. of Minnesota Press, 1980.

Toots and the Maytals. "Six and Seven Books." On *Reggae Got Soul.* Mango phonograph album, 1976.

Twain, Mark. *Adventures of Huckleberry Finn.* Ed. Walter Blair and Victor Fischer. Berkeley and Los Angeles: Univ. of California Press, 1985.

Untermeyer, Louis. Review of *Moses: Man of the Mountain.* In *Zora Neale Hurston: Critical Perspectives Past and Present,* ed. Henry Louis Gates Jr. and K. A. Appiah, 26–27. New York: Amistad, 1993.

Vail, R. G. W. "What a Young Puritan Ought to Know." *Proceedings of the American Antiquarian Society* 49 (1939): 259–66.

Vaux, J. Edward. *Church Folklore: A Record of Some Post-Reformation Usages in the English Church, Now Mostly Obsolete.* London: Griffith Farran, 1894.

Vikings, The. "Six and Seven Books of Moses." On *More Intensified! Vol. 2: Original Ska, 1963–1967.* Mango phonograph album, 1980.

W., T. "Bible and Key." *Notes and Queries,* 1st ser., vol. 2 (1 June 1850): 5.

W., W. "Inscriptions in Books." *Notes and Queries,* 1st ser., vol. 7 (30 Apr. 1853): 438.

Wallace, W. "To the Editor of the Times." *Times* (London), 3 Mar. 1928, p. 13.

Watson, Nicholas. *Richard Rolle and the Invention of Authority.* New York: Cambridge Univ. Press, 1991.

Watt, Tessa. *Cheap Print and Popular Piety, 1550–1640.* New York: Cambridge Univ. Press, 1991.

Waugh, F. W. "Canadian Folk-Lore from Ontario." *Journal of American Folklore* 31 (1918): 4–82.

Weaver, F. W. "Turning the Key and the Bible." *Notes and Queries,* 6th ser., vol. 8 (18 Aug. 1883): 130.

Weiss, Harry B. *A Book about Chapbooks: The People's Literature of Bygone Times.* Hatboro, Pa.: Folklore Associates, 1969.

———. "The Way to Wealth and Other Franklin Chapbooks." *American Book Collector* (May–June 1935): 193–95.

Welch, d'Alté A. *A Bibliography of American Children's Books Printed Prior to 1821.* Worcester, Mass.: American Antiquarian Society and Barre Publishers, 1972.

Welsh, Charles, and William H. Tillinghast. *Catalogue of English and American Chapbooks and Broadside Ballads in Harvard College Library.* 1905. Rpt. Detroit: Singing Tree Press, 1968.

Wheeler, Joseph Towne. "Booksellers and Circulating Libraries in Colonial Maryland." *Maryland Historical Magazine* 34 (1939): 111–37.

———. "Books Owned by Marylanders, 1700–1776." *Maryland Historical Magazine* 35 (1940): 337–53.

Wherry, Beatrix Albina. "Wizardry on the Welsh Border." *Folk-Lore* 15 (1904): 75–85.

Whiting, B. J., Francis W. Bradley, Richard Jente, Archer Taylor, and M. P. Tilley. "The Study of Proverbs." *Modern Language Forum* 24 (1939): 63–83.

Whiting, Bartlett Jere. *Early American Proverbs and Proverbial Phrases.* Cambridge: Belknap Press, Harvard Univ. Press, 1977.

———. *Modern Proverbs and Proverbial Sayings.* Cambridge: Harvard Univ. Press, 1989.

Whitney, Annie Weston, and Caroline Canfield Bullock. *Folklore from Maryland.* New York: American Folk-Lore Society, 1925.

Whittenbury-Kaye, Ronald D. "Book Inscriptions." *Notes and Queries,* 12th ser., vol. 11 (8 July 1922): 27.

Wieland, Darryl. "The Idea of Mystical Power in Modern Iceland." In *The Anthropology of Iceland,* ed. E. Paul Durrenberger and Gísli Pálsson, 19–38. Iowa City: Univ. of Iowa Press, 1989.

Willoughby, Harold R. *Soldiers' Bibles through Three Centuries.* Chicago: Univ. of Chicago Press, 1944.

Wilson-Kastner, Patricia. "State and Church in Iceland: Past History and Present Problems." *Lutheran Quarterly* 28 (1976): 125–39.

Winans, Robert B. *A Descriptive Checklist of Book Catalogues Separately Printed in America, 1693–1800.* Worcester, Mass.: American Antiquarian Society, 1981.

Wing, Donald. *Short-Title Catalogue of Books Printed in England, Scotland, Ireland, Wales, and British America and of English Books Printed in Other Countries, 1641–1700.* 2d ed. 3 vols. New York: Index Committee of the Modern Language Association of America, 1972–88.

Wintemberg, W. J., and Katherine H. Wintemberg. "Folk-Lore from Grey County, Ontario." *Journal of American Folklore* 31 (1918): 83–124.

"Witch Doctors to Be Banished." *Philadelphia Public Ledger,* 14 May 1904, p. 13.

Wolf, Edwin II. *The Book Culture of a Colonial American City: Philadelphia Books, Bookmen, and Booksellers.* Oxford: Clarendon Press, 1988.

———. "Report of the Librarian." *Annual Report of the Library Company of Philadelphia for 1962.* Philadelphia: Library Company of Philadelphia, 1963.

Woodhull, Frost. "Ranch Remedios." In *Man, Bird and Beast,* ed. J. Frank Dobie, 9–73. Vol. 8 of the Publications of the Texas Folklore Society. 1930. Rpt. Dallas: Southern Methodist Univ. Press, 1965.

Wright, A. R. *British Calendar Customs: England, Vol. II: Fixed Festivals, January–May, Inclusive.* Ed. T. E. Jones. London: For the Folk-Lore Society, 1938.

Yoder, Don. "Hohman and Romanus: Origins and Diffusion of the Pennsylvania German Powwow Manual." In *American Folk Medicine: A Symposium,* ed. Wayland D. Hand, 235–48. Berkeley and Los Angeles: Univ. of California Press, 1976.

Index

Aarne, Antti, *Types of the Folktale,*
xiii
Addison, Joseph, 8
Admirable secrets d'Albert le Grand,
25–26
Aesop's Fables, 100
Albertus Magnus, 26–27, 109
Albertus Parvus, Lucius, 26
Allen, Anna, 13
American Antiquarian Society, 13
Anson, George, *Lord Anson's Voyage
Round the World,* 10–11
apple, used to resuscitate dead, 76
Apuleius, *Apology,* 16
Aubrey, John, 39

Balliolensis (pseudonym), xiii
Basile, Giambattista, "The Five
Sons," 75–76; *Pentamerone,* 75
Baughman, Ernest, *Type and Motif-
Index,* xiii
Bausinger, Hermann, 75; *Folk Cul-
ture in a World of Technology,* xii
Beauchamp, William M., 91–93
Belknap, Jeremy, 10
Bergen, Fanny D., xiii–xiv
Bible, 14, 15, 21, 27–28, 30, 46, 61,
63–64, 70, 107, 109; carried to
guard against harm, 35–36; crack-
ing louse on, 29–30; slammed to

get rid of wart (motif
G271.2.5[b]), 36; sleeping with
one under bed or pillow, 34–35;
steel-plated, 36; superstitions
about, 30, 33–38; therapeutic use
of, 35–38; use in divination ritual,
29–32, 38–43. *See also* Bible and
key, New Testament, Old Testament, Pentateuch, Psalter, and
names of individual books of the
Bible
Bible and key, 41–43
Bibliomancy, 38–43
Bibliothèque bleue, x–xi, 2
biographies, 6
black book, 59–73, 94, 103, 108–10
Black School, 44–45, 65, 52, 57
blason populaire, 7, 87
bloodstopping, 22, 37–38, 42–43
Book of Mormon, 33
Book of Thoth, 15
books, burying to dispose of, 23, 34;
in Icelandic culture, 54–58; in
Philippine culture, 83–88; used as
charms, 13, 20, 82–83, 88; which
impart the knowledge of creation
(motif G224.3), 60; which tell
what's going on throughout the
world, 78–80. *See also* biographies, catechisms, chapbooks, cof-